AT HOME
with the WORD
2 0 0 1

Sunday Scriptures and Reflections

Ragan Schriver

David Philippart
Jennifer L. Willems
Bryan M. Cones

LTP

LITURGY
TRAINING
PUBLICATIONS

Reprinting from *At Home with the Word 2001*

A parish or an institution may purchase a license to reprint the Reflections (and their discussion questions), the Practices of Faith, Hope and Charity, the Prayer of the Season or the holy day boxes from *At Home with the Word 2001*. Please see page 160 for details.

If a parish or institution wishes to reproduce some or all of the scripture texts, a license must be acquired from the copyright owners (see below). When writing to copyright owners, state clearly which texts you wish to use, the number of copies to be made, and how often you'll be using the copies. There may be a license fee.

Acknowledgments

The Sunday scripture pericopes contained herein are from the New Revised Standard Version of the Bible, © 1989 Division of Christian Education of the National Council of Churches of Christ in the U.S.A. All rights reserved. Used by permission. Text emendations © 1997 Augsburg Fortress. All rights reserved.

Most Roman Catholic parishes proclaim the Sunday scriptures using the readings from the *Lectionary for Mass, Volume 1: Sundays, Solemnities and Feasts of the Lord*, copyright 1998, 1997, 1970 Confraternity of Christian Doctrine, Washington, D.C. For information on reprint permission, write: Confraternity of Christian Doctrine, 1312 Massachusetts Avenue NW, Washington DC 20005.

The English translation of the *Salve, Regina* from *A Book of Prayers* © 1993 International Committee on English in the Liturgy, Inc. (ICEL); excerpts from the English translation of *The Roman Missal* © 1973 ICEL. Used by permission. All rights reserved. For reprint permission, write: ICEL, 1522 K Street NW, Suite 1000, Washington DC 20005-1202.

The English translation of Psalm 22, 51, 63, 65, 85, 98, 100, 113, 118, 126, 131, 134, 145 and 147 from *Psalms for Praise and Worship: A Complete Liturgical Psalter*, edited by John Holbert, S T Kimbrough, Jr., and Carlton R. Young © 1992 Abingdon Press. Used by permission. All rights reserved.

The English translation of the Canticle of Zechariah © 1989 Hope Publishing Co., the Canticle of Mary © 1985 Augsburg Fortress and the Canticle of Simeon © International Consultation on English Texts. Used by permission. All rights reserved.

The art for this year's *At Home with the Word* is the work of Philadelphia artist Carolina Arentson. The cover shows the evangelist Luke, whose gospel we read all through the year 2001 (year C in the three-year cycle). Luke, according to our ancient legends, is not only a writer but a painter and a physician. Here we see him at work, perhaps writing his gospel or the Acts of the Apostles. We see an image of Mary on his easel, and images of many characters in his gospel on the wall. Through the windows, perhaps in Luke's imagination, we see some of the stories that only Luke's gospel tells: the shepherds in their fields, the prodigal son feeding the pigs. See more about Luke the writer on page 8.

The Prayers of the Season were written by Gabe Huck. The holy day commentaries were written by Peter Mazar. The reflections on pages 79, 137, 147 and 159 were written by Marian Bohen, OSU.

The design of this book is by Jill Smith. The editor was David A. Lysik, and Audrey Novak Riley was the production editor. Typesetting was by Anne Fritzinger, in Palatino and Universe. The book was printed and bound by Von Hoffmann Graphics, Inc. of Eldridge, Iowa.

AT HOME WITH THE WORD 2001 © 2000 Archdiocese of Chicago: Liturgy Training Publications, 1800 North Hermitage Avenue, Chicago IL 60622-1101; 1-800-933-1800; orders@ltp.org; fax 1-800-933-7094. All rights reserved.

See our website at www.ltp.org.

ISBN 1-56854-330-1

AHW01

How to Use At Home with the Word

This book invites you to be at home with God's word, to live *with* the Sunday scriptures in order to live *by* them.

SCRIPTURE READINGS These are the heart of *At Home with the Word.* You may want to read the scriptures before going to church, or, better yet, use this book to return to the Sunday scriptures again and again throughout the week.

Because the Sunday readings of many other Christian churches are the same as those proclaimed in Catholic communities, *At Home with the Word* has highlighted the scriptures we share. There are two minor changes that result. First, there may be a few more verses in the reading here that you'll hear proclaimed in the Sunday assembly. Also, when Roman Catholic churches observe a particular feast on a given Sunday that is not celebrated by other Christian communities, there will be two sets of readings.

REFLECTIONS Ragan Schriver is a priest of the diocese of Knoxville. He holds a degree in scriptural theology, and works for Catholic Charities.

The reflections offer background information and perhaps new things to consider. Households or small groups may share the readings and reflection weekly.

This is Year C, the year of the gospel according to Luke. Throughout Ordinary Time we will be reading most often from this gospel. See the introduction to the gospel of Luke on pages 8–9.

PRACTICE OF FAITH David Philippart practices his faith in Chicago. He is an editor, writer and catechist.

PRACTICE OF HOPE Jennifer L. Willems is associate editor of *The Catholic Voice,* newspaper of the archdiocese of Omaha. She is a cantor and a member of the RCIA team and liturgy team and liturgy committee at St. Pius X parish in Omaha.

PRACTICE OF CHARITY Bryan M. Cones is a candidate for a master's degree at Catholic Theological Union in Chicago. He is a writer and editor at LTP.

WEEKDAY READINGS Some people may want to read more than the Sunday scriptures. For each week, we've listed the verses of the books of the Bible from which the first readings for daily Mass are taken.

At Home with the Word also includes:

MORNING, EVENING AND NIGHT PRAYER These simple patterns of prayer for the home take five or ten minutes and are meant to be repeated every day. Don't be afraid of repetition; that's one way to learn.

FRIDAY AND SUNDAY PSALMS AND PRAYERS Sunday is our day of feasting, Friday our day of fasting. Both days need extra prayer and acts of discipleship. Here are psalms, a Lord's Day song and a prayer for Fridays from the U.S. bishops' letter *The Challenge of Peace.*

PRAYERS FROM THE MASS Included here are prayers and other texts from the Mass. Knowing these by heart will help you take full, conscious and active part in Sunday Mass.

SEASONAL PSALMS AND PRAYERS Each season is introduced by a page that includes an acclamation, a psalm and a short prayer. Repeating a single psalm throughout a season is a fine way to learn the psalms by heart.

CALENDAR
TABLE OF CONTENTS

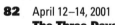

The Lectionary and At Home with the Word

by Martin F. Connell

WHAT IS A LECTIONARY? A lectionary is an ordered selection of readings, chosen from both testaments of the Bible, for proclamation in the assembly gathered for worship. Lectionaries have been used for Christian worship since the fourth century. At different times and in different places before the invention of the printing press in the fifteenth century, the orders of the readings varied a bit. The variety from church to church often reflected the different issues that were important to the local communities of the time.

For the four centuries from the Council of Trent (1545–1563) to the Second Vatican Council (1963–1965), the readings in most Catholic churches were basically the same from year to year and were proclaimed in Latin, an ancient language that many Catholics did not understand. The use of the language of the people in the liturgy and the revision of the lectionary after Vatican II have had tremendous effects on the accessibility of the Bible for Catholics. The Bible is again a vibrant source of our faith and tradition.

THE THREE-YEAR LECTIONARY CYCLE The lectionary issued by the church after the Second Vatican Council appeared in 1970. The most exciting feature of the lectionary was its basic plan. This three-year plan incorporates a fuller selection of readings from the books of the Bible. Each of the first three gospels—Matthew, Mark and Luke—corresponds with one year: Matthew for Year A, Mark for Year B and Luke for Year C. The Sunday lectionary cycle, therefore, takes three years to complete. This liturgical year 2001 is Year C, which begins on the First Sunday of Advent, December 3, 2000.

YEAR C: THE GOSPEL OF LUKE You will find that most of the gospel readings proclaimed in your Sunday assembly this year and printed in *At Home with the Word 2001* are from the gospel of Luke. This gospel will be proclaimed on most Sundays from the First Sunday of Advent to the celebration of Christ the King, November 25, 2001. The introduction to the gospel of Luke on pages 8–9 and the commentaries on the gospel each week will help you recognize and appreciate the contribution of this gospel to our faith.

THE GOSPEL OF JOHN You might ask: What about the Fourth Gospel? The gospel of John is not excluded from proclamation during the three-year cycle. Though it does not have a year during which it is highlighted, the gospel of John punctuates certain seasons and times of the year.

The readings from Year A on the third, fourth and fifth Sundays of Lent are from the gospel of John, and they are proclaimed every year in parishes celebrating the RCIA. These three wonderful stories from the gospel of John—the woman at the well (on the third Sunday), the man born blind (on the fourth Sunday) and the raising of Lazarus (on the fifth Sunday)—are important texts to accompany the celebration of the scrutinies in the process of Christian initiation.

During Years B and C, you will find two sets of readings on these Sundays in *At Home with the Word:* one set for churches celebrating the scrutinies of the RCIA and one set for parishes that are not having the initiation process during that particular liturgical year.

The gospel of John also appears for the Mass of the Lord's Supper on Holy Thursday and for the long passion reading on Good Friday. And on most of the Sundays of Easter—during the fifty days from Easter Sunday until Pentecost—the gospel of John is proclaimed at the liturgy.

THE DIFFERENCE BETWEEN THE BIBLE AND THE LECTIONARY The shape of the lectionary comes from the ancient church practice of *lectio continua,* a Latin term which describes the successive reading through books of the Bible from Sunday to Sunday. You can see such a *lectio continua* in practice if you flip through *At Home with the Word* and, for example, consider the gospel texts assigned to the Sundays from the Thirteenth Sunday in Ordinary Time, July 1, to the Feast of Christ the King, November 25. Though not every verse is included, you will notice that through these Sundays we move from chapter 9 of Luke to chapter 23.

You will find, moreover, that the first readings often echo some image, character or idea in the gospel, as is the church's intention. The second reading often stands on its own and comes from a letter of Paul or some other letter of the New Testament. You will notice, for example, that the second readings from July through November take us through Galatians, Colossians, Hebrews, First and Second Timothy and Thessalonians.

UNITY WITH OTHER CHRISTIAN CHURCHES IN THE WORD OF GOD The basic plan of the lectionary for Catholics is universal. The readings proclaimed in your church on a particular Sunday are the same as those proclaimed in Catholic churches all over the globe. The lectionary is one of the main things that makes our liturgy so "catholic," or universal.

But as time has passed, other Christian churches have adopted the Catholic lectionary also. So not only are the readings the same as those in other Catholic churches, but the revision of the Roman Catholic lectionary has been so well received that other churches have begun to follow its three-year lectionary cycle.

Catholics and their neighbors who attend other Christian churches often hear the same word of God proclaimed and preached in the Sunday gathering. Even though you may not talk about the Sunday readings with you neighbors and therefore haven't realized that your readers read the same lections and your preachers preach on the same scriptural texts, this is really a remarkable change when you consider how very far apart from one another Catholic and Protestant churches were before the Second Vatican Council.

The slight difference between the readings you'll find in *At Home with the Word 2001* and what is proclaimed on Sunday is a result of our efforts to highlight the scriptures shared by many Christian churches. The major parts of the readings will be secure, but there might be a few verses tacked on in *At Home with the Word* at the beginning or end of a reading to match those in the Revised Common Lectionary, which is used in many non–Catholic Christian churches. As always, when the page with the readings is short on space, a shorter version of a reading or two will be printed and the full citation will be provided at the end so that you can check out the fuller text in your Bible.

At the bottom of each right-hand column on the odd-numbered pages, you will find citations for the readings of the daily liturgy. When a reading is from the same book of the Bible as the reading from the day before, you will find only the citation of chapter and verse. When the book of the Bible changes from one day to the next, the full citation will be given.

We hope that your celebration of the liturgy in your parish is deepened by the preparation you will find in this book. Have a wonderful liturgical year being "at home with the Word" of God.

An Introduction to the Gospel of Luke

by Susan E. Myers

The gospel of Luke is an "orderly account" (1:3) of the birth, ministry, death and resurrection of Jesus, the Christ. The events of the gospel and its sequel, the Acts of the Apostles, take place within history, and the God who has been working among the people Israel continues to guide the Christian church. Throughout Luke and Acts, the Holy Spirit is active, guiding Jesus and empowering the church. Jesus is presented as a teacher who instructs his listeners in the life of discipleship as they travel together to Jerusalem.

AUTHORSHIP, STYLE AND PURPOSE The author of this two-part work is anonymous. The name "Luke," recalling a companion of Paul, was assigned later to give the work greater authority.

The author writes in the tradition of the Greek historians, seeking to provide a coherent account of events. The work is a unified narrative of stories gathered from other sources. The author makes the account as interesting as possible; Acts in particular reads like an adventure novel. Indeed, a good analogy might be a historical novel: facts, with details of speech and action added for greater interest. The author provides a faith account, proclaiming that Jesus is risen and exalted with God, and recounting the events that formed the Christian church. The account is not history as we know it today; Luke-Acts does not claim to be unbiased. Its goal is to move its readers to belief.

SOURCES, DATING AND RELATION TO JUDAISM The gospel of Luke was written decades after the events recounted in it. The words and deeds of Jesus were not written down at the time, and the earliest witnesses to his triumph over death did not record their experiences since they expected him to return in the near future. Instead, traditions about Jesus were transmitted orally. Eventually, some sayings of Jesus were recorded, and later, accounts of his life were written as gospels.

The author of Luke-Acts used the earlier gospel of Mark, following its general scheme and expanding it. The author used a source for sayings—often called Q—known also to the author of the gospel of Matthew, and a special source for the infancy story and a number of other unique stories. All this was skillfully woven into a compelling account of Jesus' life that draws the reader into it as a disciple of Jesus.

The gospel probably was written in the last decades of the first century (perhaps around 80). The author knows about the destruction of Jerusalem and the Temple in the year 70. The "salvation history" begun with the Hebrew people continues in the Christian community. Jerusalem is the goal of both Jesus and the reader throughout the gospel. In Acts, Jerusalem is the starting point of the proclamation of the Good News that goes even to the "ends of the earth." The author or the community he is writing to may have been "God-fearers," attracted to Judaism but not fully converted. The Judaism of Jesus and his first followers is central; this author suggests that only after the Jews rejected the gospel was it preached to the Gentiles.

THEMES OF THE GOSPEL The gospel of Luke contains many beloved stories of Jesus' life. It begins even before Jesus' birth, recounting the story of Mary and Elizabeth and providing hymns (the Magnificat and the Canticles of Zechariah and of Simeon) that have been part of the prayer life of Christians for centuries. Only in Luke-Acts do we read of the child Jesus in the Temple or of the ascension of Jesus. Several of Jesus' parables, such as the stories of the Prodigal Son and the Good Samaritan, are unique to this gospel as well.

Women figure prominently in the gospel of Luke. From this gospel we know that there were many women among Jesus' followers. Jesus visits his friends Martha and Mary, and, as in the other gospels, women are the first to find the empty tomb and to recognize that Jesus has vanquished death. Although we learn that women financially support Jesus' ministry, this gospel does not transform the lot of women. In fact, women generally appear in traditional domestic roles.

PORTRAIT OF JESUS Throughout the gospel, Jesus is a person of prayer. He often goes away to pray by himself, an act that usually precedes a decisive event. The Holy Spirit, by whom Mary conceives Jesus, descends upon him at his baptism and guides him throughout his ministry, until he bestows the Spirit upon his disciples after his exaltation with God.

Jesus is portrayed in the gospel of Luke as a man on a journey. His ministry begins in his home region of Galilee; then he sets out for the capital city of Jerusalem. On the long path to Jerusalem and his death, Jesus teaches his followers what it means to be his disciple, his student.

DISCIPLESHIP Although the gospel is set within history, Jesus teaches a certain detachment from the world to his followers. What is required is a life of total commitment, total faithfulness. Daily, the disciple of Jesus is to shoulder the cross, not as a weapon and not as a burden, but as part of the Christian journey.

CONCERN FOR THE DISENFRANCHISED The road of discipleship also involves commitment to those on the fringes of society. This gospel is very uncomfortable with the concentration of wealth in the hands of a few while others have need. All might and prestige are illusory; in the kingdom of God, the downtrodden will be rewarded and the powerful will be humbled. Justice is not simply a lofty ideal, but a demand of all who follow Jesus.

To convey this concern, the author includes a number of stories in which care and compassion are central. Jesus does not only preach compassion in such stories as the Good Samaritan, the Prodigal Son and the Rich Man and Lazarus. Indeed, he lives the ideal, comforting the women who follow his final path to death, forgiving the "good thief" on the cross and asking forgiveness for his persecutors. Being a disciple of Jesus involves living and loving as he did.

This order of prayer may be said upon waking
or before or during breakfast.

Lord, open my lips,
And my mouth will proclaim your praise.

The Sign of the Cross

In the name of the Father
and of the Son
and of the Holy Spirit.

Psalm 63:1–4, 5–8

O God, you are my God, I seek you,
I thirst for you;
my flesh faints for you,
as in a dry and weary land where no water is.
So I have looked upon you in the sanctuary,
beholding your power and glory.

Because your steadfast love is better than life,
my lips will praise you.
So I will bless you as long as I live;
I will lift up my hand and call on your name.

My mouth praises you with joyful lips,
when I think of you upon my bed,
and meditate on you in the watches of the night;
for you have been my help,
and in the shadow of your wings I sing for you.
My soul clings to you;
your right hand upholds me.

*One of the seasonal psalms throughout this book
may be prayed instead of Psalm 63.*

The Canticle of Zechariah

Bless'd be the God of Israel
who comes to set us free
and raises up new hope for us:
a Branch from David's tree.
So have the prophets long declared
that with a mighty arm
God would turn back our enemies
and all who wish us harm.

With promised mercy will God still
the covenant recall,
the oath once sworn to Abraham,
from foes to save us all;
that we might worship without fear
and offer lives of praise,
in holiness and righteousness
to serve God all our days.

My child, as prophet of the Lord
you will prepare the way,
to tell God's people they are saved
from sin's eternal sway.
Then shall God's mercy from on high
shine forth and never cease
to drive away the gloom of death
and lead us into peace.

*This canticle may be sung to the tune FOREST
GREEN or any other CMD tune, such as with the
hymn "I Sing the Almighty Power of God."*

The Lord's Prayer

*You may join hands with others or hold your
hands with palms facing upward while praying
the Lord's Prayer.*

11

E V E N I N G
prayer

This order of prayer may be said before or after dinner.

God, come to my assistance.
Lord, make haste to help me.

The Lighting of a Candle

*A candle may be lit to welcome the evening
while saying:*

Jesus Christ is the light of the world,
a light no darkness can overcome.

Psalm 113

Praise the Lord!
Praise, O servants of the Lord
praise the name of the Lord!
Blessed be the name of the Lord
from this time forth and for evermore!

From the rising of the sun to its setting
the name of the Lord is to be praised!
The Lord is high above all nations,
God's glory above the heavens!

Who is like the Lord our God,
who is seated on high,
who looks far down
upon the heavens and the earth?

God raises the poor from the dust,
and lifts the needy from the ash heap,
to make them sit with nobles,
with the nobles of God's people.

God gives the barren woman a home,
making her the joyous mother of children.
Praise the Lord!

The Canticle of Mary

My soul proclaims your greatness, Lord;
I sing my Savior's praise!
You looked upon my lowliness,
and I am full of grace.
Now ev'ry land and ev'ry age
this blessing shall proclaim—
great wonders you have done for me,
and holy is your name.

To all who live in holy fear
your mercy ever flows.
With mighty arm you dash the proud,
their scheming hearts expose.
The ruthless you have cast aside,
the lowly throned instead;
the hungry filled with all good things,
the rich sent off unfed.

To Israel, your servant blest,
your help is ever sure;
the promise to our parents made
their children will secure.
Sing glory to the Holy One,
give honor to the Word,
and praise the Pow'r of the Most High,
one God, by all adored.

*This canticle may be sung to the tune KINGSFOLD
or any other CMD tune, such as with the hymn "I
Heard the Voice of Jesus Say."*

Intercession and Lord's Prayer

*At day's end we offer our petitions in Jesus' name.
We make intercession for our church, our world,
our parish, our neighbors, our family and friends
and ourselves. We seal all our prayers with the
Lord's Prayer. In conclusion, those present may
exchange the sign of peace.*

N I G H T
p r a y e r

This order of prayer may be said before going to sleep.

God, come to my assistance.
Lord, make haste to help me.

Psalm 131

O Lord, my heart is not lifted up,
my eyes are not raised too high;
I do not occupy myself with things
too great and too marvelous for me.

But I have calmed and quieted my life,
like a weaned child with its mother;
I am like a weaned child.

O Israel, hope in the Lord
now and forever.

Or:

Psalm 134

Come, bless the Lord,
all you servants of the Lord,
who stand by night in the house of the Lord!

Lift up your hands in the holy place,
and bless the Lord!
May the Lord who made heaven and earth
bless you from Zion.

The Canticle of Simeon

Lord, now you let your servant go in peace;
your word has been fulfilled:

my own eyes have seen the salvation
which you have prepared in the sight
  of every people:

a light to reveal you to the nations
and the glory of your people Israel.

Invocation to Mary

The final prayer of the day is customarily to Mary.

Hail, holy Queen, Mother of mercy,
our life, our sweetness, and our hope!
To you we cry, the children of Eve;
to you we send up our sighs,
mourning and weeping in this land of exile.
Turn, then, most gracious advocate,
your eyes of mercy toward us;
lead us home at last
and show us the blessed fruit
of your womb, Jesus:
O clement, O loving, O sweet Virgin Mary.

Or:

Hail Mary, full of grace,
The Lord is with you!
Blessed are you among women,
and blessed is the fruit of your womb, Jesus.
Holy Mary, Mother of God,
pray for us sinners,
now and at the hour of our death.

Or during the season of Easter:

Queen of heaven, rejoice, alleluia.
The Son whom you merited to bear, alleluia,
has risen as he said, alleluia.

Rejoice and be glad, O Virgin Mary, alleluia!
For the Lord has truly risen, alleluia.

The Sign of the Cross

*We end the day the way we began it,
with the sign of the cross.*

May almighty God give us a restful night
  and a peaceful death,
the Father and the Son and the Holy Spirit.
Amen.

FRIDAY
prayer

Friday is our weekly fast day, our day of special prayer, fasting and almsgiving.

Lord, by your cross and resurrection
   you have set us free.
You are the savior of the world.

Psalm 145:13–18, 21

The Lord's words are faithful.
The Lord's deeds are gracious.
The Lord upholds all who are falling,
and raises up all who are bowed down.

The eyes of all look to you,
and you give them their food in due season.
You open your hand,
you satisfy the desire of every living thing.

All the Lord's ways are just,
all the Lord's doings are kind.
The Lord is near to all who call,
to all who call upon the Lord in truth.

My mouth will speak the praise of the Lord;
let all flesh bless God's holy name forever and ever.

Prayer of the Day

All praise be yours, God our Creator,
as we wait in joyful hope
for the flowering of justice
and the fullness of peace.

All praise for this day, this Friday.
By our weekly fasting and prayer,
cast out the spirit of war, of fear and mistrust,
and make us grow hungry for human kindness,
thirsty for solidarity
with all the people of your dear earth.

May all our prayers, our fasting and our deeds
be done in the name of Jesus. Amen.

The wedding feast of the Lamb has begun,
and his bride is prepared to welcome him.

Psalm 100

Make a joyful noise to the Lord, all the lands!
Serve the Lord with gladness!
Come into God's presence with singing!

Know that the Lord, who made us, is God.
We are the Lord's;
we are the people of God,
the sheep of God's pasture.

Enter God's gates with thanksgiving,
and God's courts with praise!
Give thanks and bless God's name!

For the Lord is good;
God's steadfast love endures for ever,
God's faithfulness to all generations.

Song of the Day

O Lord, in whom this day first dawned,
who clothe creation wondrously,
that you should clothe yourself in flesh
is yet more wonderful to see.

Now raised to heights where names all fail,
proclaimed "The Lord," O risen Christ,
in you alone we find our life,
the sun which set that we might rise.

Most Holy God, Word, Spirit: One,
outpoured in love eternally;
you love us unto death that we
might share your own divinity!

Sunday is our weekly feast day.
We rejoice in creation and
assemble to hear the word of God
and give thanks and praise.

Prayers from the Mass

Confiteor

I confess to almighty God,
and to you, my brothers and sisters,
that I have sinned through my own fault
in my thoughts and in my words,
in what I have done,
and in what I have failed to do;
and I ask blessed Mary, ever virgin,
all the angels and saints,
and you, my brothers and sisters,
to pray for me to the Lord our God.

Gloria

Glory to God in the highest,
and peace to his people on earth.
Lord God, heavenly King,
almighty God and Father,
    we worship you, we give you thanks,
    we praise you for your glory.
Lord Jesus Christ, only Son of the Father,
Lord God, Lamb of God,
you take away the sin of the world:
    have mercy on us;
you are seated at the right hand of the Father:
    receive our prayer.

For you alone are the Holy One,
you alone are the Lord,
you alone are the Most High,
    Jesus Christ,
    with the Holy Spirit,
    in the glory of God the Father. Amen.

Nicene Creed

We believe in one God,
   the Father, the Almighty,
   maker of heaven and earth,
   of all that is seen and unseen.

We believe in one Lord, Jesus Christ,
   the only Son of God,
   eternally begotten of the Father,
   God from God, Light from Light,
   true God from true God,
   begotten, not made,
     one in Being with the Father.
Through him all things were made.
For us and for our salvation
     he came down from heaven:
by the power of the Holy Spirit
     he was born of the Virgin Mary,
     and became man.
For our sake he was crucified
     under Pontius Pilate;
   he suffered, died, and was buried.
   On the third day he rose again
     in fulfillment of the scriptures;
   he ascended into heaven and is seated
     at the right hand of the Father.
He will come again in glory
     to judge the living and the dead,
     and his kingdom will have no end.

We believe in the Holy Spirit, the Lord,
     the giver of life,
   who proceeds from the Father and the Son.
   With the Father and the Son
     he is worshiped and glorified.
   He has spoken through the prophets.
We believe in one holy catholic
     and apostolic Church.
We acknowledge one baptism
     for the forgiveness of sins.
We look for the resurrection of the dead,
     and the life of the world to come.
Amen.

Preface Acclamation

Holy, holy, holy Lord, God of power and might,
heaven and earth are full of your glory.
   Hosanna in the highest.
Blessed is he who comes in the name
     of the Lord.
Hosanna in the highest.

Memorial Acclamation

Christ has died,
Christ is risen,
Christ will come again.
or:
Dying you destroyed our death,
rising you restored our life.
Lord Jesus, come in glory.
or:
When we eat this bread and drink this cup,
we proclaim your death, Lord Jesus,
until you come in glory.
or:
Lord, by your cross and resurrection
you have set us free.
You are the Savior of the world.

Lord's Prayer

Our Father, who art in heaven,
hallowed be thy name;
thy kingdom come;
thy will be done on earth as it is in heaven

Give us this day our daily bread;
and forgive us our tresspasses
as we forgive those who tresspass against us;
and lead us not into temptation,
but deliver us from evil. Amen.

Communion

Lord, I am not worthy to receive you,
but only say the word and I shall be healed.

ADVENT

Maranatha! Come, Lord Jesus!

Let me hear what God the Lord will speak,
for God will speak peace to the people,
to the faithful, to those who turn to God
    in their hearts.

Surely salvation is at hand
    for those who fear the Lord,
that glory may dwell in our land.
Steadfast love and faithfulness
    will meet;
righteousness and peace
    will kiss each other.

Faithfulness will spring up
    from the ground,
and righteousness will look down
    from the sky.
The Lord will give what is good,
and our land will yield its increase.

Righteousness will go before the Lord,
and make a path for God's footsteps.

—*Psalm 85:8–13*

In the long nights of December,
we listen, Lord, for the words you speak.
How can we hear you
when the markets and machines are so loud,
when the sellers and the entertainers
clamor for our every attention?
Still we would listen for you
and hear of wars so we may long for peace,
and hear of oppression
so we may long for justice,
and hear of hunger so we may long for you.
Then make a path, O God,
so righteousness and peace
shall meet and shall kiss
and with that kiss, with that glory,
shall we and this good creation
praise and bless your coming.

—*Prayer of the Season*

READING I *Jeremiah 33:14–16*

The days are surely coming, says the Lord, when I will fulfill the promise I made to the house of Israel and the house of Judah. In those days and at that time I will cause a righteous Branch to spring up for David, who shall execute justice and righteousness in the land. In those days Judah will be saved and Jerusalem will live in safety. And this is the name by which it will be called: "The Lord is our righteousness."

READING II *1 Thessalonians 3:9–13*

How can we thank God enough for you in return for all the joy that we feel before our God because of you? Night and day we pray most earnestly that we may see you face to face and restore whatever is lacking in your faith.

Now may that very God, our Father, and our Lord Jesus direct our way to you. And may the Lord make you increase and abound in love for one another and for all, just as we abound in love for you. And may the Lord so strengthen your hearts in holiness that you may be blameless before our God and Father at the coming of our Lord Jesus with all his saints.

[Roman Catholic: 1 Thessalonians 3:12—4:2]

GOSPEL *Luke 21:25–36*

Jesus said:

"There will be signs in the sun, the moon, and the stars, and on the earth distress among nations confused by the roaring of the sea and the waves. People will faint from fear and foreboding of what is coming upon the world, for the powers of the heavens will be shaken. Then they will see 'the Son-of-Man coming in a cloud' with power and great glory. Now when these things begin to take place, stand up and raise your heads, because your redemption is drawing near."

Then Jesus told them a parable: "Look at the fig tree and all the trees; as soon as they sprout leaves you can see for yourselves and know that summer is already near. So also, when you see these things taking place, you know that the dominion of God is near. Truly I tell you, this generation will not pass away until all things have taken place. Heaven and earth will pass away, but my words will not pass away.

"Be on guard so that your hearts are not weighed down with dissipation and drunkenness and the worries of this life, and that day does not catch you unexpectedly, like a trap. For it will come upon all who live on the face of the whole earth. Be alert at all times, praying that you may have the strength to escape all these things that will take place, and to stand before the Son-of-Man."

[Roman Catholic: Luke 21:25–28, 34–36]

Friday, December 8, 2000

IMMACULATE CONCEPTION OF THE VIRGIN MARY

Genesis 3:9–15, 20 *Eve is "the mother of the living."*

Ephesians 1:3–6, 11–12 *God chose us before the world began.*

Luke 1:26–38 *I am the servant of the Lord.*

Sin means separation from God. We believe Mary was never separated from God from the moment of her conception in her mother's womb. On this Advent feast of Mary, her "yes" undoes Eve's "no." Mary is our new Eve, the mother of the living God.

REFLECTION

Luke used several sources of information to compile his gospel. One of these sources was the earlier writing that we know as the gospel of Mark, which was probably put together before the destruction of the Temple in Jerusalem in the year 70. Luke takes the core of Mark 13 and reworks it in light of the history of his day after the destruction of the Temple.

Today's gospel passage is an example of what is known as apocalyptic literature—a particular style of writing that uses dramatic images to convey a sense of hope to readers. This passage was written at a time when the early Christians were living under Roman occupation. Luke employs a variety of images to encourage his readers: The Reign of God is at hand. Take heart! Be alert!

Apocalyptic literature provides both challenge and comfort. Jesus spent his ministry showing his followers the way to live in God's love. Luke adopts these challenges and emphasizes that the people should prepare for the coming Reign, and should not be sidetracked by the attractions or difficulties of this world. We are to remain focused on Christ's return. The coming of the Reign of God is more important than the destruction of the Jerusalem Temple. Christians are not to stay in the past but are to remain focused on the future.

The message of comfort for first-century readers involves a developing awareness of the presence of Christ shining through the distress of an oppressive political regime. Those who follow the way of Christ have nothing to fear. Others may be alarmed, but the faithful can remain steadfast in their belief that Christ the deliverer is near.

■ **What calamities do you face in your own life? What oppressive regimes do you find ruling you? How do you strive to discover the coming of Christ despite these calamities?**

■ **How can you allow Christ to ease your fears? What points of Christ's message can be a source of comfort for you in your fears?**

PRACTICE OF FAITH

STARS OF NIGHT. An ancient hymn of the Roman church welcomes the season: Creator of the stars of night,/your people's everlasting light!/O Christ, Redeemer of us all/we pray you hear us when we call.

In sorrow that the ancient curse/should doom to death a universe,/you came, O Savior, to set free/your own, in glorious liberty.

Come, Sun and Savior, to embrace/our gloomy world, its weary race./As groom to bride and bride to groom,/the wedding chamber, Mary's womb!

Learn the melody. Then go outside after dark and sing to the stars. Light one candle on your Advent wreath this week.

PRACTICE OF HOPE

BE ALERT. When I was a child, Dad and I often walked to Mass together. The problem was, he never moved fast enough for me. As I rushed along, he would just smile and say, "Where's the fire, darlin'?" It was exasperating. But now I understand what he was trying to tell me: Don't be so focused on where you're going that you forget to see who and what is around you along the way.

That has special meaning for me, especially during Advent. Children hope for Santa Claus and neat presents; adults hope they can get everything done in time and that their families will gather in peace. All of us quietly hope that Christ will come into our lives in new ways. Before we wear ourselves out this Advent, perhaps we should stop and reflect: "Where's the fire?"

PRACTICE OF CHARITY

DISTRESS AMONG NATIONS. To many who live in the nations of Africa, a plague of biblical proportions is decimating the population and leaving millions of children orphaned. According to the United Nations Children's Fund, AIDS killed some 1.4 million people in eastern and southern Africa in 1998, overtaking war as the leading cause of death in the region. Nearly 23 million people were infected with HIV in 1999. By 2005, the death toll could reach 13,000 people a day. The high cost of the drugs used to treat the illness has been an insurmountable obstacle.

For more information about AIDS in Africa, contact the Global Health Council's Global AIDS Program, 1701 K Street NW, Suite 600, Washington DC 20006; 1-202-833-5900; www.globalhealthcouncil.org.

WEEKDAY READINGS (Mo) Isaiah 2:1–5; (Tu) 11:1–10; (We) 25:6–10; (Th) 26:1–6; (Fr) Immaculate Conception, see box; (Sa) Isaiah 30:19–21, 23–26

READING I *Baruch 5:1–9*

Take off the garment of your sorrow and affliction,
  O Jerusalem,
and put on forever the beauty of the glory from God.
Put on the robe of the righteousness
    that comes from God;
put on your head the diadem of the glory
    of the Everlasting;
for God will show your splendor
    everywhere under heaven.
For God will give you evermore the name,
"Righteous Peace, Godly Glory."
Arise, O Jerusalem, stand upon the height;
    look toward the east,
and see your children gathered from west and east
    at the word of the Holy One,
    rejoicing that God has remembered them.
For they went out from you on foot,
    led away by their enemies;
but God will bring them back to you,
carried in glory, as on a royal throne.
For God has ordered that every high mountain
    and the everlasting hills be made low
    and the valleys filled up, to make level ground,
    so that Israel may walk safely in the glory of God.
The woods and every fragrant tree
    have shaded Israel at God's command.
For God will lead Israel with joy,
    in the light of divine glory,
    with the mercy and righteousness
    that come from God.
[Revised Common Lectionary: Malachi 3:1–4]

READING II *Philippians 1:3–11*

I thank my God every time I remember you, constantly praying with joy in every one of my prayers for all of you, because of your sharing in the gospel from the first day until now. I am confident of this, that the one who began a good work among you will bring it to completion by the day of Jesus Christ. It is right for me to think this way about all of you, because you hold me in your heart, for all of you share in God's grace with me, both in my imprisonment and in the defense and confirmation of the gospel. For God is my witness, how I long for all of you with the compassion of Christ Jesus.

And this is my prayer, that your love may overflow more and more with knowledge and full insight to help you to determine what is best, so that in the day of Christ you may be pure and blameless, having produced the harvest of righteousness that comes through Jesus Christ for the glory and praise of God. [Roman Catholic: Philippians 1:4–6, 8–11]

GOSPEL *Luke 3:1–6*

In the fifteenth year of the reign of Emperor Tiberius, when Pontius Pilate was governor of Judea, and Herod was ruler of Galilee, and his brother Philip ruler of the region of Ituraea and Trachonitis, and Lysanias ruler of Abilene, during the high priesthood of Annas and Caiaphas, the word of God came to John son of Zechariah in the wilderness. And John went into all the region around the Jordan, proclaiming a baptism of repentance for the forgiveness of sins, as it is written in the book of the words of the prophet Isaiah,
    "The voice of one crying out in the wilderness:
    'Prepare the way of the Lord,
        make straight the paths of the Lord.'
    'Every valley shall be filled,
        and every mountain and hill shall be made low,
    and the crooked shall be made straight,
        and the rough ways made smooth;
    and all flesh shall see the salvation of God.'"

R E F L E C T I O N

We often think of God's coming into the world either as an event of the past or as one yet to come in the distant (usually far distant) future. Our own time seems to be in between already and not yet. There is a tension between what is happening in our own lives and how we believe God's kingdom on earth will be manifested.

During Advent we are invited, even urged, to think of our lives and our place in history as opportunities for God's coming into the world. Advent has been called a second "Our Father": during Advent we joyfully look forward to the coming of God's kingdom on earth as it is in heaven. We are to remember, as the prophet Baruch exhorted the Israelites, that our sorrow and struggles are not the final word. Baruch was writing to a community that was devastated: Nebuchadnezzar had destroyed the Temple in Jerusalem and scattered the children of Israel, sending them off in all directions as slaves. Yet the Israelites are told to stand upon the height, put on a crown, and show forth the splendor of God.

Paul writes to the Philippians from prison, yet his letter overflows with joy and hope. His own confinement does not alter his conviction that Christ will bring to fruition the good work that the community has begun. We find a similar faith and hopeful expectation in the gospel. Luke carefully situates John the Baptist in a particular historical context, and several of the leaders of the day plot John's death. Yet John is not deterred from proclaiming his message. Hearkening back to the words of Isaiah, John proclaims that obstacles to the way of God will be removed. Mountains and hills will be brought low; the rough will be made smooth.

These prophecies are no less true for us today. Through the situations of our particular lives, God's plan for creation continues. We are bearers of the message of God's salvation, and in our Advent we try to show forth the splendor of God in our day and time.

■ **All of us experience pain and struggle in our lives. Imagine the prophet Baruch is speaking to you. What comforts you or transforms suffering for you?**

■ **How is hope different from optimism, or from seeing the world through rose-colored glasses? How can you cultivate the virtue of hope in your life?**

PRACTICE OF FAITH

SANTA LUCIA. This Wednesday we remember Saint Lucy, who was beheaded during the fourth-century persecutions under the emperor Diocletian, in Sicily. Her name means "light." In times past, all across northern Europe, bonfires called "Lucia fires" were burned on the night of December 13. People gathered around them and played musical instruments or banged on pots and pans to chase away the darkness and coax back the sun. Build a fire in your fireplace or barbecue. Pray for Christ to return in glory. Use these words, among the very last in the Bible: "Amen. Come, Lord Jesus!" Contemplate a flame and repeat this prayer over and over again until it flows in sync with your breathing. Light two candles on your Advent wreath.

PRACTICE OF HOPE

I THANK MY GOD. Have you heard the saying, "Gratitude is an attitude"? It's a tough attitude to get into sometimes. It's very easy to get caught up in the struggles and sorrows of life and forget the joyful little things that happen each day.

A young woman in Bristol, Indiana, was determined not to let that happen. When she was 13, Kimberley Stokely began a "gratitude journal," writing down five things she was grateful for each day. A small gesture, but it touched the lives of the people around her. It would have made a difference even if she hadn't shown it to anyone. When you seek out goodness and give thanks in a conscious way, it becomes part of your life. Once that happens, you pass it on by example. Who knows where it could lead?

PRACTICE OF CHARITY

INTERNATIONAL HUMAN RIGHTS DAY. Advent is a time of "preparing the way," of moving the world toward the reign of God. This undoubtedly includes the protection of human rights throughout the world. Today marks the anniversary of the adoption of the Universal Declaration of Human Rights by the United Nations in 1948. While the Declaration asserts some 30 universal human rights, including the rights to life, health care, education and privacy, many of the world's people suffer under systems of law or economics that prevent the exercise of their rights

Join Human Rights Watch in its effort to promote respect for human rights throughout the world: 350 5th Avenue, 34th Floor, New York, NY 10118-3299; 1-212-290-4700; www.hrw.org.

WEEKDAY READINGS (Mo) Isaiah 35:1–10; (Tu) Zechariah 2:14–17; (We) Isaiah 40:25–31; (Th) 41:13–20; (Fr) 48:17–19; (Sa) Sirach 48:1–4, 9–11

READING I *Zephaniah 3:14–20*

Sing aloud, O daughter Zion;
    shout, O Israel!
Rejoice and exult with all your heart,
    O daughter Jerusalem!
The LORD has taken away
        the judgments against you,
    and has turned away your enemies.
The Sovereign of Israel, the LORD, is in your midst;
    you shall fear disaster no more.
On that day it shall be said to Jerusalem:
Do not fear, O Zion;
    do not let your hands grow weak.
The LORD, your God, is in your midst,
    a warrior who gives victory;
the LORD will rejoice over you with gladness,
    and will renew you with love;
the LORD will exult over you with loud singing
    as on a day of festival.
I will remove disaster from you,
    so that you will not bear reproach for it.
I will deal with all your oppressors at that time.
And I will save the lame
    and gather the outcast,
and I will change their shame into praise
    and renown in all the earth.
At that time I will bring you home,
    at the time when I gather you;
for I will make you renowned and praised
    among all the peoples of the earth,
when I restore your fortunes
    before your eyes, says the LORD.
[Roman Catholic: Zephaniah 3:14–18]

READING II *Philippians 4:4–7*

Rejoice in the Lord always; again I will say, Rejoice. Let your gentleness be known to everyone. The Lord is near. Do not worry about anything, but in everything by prayer and supplication with thanksgiving let your requests be made known to God. And the peace of God, which surpasses all understanding, will guard your hearts and your minds in Christ Jesus.

GOSPEL *Luke 3:7–18*

John said to the crowds that came out to be baptized by him, "You brood of vipers! Who warned you to flee from the wrath to come? Bear fruits worthy of repentance. Do not begin to say to yourselves, 'We have Abraham as our ancestor'; for I tell you, God is able from these stones to raise up children to Abraham. Even now the ax is lying at the root of the trees; every tree therefore that does not bear good fruit is cut down and thrown into the fire."

And the crowds asked John, "What then should we do?" In reply he said to them, "Whoever has two coats must share with anyone who has none; and whoever has food must do likewise." Even tax collectors came to be baptized, and they asked him, "Teacher, what should we do?" John said to them, "Collect no more than the amount prescribed for you." Soldiers also asked him, "And we, what should we do?" He said to them, "Do not extort money from anyone by threats or false accusation, and be satisfied with your wages."

As the people were filled with expectation, and all were questioning in their hearts concerning John, whether he might be the Messiah, John answered all of them by saying, "I baptize you with water; but one who is more powerful than I is coming, the thong of whose sandals I am not worthy to untie. He will baptize you with the Holy Spirit and fire. With a winnowing fork in hand, he will clear the threshing floor and gather the wheat into his granary, burning the chaff with unquenchable fire."

So, with many other exhortations, John proclaimed the good news to the people.
[Roman Catholic: Luke 3:10–18]

REFLECTION

This passage from Luke is fashioned as a piece of prophecy. The people for whom Luke wrote his gospel were primarily Gentiles who lived outside Palestine. They were not very familiar with Jewish traditions or the religious background of the Jewish community. The prophets had been immensely important to the formation of that community, boldly calling the people back to covenant loyalty with their God. Luke provides his Gentile readers with a passage that follows in the tradition of Israelite prophecy.

The prophets of Israel typically had a personal following known as a "school" or "guild," and it seems that John the Baptist had a similar following. John's followers raise the question of whether John might be the Messiah. To counter any such notions, John contrasts the baptism he offers to that Jesus will provide, referring to Jesus as one who baptizes not just with water but with spirit and fire. It is John, then, who prepares the foundation on which Jesus shall build.

One point in this passage may ring in the ears of modern readers preparing to share food with the needy at Christmas. The prevailing thought at John's time was that any given locality was allotted only a certain amount of any particular good; no more could be expected, and what there was had to be shared. For example, if one person had three plows and two other people in the area needed plows but had none, it was expected that the person with three would share. One was to share goods with others in the area because they were one's "neighbors." When John tells his listeners to share food with those in need, he is encouraging them to develop right relationships with one another, and is planting a seed for Jesus' later expansion on who the neighbor is.

■ **Who are the prophets in your life? Who are those who call you back to a covenant with the Lord? How do you live like a prophet?**

■ **How can you expand your vision of community and neighbor in anticipation of Jesus' teachings that you will hear throughout this liturgical year?**

PRACTICE OF FAITH

O! O! O! Today the church begins the great "O!" prayers. These antiphons originally were sung at evening prayer and are ageless sighs of deep longing. Each begins with a striking name for God: O Wisdom! O Lord and Ruler! O Root of Jesse! O Key of David! O Dawn of Justice! O Desire of Nations! And finally, ultimately, "O Emmanuel." This famous name for Jesus means "God with us."

Reflect on these names for God. Each night when you pray at your evening meal, call God by one of these names. Then Christmas can be for you a season of joy and wonder—of O! O! O! instead of just Ho! Ho! Ho! Light three candles on your Advent wreath tonight.

PRACTICE OF HOPE

I WILL BRING YOU HOME. Safe, affordable housing is a challenge for many people, especially the older members of our communities who are no longer able to keep their homes. The American Province of the Notre Dame Sisters took this problem to heart—and into their motherhouse. The women decided to raze one of the buildings on their grounds in Omaha and build two housing developments for seniors on fixed incomes. The result is 77 one-bedroom apartments and a new ministry called Seven Oaks of Florence. Residents and Notre Dame Sisters say many new friendships have been forged since the first building opened in 1997. Seven Oaks has brought new life to all concerned.

PRACTICE OF CHARITY

WHOEVER HAS FOOD. The words of John the Baptist are as challenging today as they were to his hearers: "Whoever has two coats must share with anyone who has none; and whoever has food must do likewise." Two thousand years later, millions of people still lack enough food to provide them with basic nutrition, while large amounts of food are thrown away every day.

Food Not Bombs (3145 Geary Boulevard #12, San Francisco CA 94118; 1-800-884-1136) is an all-volunteer organization that provides vegetarian meals and political support to low-income and homeless people through its chapters in 50 communities in North America and Europe. Find out if there is a chapter in your area, or find another organization that is committed both to providing for the hungry in a respectful manner and to changing the structures that keep people in poverty.

WEEKDAY READINGS (Mo) Jeremiah 23:5–8; (Tu) Judges 13:2–7, 24–25; (We) Isaiah 7:10–14; (Th) Song of Solomon 2:8–14 or Zephaniah 3:14–18; (Fr) 1 Samuel 1:24–28; (Sa) Malachi 3:1–4, 23–24

READING I *Micah 5:2–5*

But you, O Bethlehem of Ephrathah,
    who are one of the little clans of Judah,
from you shall come forth for me
    one who is to rule in Israel,
whose origin is from of old,
    from ancient days.
Therefore they shall be given up until the time
    when she who is in labor has brought forth;
then the rest of the ruler's kindred shall return
    to the people of Israel.
And the ruler shall stand and feed his flock
    in the strength of the LORD,
    in the majesty of the name of the LORD his God.
And they shall live secure, for now the ruler
    shall be great
    to the ends of the earth;
and he shall be the one of peace.

READING II *Hebrews 10:5–10*

Consequently, when Christ came into the world, he said,
    "Sacrifices and offerings you have not desired,
        but a body you have prepared for me;
    in burnt offerings and sin offerings
        you have taken no pleasure.
    Then I said, 'See, God, I have come to do
        your will, O God'
    (in the scroll of the book it is written of me)."
    When Christ said above, "You have neither desired nor taken pleasure in sacrifices and offerings and burnt offerings and sin offerings" (these are offered according to the law), then he added, "See, I have come to do your will." Christ abolishes the first in order to establish the second. And it is by God's will that we have been sanctified through the offering of the body of Jesus Christ once for all.

GOSPEL *Luke 1:39–55*

In those days Mary set out and went with haste to a Judean town in the hill country, where she entered the house of Zechariah and greeted Elizabeth. When Elizabeth heard Mary's greeting, the child leaped in her womb. And Elizabeth was filled with the Holy Spirit and exclaimed with a loud cry, "Blessed are you among women, and blessed is the fruit of your womb. And why has this happened to me, that the mother of my Lord comes to me? For as soon as I heard the sound of your greeting, the child in my womb leaped for joy. And blessed is she who believed that there would be a fulfillment of what was spoken to her by the Lord."
And Mary said,
    "My soul magnifies the Lord,
    and my spirit rejoices in God my Savior,
    who has looked with favor on me, a lowly servant.
    Surely, from now on all generations
        will call me blessed;
    for the Mighty One has done great things for me:
    holy is the name of the Lord,
    whose mercy is for the God-fearing
    from generation to generation.
    The arm of the Lord is filled with strength,
    scattering the proud in the thoughts
        of their hearts.
    God has brought down the powerful
        from their thrones,
    and lifted up the lowly;
    God has filled the hungry with good things,
    and sent the rich away empty.
    God has helped Israel, the Lord's servant,
    in remembrance of mercy,
    according to the promise God made
        to our ancestors,
    to Abraham and to his descendants forever."
[Roman Catholic: Luke 1:39–45]

REFLECTION

The gospel passage today is a literary masterpiece that holds an important place in the tradition of the church. Elizabeth's greeting is the root from which the prayer commonly referred to as the "Hail Mary" grew. The hymn that Mary proclaims is the Magnificat, a title that comes from the Latin for the first line. This passage is an integral part of the Evening Prayer of the church and is recited each evening by many people all over the world.

This hymn is a song of reversal, challenging to the powerful and mighty of this world. In fact, it is so challenging to the leaders of some South American countries that its public recitation has been banned in some places. The song proclaims the reversal of Mary's state from lowliness to exaltation, then exalts God's involvement in other such reversals in the past and present. The hymn climaxes with a declaration of God's mercy in the fulfillment of the promise that was made to Abraham so long ago. In a way, Mary herself embodies the history of the Israelites: God's mercy has taken her out of the desert of her own poverty and made her the promised land in which the seed of God takes life.

For a modern perspective, take a walk in Mary's sandals. Imagine a pregnant young woman whose family sends her to stay with her cousin for a while. It would have taken Mary four days to walk from Nazareth in Galilee to a village in Judea. Luke states that she was alone in this trek, which was quite unusual for a female in that place and time. This solitude amplifies Mary's loneliness and fear. She must have felt alone, frightened and abandoned on the long trek to see Elizabeth, but upon arrival her despondency turns into joy. Elizabeth's child leaps as the two women meet, just as David leapt before the ark of the covenant. Elizabeth and her unborn baby recognize the Christ within the young Mary. Because of Elizabeth's hospitality and joy, Mary realizes the role of God in her life. It is this realization that makes her burst into song, proclaiming the greatness of the Lord. Mary and Elizabeth have such a special relationship that God is proclaimed within it.

■ Is there a specific prayer that is special to you? How can your prayer bring a reversal in your life?

■ Who would you travel so far to see? Who helps you see Jesus in yourself? Who is your Elizabeth?

PRACTICE OF FAITH

GIVING GIFTS. Gift-giving at Christmas is an ancient custom. Some say it comes from the magi themselves—those mysterious strangers who brought to Christ gifts of gold, frankincense and myrrh. In a consumer culture, gift-giving sometimes becomes a frenzy of tearing open piles of stuff. But there's more to it! Giving the gift, savoring it, and thanking the giver are all parts of this great experience.

If you can, decide with your household or friends that you will exchange one gift (maybe two) tonight and then again every day until they are all opened or until January 6, whichever comes first. If this can't work, at least make sure that everyone—especially the children—opens each gift carefully and thanks the giver before going on to the next package. Light all four candles on your Advent wreath tonight.

PRACTICE OF HOPE

THEY SHALL LIVE SECURE. In preparation for Jubilee 2000, we were asked to consider taking a pledge for charity, justice and peace, developed by the U.S. bishops. If you haven't taken it—or haven't heard of it yet—there is still time, since the jubilee will be observed through the first weekend in January 2001. The pledge is worthwhile even beyond that date, however. It asks people to pray for greater justice and peace, to reach out across boundaries of religion, race and gender, to live justly, and to serve those who are poor and vulnerable. Not only can these actions make a difference in our lives, but they also can give new hope and life to people we do not know. For more information on the Jubilee Pledge and opportunities for action, visit www.nccbuscc.org.

PRACTICE OF CHARITY

LIFTING UP THE LOWLY. Mary's words are a challenge to any society that does not provide for the poor. Her hymn is hard to misunderstand: God stands with the poor and brings down the powerful.

The Catholic Campaign for Human Development reports that 7.7 million American families, one in nine, live below the poverty line, while 9.5 million Americans work full- or part-time and still live below the poverty line. Support legislation in your area that mandates a living wage, considered to be approximately $7.60 an hour in 1999. Write your elected representatives in support of an increase in the federal minimum wage. Your representative can be reached at the U.S. House of Representatives, Washington DC 20515; the address for senators is U.S. Senate, Washington DC 20510.

WEEKDAY READINGS (Mo) Christmas; (Tu) Acts 6:8–10; 7:54–59; (We) 1 John 1:1–4; (Th) 1:5—2:2; (Fr) 2:3–11; (Sa) 2:12–17

CHRISTMAS

All creatures a choir!

O sing to the Lord a new song,
for the Lord has done marvelous things!
God's right hand and holy arm
have gotten the victory.

The Lord has remembered
   steadfast love and faithfulness
to the house of Israel.
All the ends of the earth have seen
the victory of our God.

Make a joyful noise to the Lord,
   all the earth;
break forth into joyous song
   and sing praises!
Sing praises to the Lord with the lyre,
with the lyre and the sound of melody!
With trumpets and the sound
   of the horn
make a joyful noise before the Ruler,
   the Lord!

Let the sea roar, and all that fills it;
the world and those who dwell in it!
Let the floods clap their hands;
let the hills sing for joy together
   before the Lord.

—Psalm 98:1, 3–8

When people witness deeds like these —
mercy winning victories
and justice welcomed
   in the public places—
then the earth itself will be an orchestra
and all creatures a choir,
and we shall sing together a song
that announces you,
God of poor shepherds and stargazers.
Rehearse us now in that Christmas song:
Like those shepherds may we know where
   to look,
like the magi may we know
   when to listen to the powerful
and when to mere dreams.
Come, Lord, and lift us up in song.

— Prayer of the Season

READING I *Isaiah 9:2–7*

The people who walked in darkness
  have seen a great light;
those who lived in a land of deep darkness—
  on them light has shined.
You have multiplied the nation,
  you have increased its joy;
they rejoice before you
  as with joy at the harvest,
  as people exult when dividing plunder.
For the yoke of their burden,
  and the bar across their shoulders,
  the rod of their oppressor,
  you have broken as on the day of Midian.
For all the boots of the tramping warriors
  and all the garments rolled in blood
  shall be burned as fuel for the fire.
For a child has been born for us,
  a son given to us;
authority rests upon his shoulders;
  and he is named
  Wonderful Counselor, Mighty God,
  Everlasting Father, Prince of Peace.

His authority shall grow continually,
  and there shall be endless peace
for the throne and dominion of David,
  to establish and uphold it
with justice and with righteousness
  from this time onward and forevermore.
The zeal of the LORD of hosts will do this.

READING II *Titus 2:11–14*

The grace of God has appeared, bringing salvation to all, training us to renounce impiety and worldly passions, and in the present age to live lives that are self-controlled, upright, and godly, while we wait for the blessed hope and the manifestation of the glory of our great God and Savior, Jesus Christ.

It is Jesus Christ who gave himself for us to might redeem us from all iniquity and purify for himself a people of his own who are zealous for good deeds.

GOSPEL *Luke 2:1–14*

In those days a decree went out from Emperor Augustus that all the world should be registered. This was the first registration and was taken while Quirinius was governor of Syria. All went to their own towns to be registered. Joseph also went from the town of Nazareth in Galilee to Judea, to the city of David called Bethlehem, because he was descended from the house and family of David. He went to be registered with Mary, to whom he was engaged and who was expecting a child. While they were there, the time came for her to deliver her child. And she gave birth to her firstborn son and wrapped him in bands of cloth, and laid him in a manger, because there was no place for them in the inn.

In that region there were shepherds living in the fields, keeping watch over their flock by night. Then an angel of the Lord stood before them, and the glory of the Lord shone around them, and they were terrified.

But the angel said to them, "Do not be afraid; for see—I am bringing you good news of great joy for all the people: to you is born this day in the city of David a Savior, who is the Messiah, the Lord. This will be a sign for you: you will find a child wrapped in bands of cloth and lying in a manger." And suddenly there was with the angel a multitude of the heavenly host, praising God and saying, "Glory to God in the highest heaven, and on earth peace among those whom God favors!"

REFLECTION

Who ever heard of light coming from darkness? Who would think of a heavy yoke being broken? What sort of little child would be addressed as Mighty God? These images of reversal from the first reading pave the way for the amazing reversals in the gospel. The shepherds we hear of in the gospel were the lowly underclass, often considered thieves because they grazed their animals on other people's property. They rarely bathed, and they spent long periods away from their families taking care of the sheep. The gospel passage unites this earthy lot with the unearthly angelic messengers. The manger, the place where animals were fed, is united with a family of dignity, a family of the royal house of David. A newborn baby is identified as the Messiah. Even popular images of the Christmas event depict opposites uniting. Donkeys would never be stabled with cattle, yet most of our manger scenes have both animals happily together. The coming together of supposed opposites highlights the significance of God becoming human. It makes clear that with God, all things are possible.

This particular gospel passage is one of the most well-known among Christians, and this familiarity makes it very difficult to recall what Luke's intentions are with this story. It is important to remember that Luke does not intend to convey historical accuracy but rather the revelation of the Son of God. He is weaving a story that, among other things, places the birth of Jesus in the city of David, which is important because it adds to the list of Jesus' "messianic credentials." There is absolutely nothing glamorous about this birth as it is told, which is true to Luke's goal of pointing out God's involvement in human, earthly events.

One final point about Luke's narration is that the story of Jesus' birth is told in the shadow of the cross. The infant Jesus is wrapped in cloth and placed in a manger, foreshadowing the time when Jesus is wrapped in cloth and placed in a tomb. The presence of the child Jesus in the wooden manger will lead to the presence of Christ on the wood of the cross. The paschal mystery encompasses every part of Jesus' life.

■ **How do you see the Lord active in the events of your life? How is the Lord involved in your story?**

PRACTICE OF FAITH

TREE OF LIFE. Have you ever noticed how many times trees are mentioned in the Bible? In the center of the first garden, God planted the tree of life (Genesis 2:9). Biblical father Jesse is likened to a root and a stump from which a new tree with many branches grows (Isaiah 11:1). When God comes to save us, the trees of the forest will clap their hands (Psalm 96). Jesus—whose very name in Hebrew means "God saves"—brings life eternal by dying on the tree (Acts 10:39). And in the middle of the New Jerusalem, on either side of the river of life, is the tree of life, restored to us now with 12 kinds of fruits, enough food for all the tribes of humanity (Revelation 22:2). No wonder we use a tree to celebrate Christ's birth. Keep your tree up and lit (and watered!) until the Christmas season ends—January 7th this year.

PRACTICE OF HOPE

LIGHT HAS SHINED. When the world seems to be its darkest and coldest, light comes into our lives. On trees, on bushes, on windows, on balconies and porches, bits of color brighten the night. Christmas tree lights have a way of lightening the spirit, too. A hard day at work doesn't seem so bad after a drive home through neighborhoods blazing with color.

In my neighborhood, there is one tree in particular that everyone admires. The tallest tree in the area, it can be seen for blocks, its many bright lights sparkling like stars. Looking at this invitation to joy gives you the feeling that anything is possible. That is the hope we seek and celebrate tonight. Jesus, the brightest light that ever shined, makes all things new, all things possible. Even eternal life. There is no greater hope.

PRACTICE OF CHARITY

SHEPHERDS LIVING IN THE FIELDS. The celebration of Jesus' birth is often observed with food and wine in abundance, gifts for everyone, and the company of friends and family. How ironic, then, that those who saw the newborn Christ on his first night were homeless! Mary and Joseph could find no room at the inn; the shepherds lived in the fields with their flocks. Our observation of Christmas would be inauthentic if we did not let this incongruity disturb us a little. Many people do most of their charitable giving at this time of year, out of generous hearts and perhaps a little guilt. Find an organization in your area that provides meals or gifts to poor people and contribute your time and talent in this holiday season. Take the next step as well, and establish a relationship with that organization, volunteering your time, talent and treasure year-round.

READING I *1 Samuel 1:20–22, 24–28*

In due time Hannah conceived and bore a son. She named him Samuel, for she said, "I have asked him of the LORD." The man Elkanah and all his household went up to offer to the LORD the yearly sacrifice and to pay his vow. But Hannah did not go up, for she said to her husband, "As soon as the child is weaned, I will bring him, that he may appear in the presence of the LORD, and remain there forever; I will offer him as a nazirite for all time."

When she had weaned him, she took him up with her, along with a three-year-old bull, an ephah of flour, and a skin of wine. She brought him to the house of the LORD at Shiloh; and the child was young. Then they slaughtered the bull, and they brought the child to Eli. And she said, "Oh, my lord! As you live, my lord, I am the woman who was standing here in your presence, praying to the LORD. For this child I prayed; and the LORD has granted me the petition that I made. Therefore I have lent him to the LORD; as long as he lives, he is given to the LORD." She left him there for the LORD.

[Revised Common Lectionary: 1 Samuel 2:18–20, 26]

READING II *1 John 3:1–2, 21–24*

See what love the Father has given us, that we should be called children of God; and that is what we are. The reason the world does not know us is that it did not know God. Beloved, we are God's children now; what we will be has not yet been revealed. What we do know is this: when it is revealed, we will be like God, for we will see God as God is.

Beloved, if our hearts do not condemn us, we have boldness before God; and we receive from God whatever we ask, because we obey the commandments and do what pleases God.

And this is God's commandment, that we should believe in the name of Jesus Christ, the Son of God, and love one another, just as Jesus has commanded us. All who obey God's commandments abide in God, and God abides in them. And by this we know that God abides in us, by the Spirit that God has given us.

[Revised Common Lectionary: Colossians 3:12–17]

GOSPEL *Luke 2:41–52*

Now every year Jesus' parents went to Jerusalem for the festival of the Passover. And when he was twelve years old, they went up as usual for the festival. When the festival was ended and they started to return, the boy Jesus stayed behind in Jerusalem, but his parents did not know it. Assuming that he was in the group of travelers, they went a day's journey. Then they started to look for him among their relatives and friends. When they did not find him, they returned to Jerusalem to search for him.

After three days they found Jesus in the temple, sitting among the teachers, listening to them and asking them questions. And all who heard Jesus were amazed at his understanding and his answers. When his parents saw him they were astonished; and his mother said to him, "Child, why have you treated us like this? Look, your father and I have been searching for you in great anxiety." Jesus said to them, "Why were you searching for me? Did you not know that I must be in my Father's house?" But they did not understand what he said to them.

Then Jesus went down with them and came to Nazareth, and was obedient to them. His mother treasured all these things in her heart. And Jesus increased in wisdom and in years, and in divine and human favor.

Monday, January 1, 2001

MARY, MOTHER OF GOD

Numbers 6:22–27 *The Lord's face shines on you!*

Galatians 4:4–7 *You are no longer slaves but children of God.*

Luke 2:16–21 *Mary pondered these things in her heart.*

Our merry Christmastime unfolds with the blessing of the new year, with the astonishing good news of peace on earth, and with the treasures that Mary pondered within her heart.

REFLECTION

The gospel passage follows a literary form common to Greek biographies of the first century, the legend. This story serves as a bridge from the infancy account to the stories of Jesus' adulthood. This same type of bridge is employed in *Life of Appolonias of Tyana* and Philo's *Life of Moses*. The primary purpose of a legend in the Bible is to present not historical information but theological reflection. However, today's gospel does offer a few historical tidbits: the Holy Family's devout observance of the Passover customs; the impact Jesus made on his mother; and the natural physical growth of Jesus. The story could possibly be based on the story of Samuel's childhood.

It is important for a modern reader to remember that the gospel was written after Christ's death, resurrection and ascension. The author, having knowledge of the course of Jesus' ministry, makes use of foreshadowing in this particular story to hint at future events. The use of symbols brings this foreshadowing to life.

In the story, Jesus is lost. This state of being lost is a foreshadowing of death. Jesus' parents and their company must have felt shock, sorrow and fear at the loss of their son, as if they were mourning one who had died. Being found on the third day, with the attendant reaction of joy and elation mixed with some confusion, speaks of coming to new life.

These techniques of foreshadowing used by the author at this point set the tone for the whole gospel. Jesus' entire mission is understood as bringing those who are lost, disenfranchised, marginalized and even dead, back to a place in the community, back to life.

■ In today's gospel, we get a glimpse of Jesus' mission to overcome death. In what ways do you get a glimpse of your destiny, the kingdom of God?

■ Have you ever been separated from those you were with, or lost? How did it feel? Contrast that with the feeling of finding your way, of knowing where you are. Where are you lost, and where are you found, on your personal spiritual journey?

PRACTICE OF FAITH

TEENS. Jesus, Mary and Joseph—the Holy Family—point to the very life of God. By baptism we come to know God as Holy Trinity—Father, Son and Holy Spirit. We are children of the Father, born of the Holy Spirit, brothers and sisters of the firstborn, Christ. So we contemplate the Holy Family as a sign of God-in-the-flesh. And what we see is an adolescent who wanders off to do what he has to do, worrying his parents sick!

This week, take a long loving look at a teenager. What do you see of God in this young person? Say a prayer for all the teenagers you know. Ask God to keep them safe and strong within holy families.

PRACTICE OF HOPE

CLOTHE YOURSELVES WITH LOVE. Here in northeast Nebraska, we have seen many centennial celebrations in recent years. One of the more memorable of these featured a wedding gown fashion show. The idea was to make clear what a century looks like, but it revealed so much more. The church was packed as these beaming women walked down the aisle again. It wasn't the gowns that made them beautiful, but the love these dresses represented. That love built the families on which the parish community was built. Sometimes love is taken for granted. The fashion show gave the parishioners an opportunity to wear their hearts on their sleeves for all to see.

PRACTICE OF CHARITY

HOLY AND HUMAN FAMILIES. The gospel passage recounted today recalls the fear, misunderstandings and hurt feelings of a very human and very holy family. Mary and Joseph cannot imagine why Jesus would have left the group as it traveled home; Jesus cannot understand why his parents did not know where he would be. This wasn't the first of the Holy Family's misunderstandings: At one point in his ministry, Jesus' family thought he was crazy! Yet this family, in all its humanity, was indeed holy, as are our families, as troubled and wonderful as they can be. Reach out to a member of your family you are estranged from. Try to clear up misunderstandings; forgive and be reconciled. If this is not possible, say a prayer for that person; praying is a great act of charity that can heal deep wounds.

WEEKDAY READINGS (Mo) Mary, Mother of God, see box; (Tu) 1 John 2:29—3:6; (We) 2:29—3:6; (Th) 3:7–10; (Fri) 3:11–21; (Sa) 5:5–13

READING I *Isaiah 60:1–6*

Arise, shine; for your light has come,
   and the glory of the LORD has risen upon you.
For darkness shall cover the earth,
   and thick darkness the peoples;
but the LORD will arise upon you,
   and the glory of the LORD will appear over you.
Nations shall come to your light,
   and rulers to the brightness of your dawn.
Lift up your eyes and look around;
   they all gather together, they come to you;
your sons shall come from far away,
   and your daughters shall be carried on their
      nurses' arms.
Then you shall see and be radiant;
   your heart shall thrill and rejoice,
because the abundance of the sea shall be brought
      to you,
   the wealth of the nations shall come to you.
A multitude of camels shall cover you,
   the young camels of Midian and Ephah;
   all those from Sheba shall come.
They shall bring gold and frankincense,
   and shall proclaim the praise of the LORD.

READING II *Ephesians 3:2–3, 5–6*

Surely you have already heard of the commission
of God's grace that was given me for you, and how
the mystery of Christ was made known to me by
revelation.

   In former generations this mystery was not made
known to humankind, as it has now been revealed
to his holy apostles and prophets by the Spirit: that
is, the Gentiles have become heirs with us, members
of the same body, and sharers in the promise in
Christ Jesus through the gospel.

GOSPEL *Matthew 2:1–12*

In the time of King Herod, after Jesus was born in
Bethlehem of Judea, magi from the East came to
Jerusalem, asking, "Where is the child who has been
born king of the Jews? For we observed his star at
its rising, and have come to pay him homage."

   When King Herod heard this, he was frightened,
and all Jerusalem with him; and calling together all
the chief priests and scribes of the people, he inquired
of them where the Messiah was to be born. They
told him, "In Bethlehem of Judea; for so it has been
written by the prophet:

   'And you, Bethlehem, in the land of Judah,
      are by no means least
      among the rulers of Judah;
   for from you shall come a ruler
      who is to shepherd my people Israel.' "

Then Herod secretly called for the magi and learned
from them the exact time when the star had
appeared. Then he sent them to Bethlehem, saying,
"Go and search diligently for the child; and when
you have found him, bring me word so that I may
also go and pay him homage."

   When they had heard the king, they set out; and
there, ahead of them, went the star that they had
seen at its rising, until it stopped over the place
where the child was. When they saw that the star
had stopped, they were overwhelmed with joy. On
entering the house, they saw the child with Mary his
mother; and they knelt down and paid him homage.
Then, opening their treasure chests, they offered him
gifts of gold, frankincense, and myrrh.

   And having been warned in a dream not to
return to Herod, they left for their own country by
another road.

REFLECTION

We have many images of the Magi who came to visit the Messiah. Typically, they are depicted as three kings wearing royal robes and crowns, and bearing unusual gifts. Tradition has named the visitors Gaspar (or Caspar), Melchior and Balthasar. However, the gospel itself provides no specifics about name, number or royal rank. The term "magi" may indicate that they were magicians or possibly astrologers. They brought gifts that were unusual for an infant, but very appropriate for a deity. These visitors from far away came bearing various forms of incense with which to honor a god or a human of great and royal stature.

It is perplexing why Matthew included this narrative in his gospel. His purpose in writing was to rally the Jews, that is, to encourage them to see Jesus as the Messiah. To this end, he employs many allusions to Jewish life and customs. Therefore, it seems odd that he would include foreigners in his story. Apparently, Matthew is subtly encouraging his Jewish audience to be inclusive of those who were not Jews.

Not only are the Magi an example of inclusion and universality, they also present a lesson of conversion. The Magi arrive on the scene, converse with Herod in his royal household, and even ally themselves with him. Yet, after meeting Jesus they go home by a different route. They no longer want to be involved with Herod, now that they have met the real King. They have been changed; their lives have been touched in a unique way. The gifts they offer may also be evidence of their conversion. Gold, frankincense and myrrh may have been used in magic or astronomy. In offering these to Jesus, the Magi are leaving behind their former ways in order to devote themselves to the new King.

■ **How do you experience the universality of Christ in your life? In your parish? How can you convey this universality to others?**

■ **In what areas of your life do you need to undergo some form of conversion? What does conversion mean to you? What aspects of your life do you need to leave behind?**

PRACTICE OF FAITH

ENTERING THE HOUSE. An ancient European custom is to bless your home on Epiphany. Here's how: Mark in your Bible the passage Matthew 2:1–12. Get a piece of chalk and a sturdy stool or ladder. Gather everyone at the front door. Listen to the reading from Matthew. Then someone writes with the chalk above the door: 20 + C + M + B + 01. Then all sing "We Three Kings" (and you can move on to the next door to the house, or to all the bedroom doors, and repeat the process.) The numbers stand for the year. The letters may stand for the traditional names of the Magi—Caspar, Melchior and Balthasar. They are also shorthand for *Christus mansionem benedicat,* Latin for "Christ bless this house."

PRACTICE OF HOPE

ARISE, SHINE. Some fortunate dioceses have enough priests to meet current needs. Many don't, however, and this has prompted a variety of creative responses. In the diocese of Great Falls–Billings, Montana, for example, men and women are being trained to serve as lay preachers. They go through a two-year training program that involves the diocese's offices of worship and lay ministry and a national organization called Partners in Preaching. The first commissioning service sent 80 people to proclaim the gospel in eastern Montana. It just goes to show that no matter what happens, the Word of God finds a way to be heard. And who knows how many good things can happen when people hear God's call and respond?

PRACTICE OF CHARITY

PROCLAIMING JUBILEE. Epiphany marks the end of the Jubilee observance that began on Christmas Eve, 1999. Among the themes of the Jubilee year was debt relief for the world's poorest nations. In sub-Saharan Africa, governments owe an average of $400 for every man, woman and child. Zambia alone owed $7.1 billion in 1999; seventy percent of its population lives below the poverty line. Interest payments to creditor nations force currency devaluation and reductions in government subsidies, leaving most of the populations of heavily-indebted nations in poverty. Although movements such as Jubilee 2000 met some success, the work of proclaiming Jubilee cannot end with Epiphany. To learn more about international debt, its causes and effects, contact Bread for the World, National Office, 1100 Wayne Ave., Suite 1000, Silver Spring MD 20910; 1-800-82-BREAD; www.bread.org.

WEEKDAY READINGS (Mo) Isaiah 42:1-4, 6–7; (Tu) Hebrews 2:5–12; (We) 2:14–18; (Th) 3:7-14; (Fr) 4:1–5, 11; (Sa) 4:12–16

READING I *Isaiah 43:1–7*

But now thus says the LORD,
   the one who created you, O Jacob,
   the one who formed you, O Israel:
Do not fear, for I have redeemed you;
   I have called you by name, you are mine.
When you pass through the waters,
   I will be with you;
   and through the rivers,
     they shall not overwhelm you;
when you walk through fire you shall not be burned,
   and the flame shall not consume you.

For I am the LORD your God,
   the Holy One of Israel, your Savior.
I give Egypt as your ransom,
   Ethiopia and Seba in exchange for you.
Because you are precious in my sight,
   and honored, and I love you,
I give people in return for you,
   nations in exchange for your life.

Do not fear, for I am with you;
   I will bring your offspring from the east,
   and from the west I will gather you;
I will say to the north, "Give them up,"
   and to the south, "Do not withhold;
bring my sons from far away
   and my daughters from the end of the earth—
everyone who is called by my name,
   whom I created for my glory,
   whom I formed and made."

READING II *Acts 8:14–17*

Now when the apostles at Jerusalem heard that Samaria had accepted the word of God, they sent Peter and John to them. The two went down and prayed for them that they might receive the Holy Spirit (for as yet the Spirit had not come upon any of them; they had only been baptized in the name of the Lord Jesus). Then Peter and John laid their hands on them, and they received the Holy Spirit.

GOSPEL *Luke 3:15–17, 21–22*

As the people were filled with expectation, and all were questioning in their hearts concerning John, whether he might be the Messiah, John answered all of them by saying, "I baptize you with water; but one who is more powerful than I is coming, the thong of whose sandals I am not worthy to untie. He will baptize you with the Holy Spirit and fire. With a winnowing fork in hand, he will clear the threshing floor and gather the wheat into his granary, burning the chaff with unquenchable fire."

Now when all the people were baptized, and when Jesus also had been baptized and was praying, the heaven was opened, and the Holy Spirit descended upon him in bodily form like a dove. And a voice came from heaven, "You are my Son, the Beloved; with you I am well pleased."

REFLECTION

There must be hundreds of images that could represent the Spirit of God. An eagle, a majestic ray of light coming from the sky, or even a gust of wind would have been suitable ways to represent the Spirit at the grand event of the baptism of Jesus. However, the image of a dove was chosen. It seems odd that a dove would be chosen to signify the Holy Spirit. The dove was what the poor offered for sacrifice in the Temple. Only those who could not afford anything else purchased the cheap and otherwise useless dove. Even today, no one wants doves to congregate at their bird feeders, keeping away the prettier birds.

But the dove can serve here to remind us of how Noah sent out a dove after the flood to scout for land. The dove becomes the bearer of the sign of new life, an olive branch (Genesis 8:9). This same dove hovers over the waters of baptism just as God's Spirit hovered over the waters of chaos at the creation (Genesis 1:4). It seems that this bird, considered so worthless, has become the symbol of priceless new life, not just the new life after the flood, or the new life at the creation, but the new life brought by baptism. It is often the least likely thing, image or person that brings an awareness of God's spirit and the life it provides. Even a dove can point to the presence of the divine in our world.

The proclamation of the voice from heaven that Jesus is "my son with whom I am well pleased" is extremely important. The voice makes clear that Jesus is the Son of God. But for the first-century readers, the voice's declaration has another very important dimension. In a time before DNA testing or other advanced scientific proof of paternity, public acknowledgement of paternity was proof. Public acknowledgment gave the child legitimacy and a measure of social standing within the community. It also served as a public announcement of the father's responsibility for the child. The modern ear hears this text as a theological statement of who Jesus is for the believer. The audience of 2000 years ago also heard it as an explanation of relationships, of how Jesus and the baptized Christian fit into the society of their time.

■ **What does baptism mean to you? How can it bring new life?**

■ **What images of God speak loudest to you? Are there any images that surprise you? How does the proclamation of Jesus as beloved son touch you and relate to your image of God?**

PRACTICE OF FAITH

PASS THROUGH THE WATERS. When Jesus comes up from the waters of the Jordan, the voice of God says "You are my Beloved."

Listen for this voice every time you "come up from the waters"—when you step out of the shower, gulp down a glass of water, or finish washing the dishes. Revive the custom of the Saturday night bath: Fill the tub with warm water, use bath salts and soak. Anoint yourself with baby oil and bundle up in your favorite pajamas or bathrobe. Hear the voice?

On your new calendar, mark the date of your baptism. (Ask a relative or call the church of your baptism if you don't know the date.) Resolve to keep the anniversary this year—by taking a good long bath and joining in the celebration of the eucharist.

PRACTICE OF HOPE

I AM WITH YOU. We know that God is always near. Sometimes we are reminded of just how close God is through other people.

A missionary who recently visited our parish told us about her friend, a nurse who worked with the poor in India. One of the children the nurse worked with looked at her and said, "You are God." She tried to correct the child, but he persisted: "You are God." She tried one last time to tell her young companion that she was a nurse, not God, but he said, "I can't see God. I can see you. You are God."

We don't always recognize the "God moments" in our lives, but that doesn't stop God. We give and receive hope by being Christ for one another.

PRACTICE OF CHARITY

WATER. Today's feast reminds us of the role water plays in our religious life. The Israelites passed through the waters of the Red Sea in the Exodus; the prophet Elijah instructed Naaman the Syrian to bathe in the waters of the Jordan; Jesus himself was baptized in the same waters; and Christians enter the community of the faithful through the waters of baptism.

Yet, for all its religious significance, water itself is also a source of conflict. Many of the world's people live without adequately purified drinking water, resulting in outbreaks of cholera and high infant mortality. Support Children's Cup, an organization committed to providing safe drinking water for all the world's people; PO Box 400, Prairieville LA 70769-0400; 1-225-673-4505; www.childrenscup.org.

WEEKDAY READINGS (Mo) Isaiah 42:1–4, 6–7; (Tu) Hebrews 2:5–12; (We) 2:14–18; (Th) 3:7–14; (Fr) 4:1–5, 11; (Sa) 4:12–16

WINTER ORDINARY TIME

Blessed are you in the sleep of winter!

Praise the Lord, O Jerusalem!
Praise your God, O Zion!
The Lord strengthens the bars
    of your gates,
blesses your children among you,
makes peace in your borders,
fills you with the finest wheat.

The Lord sends out commands
    to the earth;
the word of God runs swiftly.
The Lord sends snow like wool,
scatters hoarfrost like ashes,
throws out ice like crumbs;
who can withstand its cold?

The Lord sends forth the word
    and melts them;
makes the wind blow,
    and the waters flow.
The Lord declares the divine word to Jacob,
divine statutes and ordinances to Israel.
Praise the Lord!

—Psalm 147:12–19

Shall we praise you, hail-hurling God,
in winter's splendor,
in the grace of snow
that covers with brightness
and reshapes both your creation and ours?
Or shall we curse the fierce cold
that punishes homeless people
and shortens tempers?
Blessed are you
in the earth's tilt and course.
Blessed are you in the sleep of winter
and in the oncoming lenten spring.
Now and then and always,
fill these lands with peace.

—Prayer of the Season

41

READING I *Isaiah 62:1–5*

For Zion's sake I will not keep silent,
    and for Jerusalem's sake I will not rest,
until its vindication shines out like the dawn,
    and its salvation like a burning torch.
The nations shall see your vindication,
    and all the rulers your glory;
and you shall be called by a new name
    that the mouth of the LORD will give.

You shall be a crown of beauty in the hand
        of the LORD,
    and a royal diadem in the hand of your God.
You shall no more be termed Forsaken,
    and your land shall no more be termed Desolate;
but you shall be called My Delight,
    and your land Married;
for the LORD delights in you,
    and your land shall be married.
For as a young man marries a young woman,
    so shall your builder marry you,
and as one rejoices in marrying one's beloved,
    so shall your God rejoice over you.

READING II *1 Corinthians 12:1–11*

Now concerning spiritual gifts, brothers and sisters,
I do not want you to be uninformed. You know that
when you were pagans, you were enticed and led
astray to idols that could not speak. Therefore I want
you to understand that no one speaking by the Spirit
of God ever says "Let Jesus be cursed!" and no one
can say "Jesus is Lord" except by the Holy Spirit.

Now there are varieties of gifts, but the same
Spirit; and there are varieties of services, but the same
Lord; and there are varieties of activities, but it is the
same God who activates all of them in everyone. To
each is given the manifestation of the Spirit for the
common good. To one is given through the Spirit the
utterance of wisdom, and to another the utterance
of knowledge according to the same Spirit, to another
faith by the same Spirit, to another gifts of healing by
the one Spirit, to another the working of miracles, to
another prophecy, to another the discernment of spirits, to another various kinds of tongues, to another
the interpretation of tongues. All these are activated
by one and the same Spirit, who allots to each one
individually just as the Spirit chooses.
[Roman Catholic: 1 Corinthians 12:4–11]

GOSPEL *John 2:1–11*

On the third day there was a wedding in Cana of
Galilee, and the mother of Jesus was there. Jesus and
his disciples had also been invited to the wedding.
When the wine gave out, the mother of Jesus said to
him, "They have no wine." And Jesus said to her,
"Woman, what concern is that to you and to me? My
hour has not yet come." His mother said to the servants, "Do whatever he tells you."

Now standing there were six stone water jars for
the Jewish rites of purification, each holding twenty
or thirty gallons. Jesus said to them, "Fill the jars
with water." And they filled them up to the brim. He
said to them, "Now draw some out, and take it to
the chief steward." So they took it. When the steward tasted the water that had become wine, and did
not know where it came from (though the servants
who had drawn the water knew), the steward called
the bridegroom and said to him, "Everyone serves
the good wine first, and then the inferior wine after
the guests have become drunk. But you have kept
the good wine until now."

Jesus did this, the first of his signs, in Cana of
Galilee, and revealed his glory; and his disciples
believed in him.

REFLECTION

One of the purposes of the gospel of John was to invite Greek-speaking Jews to convert to Christianity. This conversion required the convert to replace long-held ideologies with new, often difficult, notions of how life is to be lived. It is through the power of Jesus that people find the strength to convert. Today's gospel highlights Jesus as an agent of change.

This change is suggested in the reference to the jars used "for Jewish rites of purification" and through Jesus' words to his mother. The common Jewish rite of cleansing is replaced by the purification Jesus will accomplish on the cross. Jesus tells his mother that his "hour has not yet come," which is a hint of the greater hour of Christ's revelation on the cross. The cross is the ultimate image of change; conversion in that death becomes the gateway to new life. Just as Christ replaced the old purification rites with messianic cleansing at the crucifixion, he renews the world in which we live even today.

It is interesting that this passage is introduced with the phrase "on the third day." This phrase is much more than just a calendar reference; it is an important theological reference. The third day is the day of victory, a day of newness. Recall that various Old Testament events involved some sort of a revitalization on the third day (for example, Jonah was spewed onto the shore on the third day).

■ What areas of your life need to experience conversion? What role does Christ play in your conversion?

■ People are often fearful of change. How do you feel about changes in your life? How can the Lord comfort you in times of change?

PRACTICE OF FAITH

THERE WAS A WEDDING. Though there is no guarantee that the marriage will be smooth, we gather around a couple and celebrate their wedding as if heaven has come down to earth. And in a sense it has. When baptized people marry, their union is a sign that points to and makes present the love that Christ has for us. If the names of those to be married at your parish are published in the bulletin (the "banns"), clip them out and stick them in this book. Pray that Christ will come as guest and gift to their wedding. When you attend a wedding, participate fully in the liturgy. Sing the songs and make the responses. (Don't waste your time fiddling with cameras or video recorders.)

PRACTICE OF HOPE

A CROWN OF BEAUTY. Most of us will never know what it is like to wear a crown. Unless you are born into a royal family—or marry into one—that kind of headgear just does not figure into everyday life. For us commoners, our hair is our crown. But even this is not an option for children who are suffering hair loss due to chemotherapy or other medical conditions.

A not-for-profit organization called Locks of Love strives to return that bit of dignity and hope to these children through custom-fitted hairpieces. Donations of money and hair make this possible. Officials note that 75 percent of the donors are children. The recipients get the hairpieces without charge, or pay according to a sliding scale. The smiles of those who receive these gifts are priceless. To learn more about the Florida-based organization, visit www.locksoflove.org or call (561) 963-1677.

PRACTICE OF CHARITY

I WILL NOT KEEP SILENT. Tomorrow marks the anniversary of the birth of Dr. Martin Luther King, Jr., in 1929. His refusal to be silent about racial injustice in the United States marks him as a prophet for all times. Despite many victories, Dr. King's work to promote racial justice is yet unfinished; people of color continue to struggle with racism in its myriad forms. Read the U.S. bishops' document *Brothers and Sisters to Us,* available from the United States Catholic Conference, Office for Publishing and Promotion Services, 3211 4th Street NE, Washington DC 20017-1194; 1-800-235-8722; www.nccbuscc.org. Consider beginning or participating in a group committed to promoting racial justice in your parish.

WEEKDAY READINGS (Mo) Hebrews 5:1–10; (Tu) 6:10–20; (We) 7:1–3, 15–17; (Th) 7:25—8:6; (Fr) 8:6–13; (Sa) 9:2–3, 11–14

JANUARY 21, 2001 Third Sunday in Ordinary Time
Third Sunday after the Epiphany

READING I *Nehemiah 8:1–3, 5–6, 8–10*

When the seventh month came—the people of Israel being settled in their towns—all the people gathered together into the square before the Water Gate. They told the scribe Ezra to bring the book of the law of Moses, which the LORD had given to Israel. Accordingly, the priest Ezra brought the law before the assembly, both men and women and all who could hear with understanding. This was on the first day of the seventh month. Ezra read from it facing the square before the Water Gate from early morning until midday, in the presence of the men and the women and those who could understand; and the ears of all the people were attentive to the book of the law.

And Ezra opened the book in the sight of all the people, for he was standing above all the people; and when he opened it, all the people stood up. Then Ezra blessed the LORD, the great God, and all the people answered, "Amen, Amen," lifting up their hands. Then they bowed their heads and worshiped the LORD with their faces to the ground. So the Levites read from the book, from the law of God, with interpretation. They gave the sense, so that the people understood the reading.

And Nehemiah, who was the governor, and Ezra the priest and scribe, and the Levites who taught the people said to all the people, "This day is holy to the LORD your God; do not mourn or weep." For all the people wept when they heard the words of the law. Then Ezra said to them, "Go your way, eat the fat and drink sweet wine and send portions of them to those for whom nothing is prepared, for this day is holy to our LORD; and do not be grieved, for the joy of the LORD is your strength."

READING II *1 Corinthians 12:12–14, 27*

For just as the body is one and has many members, and all the members of the body, though many, are one body, so it is with Christ. For in the one Spirit we were all baptized into one body—Jews or Greeks, slaves or free—and we were all made to drink of one Spirit.

Indeed, the body does not consist of one part but of many.

Now you are the body of Christ and individually parts of it.

[Complete reading: 1 Corinthians 12:12–31]

GOSPEL *Luke 1:1–4; 4:14–21*

Since many have undertaken to set down an orderly account of the events that have been fulfilled among us, just as they were handed on to us by those who from the beginning were eyewitnesses and servants of the word, I too decided, after investigating everything carefully from the very first, to write an orderly account for you, most excellent Theophilus, so that you may know the truth concerning the things about which you have been instructed.

Then Jesus, filled with the power of the Spirit, returned to Galilee, and a report about him spread through all the surrounding country. He began to teach in their synagogues and was praised by everyone.

When Jesus came to Nazareth, where he had been brought up, he went to the synagogue on the sabbath day, as was his custom. He stood up to read, and the scroll of the prophet Isaiah was given to him. He unrolled the scroll and found the place where it was written:

"The Spirit of the Lord is upon me,
  because the Lord has anointed me
  to bring good news to the poor.
The Lord has sent me to proclaim release
    to the captives
  and recovery of sight to the blind,
  to let the oppressed go free,
to proclaim the year of the Lord's favor."

And Jesus rolled up the scroll, gave it back to the attendant, and sat down. The eyes of all in the synagogue were fixed on him. Then he began to say to them, "Today this scripture has been fulfilled in your hearing."

[Revised Common Lectionary: Luke 4:14–21]

REFLECTION

The gospel of Luke is the only one of the four gospels that is addressed to a particular individual. In the opening lines the work is addressed to "Theophilus" (Greek for "friend of God"). Scholars debate whether this is the name of a particular historical individual or a unique term inviting all readers to befriend Jesus.

The gospel reading for today answers several questions that may arise in a reader's mind. The primary question is: "Who is Jesus for me?" Jesus answers this question for all of us by quoting the "servant song" from Isaiah. Jesus is telling us that he is a prophet. In the Hebrew sense, a prophet is one who is called, and Jesus makes clear that he has been called, too. Through his selection of this particular quotation from Isaiah, Jesus explains himself as a servant and a prophet, one who is called to serve.

This answers the question of who Jesus is, but who is he called to serve? The Spirit has called him to serve the *anawim,* a term for all those who have been marginalized, impoverished or excluded from human fellowship and community.

The third question that may come to mind is "When will Christ come to serve the *anawim?*" The answer comes loud and clear in the last line of this passage: Today! This term is not limited to some particular day 2000 years ago. It includes this moment, today. On this day, in this moment, Jesus Christ is called by the Spirit to be in a special relationship with all people, even the lowest of society.

■ **How do you know where the Spirit is calling you? How can you know the Spirit's call?**

■ **Do you identify with the poor, the blind, the oppressed?**

■ **How has Christ, through his relationship with you, brought good news, restored your sight, or set you free?**

PRACTICE OF FAITH

GO YOUR WAY. Look again at the first reading. First, the people who had been exiled gather by the Water Gate. Then they listen to the Word of God, proclaimed and preached. They weep for all their failings and for all the good that God has done. Then the prophet tells them to go their way, to "eat the fat and drink sweet wine." But this is no mere "eat, drink and be merry." For the people are told to share with those who have nothing.

Are ministers of the eucharist sent out each Sunday to share communion with the homebound, the hospitalized and the imprisoned? (Might God be calling you to this service?) Do you like to go out for brunch after Sunday Mass? How about inviting a widow, or a newly arrived parishioner, someone who is lonely or who otherwise would go without?

PRACTICE OF HOPE

DO NOT BE GRIEVED. One of the hardest things I ever did also turned out to be one of the greatest blessings of my life. I stayed with my father and helped care for him as he died. He was not able to talk much in those last days, so I take comfort in the conversation we had when he called to tell me he did not have very long to live. There was shock, fear and sadness, but ultimately we agreed that we were lucky. As people of faith, we knew that death was not really the end. New life awaited Dad. As we helped him prepare for that new life in Christ, we drew strength from our faith and the friends and prayers that surrounded us. We were never alone. As members of the one Body of Christ, we never will be.

PRACTICE OF CHARITY

BAPTIZED INTO ONE BODY. The readings draw our attention to the Octave of Christian Unity (January 18–25). The second reading highlights the many different ministries of the Body of Christ; the gospel highlights our common mission. All Christians are called "to bring good news to the poor . . . to proclaim release to captives and recovery of sight to the blind, to let the oppressed go free, to proclaim the year of the Lord's favor."

Attend a local Protestant or Orthodox church during these days, or volunteer at the soup kitchen or other ministry of a local congregation other than your own. Praying and working together can only strengthen our common commitment to the gospel and draw us closer together.

WEEKDAY READINGS (Mo) Hebrews 9:15, 24–28; (Tu) 10:1–10; (We) 10:11–18; (Th) Acts 22:3–16; (Fr) 2 Timothy 1:1–8 or Titus 1:1–5; (Sa) Hebrews 11:1–2, 8–19

READING I *Jeremiah 1:4–5, 17–19*

Now the word of the LORD came to me saying, "Before I formed you in the womb, I knew you, and before you were born, I consecrated you; I appointed you a prophet to the nations.

"Therefore, gird up your loins; stand up and tell the people everything that I command you. Do not break down before them, or I will break you before them. And I for my part have made you today a fortified city, an iron pillar, and a bronze wall, against the whole land—against the kings of Judah, its princes, its priests, and the people of the land.

"They will fight against you; but they shall not prevail against you, for I am with you, says the LORD, to deliver you."

[*Revised Common Lectionary: Jeremiah 1:4–10*]

READING II *1 Corinthians 12:31–13:13*

Brothers and sisters, strive for the greater gifts. And I will show you a still more excellent way.

If I speak in the tongues of mortals and of angels, but do not have love, I am a noisy gong or a clanging cymbal. And if I have prophetic powers, and understand all mysteries and all knowledge, and if I have all faith, so as to remove mountains, but do not have love, I am nothing. If I give away all my possessions, and if I hand over my body so that I may boast, but do not have love, I gain nothing.

Love is patient; love is kind; love is not envious or boastful or arrogant or rude. It does not insist on its own way; it is not irritable or resentful; it does not rejoice in wrongdoing, but rejoices in the truth. It bears all things, believes all things, hopes all things, endures all things.

Love never ends. But as for prophecies, they will come to an end; as for tongues, they will cease; as for knowledge, it will come to an end. For we know only in part, and we prophesy only in part; but when the complete comes, the partial will come to an end. When I was a child, I spoke like a child, I thought like a child, I reasoned like a child; when I became an adult, I put an end to childish ways. For now we see in a mirror, dimly, but then we will see face to face. Now I know only in part; then I will know fully, even as I have been fully known. And now faith, hope, and love abide, these three; and the greatest of these is love.

GOSPEL *Luke 4:21–30*

Then Jesus began to say to all in the synagogue in Nazareth, "Today this scripture has been fulfilled in your hearing." All spoke well of him and were amazed at the gracious words that came from his mouth. They said, "Is not this Joseph's son?" Jesus said to them, "Doubtless you will quote to me this proverb, 'Doctor, cure yourself!' And you will say, 'Do here also in your hometown the things that we have heard you did at Capernaum.'" And he said, "Truly I tell you, no prophet is accepted in the prophet's hometown. But the truth is, there were many widows in Israel in the time of Elijah, when the heaven was shut up three years and six months, and there was a severe famine over all the land; yet Elijah was sent to none of them except to a widow at Zarephath in Sidon. There were also many lepers in Israel in the time of the prophet Elisha, and none of them was cleansed except Naaman the Syrian."

When they heard this, all in the synagogue were filled with rage. They got up, drove Jesus out of the town, and led him to the brow of the hill on which their town was built, so that they might hurl him off the cliff. But Jesus passed through the midst of them and went on his way.

REFLECTION

The passage from the gospel of Luke is the second part of what has been called the sermon in the synagogue at Nazareth. The first segment was proclaimed during last Sunday's liturgy.

Luke's presentation in today's selection was jolting to the first-century Jewish reader. Jesus aligns himself with the many prophets who came before him to call the people back to the covenant, and reminds the people that a prophet is not accepted in his own home, Israel. In years past, the Israelites did not want to hear about returning to covenant loyalty with the Lord, and therefore treated some of the prophets badly. Jesus uses this history to make a similar point about himself.

In addition, the Israelites had become extremely nationalistic, unable to see their God as one who would care for those outside the boundaries of Israel. Jesus plays on this nationalist sentiment to make another point. Jesus refers to the prophet Elijah's mission to a widow at Zarephath in Sidon, and to the prophet Elisha's miraculous healing of Naaman the Syrian. By this, Jesus proclaims that his ministry, too, is not just to Israel, but to all people. Even more, Jesus is saying that those who are "outsiders" are the ones who will recognize Jesus' status as the anointed of God.

This angers the listeners, but Jesus passes through the sea of their angry self-righteousness. This passing recalls the way Moses passed through the Red Sea. Jesus is the new Moses, come to set all people free, not just the members of one group.

This message is well-suited to the Gentile Christian audience for whom Luke was writing. This passage would most likely be interpreted as a welcome by these Gentile believers, while challenging any Jewish readers to be open to the inclusion of a variety of people into the community of believers in Jesus.

■ How have you been narrow-minded in your understanding of the salvation offered by Jesus? When have you been judgmental, or at least less open, toward those of different faiths? Races? Or economic or social classes?

■ Are there teachings of Jesus that make you angry? In what ways can you allow Christ to walk through your own anger?

PRACTICE OF FAITH

CANDLES. Friday, February 2, is the feast of the Presentation of the Lord in the Temple. (See Luke 2:21–39.) This is a day—40 days after Christmas—to light candles and give thanks to God for the gift of light shining in the dark. Set candles on the dinner table. After everything is in place and everyone is seated, turn off the electric lights. Sit for a moment and appreciate the twilight. Then strike a match and light the candles. As you light the candles sing (if you remember from last Easter Vigil) or say: "Christ our Light! Thanks be to God!"

PRACTICE OF HOPE

TO BUILD AND TO PLANT. In Sierra Leone deforestation of the hillsides around the capital city of Freetown leads to a deadly chain reaction during the rainy season. The downpours on the bare slopes result in erosion, which causes flooding, which has destroyed houses and lives. In an attempt to restore some balance, Catholic Relief Services donated more than 240,000 seedlings to a government reforestation project. The goal is to get local farmers involved in planting and caring for the new acacia trees. Once again, CRS has created a win-win situation that enables the people of Sierra Leone and their government to work together for the good of the environment.

PRACTICE OF CHARITY

BEFORE YOU WERE BORN. The words of God to the prophet Jeremiah are testimony to the intimate connection of God with human life in all its stages and forms. These words also lend scriptural force to the Catholic church's prohibition of abortion. Yet, so often, abortion foes and proponents engage in recriminating rhetoric that neither prevents abortion nor helps women in crisis.

Many organizations, however, are quietly working to help both pregnant women and women who have had abortions. Among these is Project Rachel, a program now operating in 135 Catholic dioceses that helps women grieve, accept forgiveness and heal after an abortion. Project Rachel's specially-trained priests, therapists and volunteer counselors provide a crucial service to women. Volunteer your time, or make a contribution to this or a similar ministry. The National Office of Post-Abortion Reconciliation and Healing, of which Project Rachel is the Catholic ministry, can be reached at PO Box 07477, Milwaukee WI 53207-0477; 1-800-5WE-CARE; www.marquette.edu/rachel.

WEEKDAY READINGS (Mo) Hebrews 11:32–40; (Tu) 12:1–4; (We) 12:4–7, 11–15; (Th) 12:18–19, 21–24; (Fr) Malachi 3:1–4; (Sa) Hebrews 13:15–17, 20–21

READING I *Isaiah 6:1–8*

In the year that King Uzziah died, I saw the Lord sitting on a throne, high and lofty; and the hem of the Lord's robe filled the temple. Seraphs were in attendance above the Lord; each had six wings: with two they covered their faces, and with two they covered their feet, and with two they flew. And one called to another and said:

"Holy, holy, holy is the LORD of hosts;
the whole earth is full of the glory of the LORD."

The pivots on the thresholds shook at the voices of those who called, and the house filled with smoke. And I said: "Woe is me! I am lost, for I am a man of unclean lips, and I live among a people of unclean lips; yet my eyes have seen the Sovereign, the LORD of hosts!"

Then one of the seraphs flew to me, holding a live coal that had been taken from the altar with a pair of tongs. The seraph touched my mouth with it and said: "Now that this has touched your lips, your guilt has departed and your sin is blotted out." Then I heard the voice of the Lord saying, "Whom shall I send, and who will go for us?" And I said, "Here am I; send me!"

READING II *1 Corinthians 15:1–11*

Now I would remind you, brothers and sisters, of the good news that I proclaimed to you, which you in turn received, in which also you stand, through which also you are being saved, if you hold firmly to the message that I proclaimed to you—unless you have come to believe in vain.

For I handed on to you as of first importance what I in turn had received: that Christ died for our sins in accordance with the scriptures, and that he was buried, and that he was raised on the third day in accordance with the scriptures, and that he appeared to Cephas, then to the twelve. Then he appeared to more than five hundred brothers and sisters at one time, most of whom are still alive, though some have died. Then he appeared to James,

then to all the apostles. Last of all, as to one untimely born, Christ appeared also to me. For I am the least of the apostles, unfit to be called an apostle, because I persecuted the church of God. But by the grace of God I am what I am, and God's grace toward me has not been in vain. On the contrary, I worked harder than any of them—though it was not I, but the grace of God that is with me. Whether then it was I or they, so we proclaim and so you have come to believe.

GOSPEL *Luke 5:1–11*

Once while Jesus was standing beside the lake of Gennesaret, and the crowd was pressing in on him to hear the word of God, he saw two boats there at the shore of the lake; those who were fishing had gone out of the boats and were washing their nets. Jesus got into one of the boats, the one belonging to Simon, and asked him to put out a little way from the shore. Then he sat down and taught the crowds from the boat.

When Jesus had finished speaking, he said to Simon, "Put out into the deep water and let down your nets for a catch." Simon answered, "Master, we have worked all night long but have caught nothing. Yet if you say so, I will let down the nets." When they had done this, they caught so many fish that their nets were beginning to break. So they signaled their partners in the other boat to come and help them. And they came and filled both boats, so that they began to sink. But when Simon Peter saw it, he fell down at Jesus' knees, saying, "Go away from me, Lord, for I am a sinful man!" For Simon and all who were with him were amazed at the catch of fish that they had taken; and so also were James and John, sons of Zebedee, who were partners with Simon. Then Jesus said to Simon, "Do not be afraid; from now on you will be catching human beings." When they had brought their boats to shore, they left everything and followed Jesus.

REFLECTION

Jesus is presented as a teacher in today's gospel passage. But he is not a teacher who lectures from a podium: He teaches through his connection with the people with whom he lives, as well as by his own actions.

In the first century, fishing was usually done at night or in the early morning. After a night at work, the fishers then had to clean their nets and ready the boat for the next outing. Many in Israel looked down on those who fished for a living, saying that they were never at home taking care of their families. Friends and relatives who would gather at the shore to be with the fishers would also have been looked down on. Knowing something about Jesus' audience helps us to understand more deeply who Jesus is.

It is interesting that Luke does not go into any detail about what Jesus taught on that day he spent with the fishers. Luke does, however, tell us about Jesus' actions, and therein is a lesson. Jesus tells the fishers to go out deeper and cast their nets. This may well be understood as a metaphor for going deeper into life, going deeper into relationship with others, going deeper into love with the Lord and experiencing rewards that will be astonishing. This challenge to experience life more deeply ends with the disciples responding to Jesus' invitation to follow him.

■ **In what ways can you identify with the fishers? When have you felt ostracized by your community? When and how has Christ taught you to feel differently about yourself?**

■ **What areas of your life do you need to explore more deeply? How can you cast your nets deeper into those areas?**

PRACTICE OF FAITH

CATCHING HUMAN BEINGS. Among all that has changed about welfare and assistance to the poor these past several years, have you heard much talk about "safety nets"—assistance programs that are supposed to "catch" the poorest among us from "falling through the cracks"? Search the newspapers, the library or the Internet this week for information about the poor in your area. What safety nets are in place? Are they working? Have we truly reformed welfare, or simply stopped helping people who are still in need? Join your parish St. Vincent de Paul Society or volunteer to work once a month at a soup kitchen. Loving service is the best way to bring people to faith in Christ.

PRACTICE OF HOPE

SEND ME. When it comes to helping others, you don't have to ask the students at Marquette University twice. Each year since 1990, volunteers from the Wisconsin school have planted flowers, painted walls and picked up trash as part of Hunger Cleanup Day. In addition to the physical labor, money is raised to assist local charities. Marquette officials note that their university has more volunteers participating in the day than any other university in the country.

Pride in one's school is good motivation, but it doesn't make for long-term success. People only step forward this way when service is a part of who they are as individuals and as a community. That's when they can say: "Here I am. Send me."

PRACTICE OF CHARITY

BLACK HISTORY MONTH. February is customarily observed as Black History Month in the United States. Although the study of African American history should not be limited to any period of time, February offers an opportunity to highlight what has often been neglected in history books and schools: the stories of African American women and men—people like Sojourner Truth, Frederick Douglass, Crispus Attucks, Malcolm X. Find out what programs, lectures or cultural events are being offered in your community during February; commit to attending one or several of them with your family and friends. Participate in discussion groups in your parish or neighborhood. This month-long celebration of history and culture can contribute to a dialogue among races that lasts all year.

WEEKDAY READINGS (Mo) Genesis 1:1–19; (Tu) 1:20—2:4; (We) 2:4–9, 15–17; (Th) 2:18–25; (Fr) 3:1–8; (Sa) 3:9–24

READING I *Jeremiah 17:5–10*

Thus says the LORD:

Cursed are those who trust in mere mortals
   and make mere flesh their strength,
   whose hearts turn away from the LORD.
They shall be like a shrub in the desert,
   and shall not see when relief comes.
They shall live in the parched places
      of the wilderness,
   in an uninhabited salt land.

Blessed are those who trust in the LORD,
   whose trust is the LORD.
They shall be like a tree planted by water,
   sending out its roots by the stream.
It shall not fear when heat comes,
   and its leaves shall stay green;
in the year of drought it is not anxious,
   and it does not cease to bear fruit.

The heart is devious above all else;
   it is perverse—
who can understand it?
I the LORD test the mind
   and search the heart,
to give to all according to their ways,
   according to the fruit of their doings.

[Roman Catholic: Jeremiah 17:5–8]

READING II *1 Corinthians 15:12–20*

Now if Christ is proclaimed as raised from the dead, how can some of you say there is no resurrection of the dead? If there is no resurrection of the dead, then Christ has not been raised; and if Christ has not been raised, then our proclamation has been in vain and your faith has been in vain. We are even found to be misrepresenting God, because we testified of God that God raised Christ—whom God did not raise if it is true that the dead are not raised. For if the dead are not raised, then Christ has not been raised. If Christ has not been raised, your faith is futile and you are still in your sins. Then those also who have died in Christ have perished. If for this life only we have hoped in Christ, we are of all people most to be pitied.

But in fact Christ has been raised from the dead, the first fruits of those who have died.

[Roman Catholic: 1 Corinthians 15:12, 16–20]

GOSPEL *Luke 6:17–26*

Jesus came down with the twelve and stood on a level place, with a great crowd of his disciples and a great multitude of people from all Judea, Jerusalem, and the coast of Tyre and Sidon. They had come to hear him and to be healed of their diseases; and those who were troubled with unclean spirits were cured. And all in the crowd were trying to touch him, for power came out from him and healed all of them.

Then Jesus looked up at his disciples and said:

"Blessed are you who are poor,
   for yours is the dominion of God.
"Blessed are you who are hungry now,
   for you will be filled.
"Blessed are you who weep now,
   for you will laugh.

"Blessed are you when people hate you, and when they exclude you, revile you, and defame you on account of the Son-of-Man. Rejoice in that day and leap for joy, for surely your reward is great in heaven; for that is what their ancestors did to the prophets.

"But woe to you who are rich,
   for you have received your consolation.
"Woe to you who are full now,
   for you will be hungry.
"Woe to you who are laughing now,
   for you will mourn and weep.

"Woe to you when all speak well of you, for that is what their ancestors did to the false prophets."

[Roman Catholic: Luke 6:17, 20–26]

REFLECTION

Luke, writing to a primarily Gentile audience, gives a spare account of the beatitudes. This is a difference from Matthew's version: Matthew fleshes out his presentation of the beatitudes with references to the rabbinic tradition that would be familiar to his primarily Jewish-Christian audience. Luke, on the other hand, presents the beatitudes as a set of moral guidelines for a renewed people of God.

There are many differences between Matthew's and Luke's descriptions of Jesus' great sermon. In Matthew, Jesus is presented as giving the sermon on a mountain top, not necessarily as a point of historical information but to indicate that the teachings of Jesus are the new law built on the original law given on the mountain of Sinai. In Luke, Jesus speaks on level ground, and his sermon is addressed to the disciples while the gathered crowds listen in. This is apparently Luke's way of indicating that these commands are for those who have already chosen to follow Christ. Also, in Luke, community support is necessary to live the message of the beatitudes.

In many ways, these verses are the most difficult in the gospel. They take the lid off the moral code. No Christian can be smug about how well they follow the law simply because they "did not steal" or they "did not kill"; now they must consider justice and equity. If Jesus' statements are taken seriously they lead the follower of Christ to see life as something different than an opportunity to amass goods without regard to the needs of others. The beatitudes in the gospel of Luke invite believers to evaluate their lives in terms of the values of the Reign of God.

■ **Which beatitude strikes the closest to home? How can this teaching be lived out in your life?**

■ **How do you endure difficulty in your commitment to Christ? Which beatitudes are the most difficult for you to follow? How can you endure these difficulties?**

PRACTICE OF FAITH

SAINT VALENTINE. Wednesday is Valentine's Day! Most churches do not observe it as a religious memorial, but there are actually two historical figures named Valentine who died for their Christian faith in the early centuries of the church. Their biographical details tended to get mixed up. Both apparently wrote notes—one from his prison cell to people who asked for his prayers, and one to the daughter of the judge who condemned him to death. The Romans used to play a game on February 14 where young women would write love poems, sign them and drop them in an urn. Young men would then pick one and court the woman whose name he drew. So there seems to be a long association with writing love notes on this day. Not a bad practice of faith!

PRACTICE OF HOPE

TRUST IN THE LORD. When times are tough, it is easy to say, "Trust in the Lord." It is harder to actually do it, however. As humans we need reassurance—a pat on the shoulder, a hug, a comforting word.

I recently read of a youth group that found a tangible way to turn their troubles over to God. They created "God cans." These decorated soda cans serve as receptacles for life's tough questions and problems, which are written on slips of paper. Their thinking: Even if they can't come up with an answer, "God can." The scriptures encourage us to trust God. Do we let God help us? Comfort us? Save us? We must remember that God can.

PRACTICE OF CHARITY

WOE TO YOU RICH. The beatitudes are recounted today in the gospel. Luke's account is a nuts-and-bolts call to justice: Blessed are the poor, woe to the rich; blessed are the hungry, woe to the full.

These words are especially cogent in view of today's global economy. Great wealth and abject poverty are being institutionalized under the influence of gigantic multinational corporations. Catholic social teaching dictates that the purpose of the economy is not the production of wealth, but the integral development of the human person on all levels. Read *Economic Justice for All,* the 1986 pastoral letter of the U. S. Bishops. It is available from the United States Catholic Conference, Office for Publishing and Promotion Services, 3211 4th St. NE, Washington DC 20017-1194; 1-800-235-8722; www.nccbuscc.org.

WEEKDAY READINGS (Mo) Genesis 4:1–15, 25; (Tu) 6:5–8; 7:1–5, 10; (We) 8:6–13, 20–22; (Th) 9:1–13; (Fr) 11:1–9; (Sa) Hebrews 11:1–7

READING I *1 Samuel 26:23–25*

David called aloud to Saul, "The LORD rewards everyone for his righteousness and his faithfulness; for the LORD gave you into my hand today, but I would not raise my hand against the LORD's anointed. As your life was precious today in my sight, so may my life be precious in the sight of the LORD, and may he rescue me from all tribulation."

Then Saul said to David, "Blessed be you, my son David! You will do many things and will succeed in them." So David went his way, and Saul returned to his place.

[Complete Roman Catholic: 1 Samuel 26:2, 7–9, 12–13, 22–23]

[Revised Common Lectionary: Genesis 45:3–11, 15]

READING II *1 Corinthians 15:35, 42–50*

But someone will ask, "How are the dead raised? With what kind of body do they come?"

What is sown is perishable, what is raised is imperishable. It is sown in dishonor, it is raised in glory. It is sown in weakness, it is raised in power. It is sown a physical body, it is raised a spiritual body. If there is a physical body, there is also a spiritual body. Thus it is written, "The first Adam became a living being"; the last Adam became a life-giving spirit. But it is not the spiritual that is first, but the physical, and then the spiritual. The first human was from the dust of the earth; the second human is from heaven. As was the one made of dust, so are those who are of the dust; and as is the one of heaven, so are those who are of heaven. Just as we have borne the image of the one of dust, we will also bear the image of the one of heaven.

What I am saying, brothers and sisters, is this: flesh and blood cannot inherit the dominion of God, nor does the perishable inherit the imperishable.

[Roman Catholic: 1 Corinthians 15:45–49]

[Revised Common Lectionary: 1 Corinthians 15:35–38, 42–50]

GOSPEL *Luke 6:27–38*

Jesus said:

"But I say to you that listen, Love your enemies, do good to those who hate you, bless those who curse you, pray for those who abuse you. If anyone strikes you on the cheek, offer the other also; and from anyone who takes away your coat do not withhold even your shirt. Give to everyone who begs from you; and if anyone takes away your goods, do not ask for them again. Do to others as you would have them do to you.

"If you love those who love you, what credit is that to you? For even sinners love those who love them. If you do good to those who do good to you, what credit is that to you? For even sinners do the same. If you lend to those from whom you hope to receive, what credit is that to you? Even sinners lend to sinners, to receive as much again. But love your enemies, do good, and lend, expecting nothing in return. Your reward will be great, and you will be children of the Most High, who is kind to the ungrateful and the wicked. Be merciful, just as your Father is merciful.

"Do not judge, and you will not be judged; do not condemn, and you will not be condemned. Forgive, and you will be forgiven; give, and it will be given to you. A good measure, pressed down, shaken together, running over, will be put into your lap; for the measure you give will be the measure you get back."

REFLECTION

Human beings seem to have an innate need to go along with the crowd. This human tendency was alive and well in the first-century Mediterranean world in which Jesus lived. Jesus consistently challenged such behavior, as he does in this section of the Sermon on the Plain. Those listening to Jesus' words would have been solidly convinced that they were to hate their enemies (that is, foreigners). People in the agricultural society of Jesus' time dealt with strangers either through trade or taxation. Neither led to good relations between the people on either side of the exchange.

It would have been quite a jolt to the Israelites of Jesus' time to hear that they were to love the stranger, the foreigner. They were used to dealing with strangers as adversaries. Love, as Jesus speaks of it, indicates an attachment to the other similar to the attachment between family members, and includes forgiveness, mercy and kindness.

This teaching is probably quite a jolt to the modern reader as well. It challenges our thoughts and actions toward those of other races, nationalities and classes. Christ's words continue to challenge throughout time.

■ Who are your "enemies"? Who do you feel attached to? How can you best deal with enemies as Christ expects you to?

■ How can you love as Jesus loved? How can your love of others take the form the gospel expects?

PRACTICE OF FAITH

DO GOOD TO EACH. The love to which we are challenged is not a feeling as much as it is an act of will, a choice to try tricky paths of reconciliation, to defuse hatred instead of reflecting it back. It is also difficult to love our enemies when we are not even aware of them. Sure, we know who our individual enemies are. But the institutions to which we belong—our nation, our community, even the church—have enemies. We block shipments of food and medicines to Cuba and Iraq because of their leaders, and innocent children suffer. We deposit money in a bank that won't give minorities mortgages. And we are always trying to send some group to hell because they don't think like we do. This week, make a list of your enemies, chosen and inherited. Then do good to each, one by one.

PRACTICE OF HOPE

LOVE YOUR ENEMIES. Bud Welch lost his daughter, Julie, in the Oklahoma City bombing in 1995. Long opposed to the death penalty, he faced some dark days after the explosion. Healing began when he realized the pain of Bill McVeigh, the father of Timothy McVeigh, the man convicted of the bombing. Welch eventually met with McVeigh and his daughter, Jennifer. He assured them that he did not want Timothy McVeigh to be put to death and would do whatever he could to prevent it. Welch continues to speak out against the death penalty. He demonstrates in a powerful way that forgiveness is possible. The first step is moving past hate and anger.

PRACTICE OF CHARITY

THOSE WHO ABUSE YOU. February 19 is the second anniversary of the brutal beating death of Billy Jack Gaither, a gay man from Alabama who was murdered by two acquaintances because, they claimed, he had made a sexual advance toward them. The brutality of Gaither's murder highlighted the continued hatred and fear of gay men and lesbians held by some in our society. No matter what their position on homosexual relationships, the churches are unanimous that no person should be the victim of violence for any reason, including sexual orientation. Read *Always Our Children,* a document of the U.S. Bishops' Committee on Family Life (U. S. Catholic Conference, 3211 4th St. NE, Washington DC 20017-1194; 1-800-235-8722; www.nccbuscc.org), to gain a sense of the church's current understanding of homosexuality. Commit yourself to opposing ignorant or hateful language about any person for any reason.

WEEKDAY READINGS (Mo) Sirach 1:1–10; (Tu) 2:1–11; (We) 4:11–19; (Th) 1 Peter 5:1–4; (Fr) Sirach 6:5–17; (Sa) 17:1–15

READING I *Sirach 27:4–7*

When a sieve is shaken, the refuse appears;
  so do people's faults when they speak.
The kiln tests the potter's vessels;
  so the test of a person is in conversation.
Its fruit discloses the cultivation of a tree;
  so one's speech discloses the cultivation
    of one's mind.
Do not praise people before he speaks,
  for this is the way people are tested.

READING II *1 Corinthians 15:54–58*

When this perishable body puts on imperishability,
and this mortal body puts on immortality, then the
saying that is written will be fulfilled:

  "Death has been swallowed up in victory."
  "Where, O death, is your victory?
    Where, O death, is your sting?"

The sting of death is sin, and the power of sin is the
law. But thanks be to God, who gives us the victory
through our Lord Jesus Christ.

  Therefore, my beloved, be steadfast, immovable,
always excelling in the work of the Lord, because
you know that in the Lord your labor is not in vain.

GOSPEL *Luke 6:39–45*

Jesus also told them a parable:

  "Can a blind person guide a blind person? Will
not both fall into a pit? A disciple is not above the
teacher, but everyone who is fully qualified will be
like the teacher. Why do you see the speck in your
neighbor's eye, but do not notice the log in your
own eye? Or how can you say to your neighbor,
'Friend, let me take out the speck in your eye,' when
you yourself do not see the log in your own eye?
You hypocrite, first take the log out of your own eye,
and then you will see clearly to take the speck out
of your neighbor's eye.

  "No good tree bears bad fruit, nor again does a
bad tree bear good fruit; for each tree is known by
its own fruit. Figs are not gathered from thorns, nor
are grapes picked from a bramble bush. The good
person out of the good treasure of the heart produces good, and the evil person out of evil treasure
produces evil; for it is out of the abundance of the
heart that the mouth speaks."

Wednesday, February 28, 2001

ASH WEDNESDAY

Joel 2:12–18 *Proclaim a fast. Rend your hearts.*

2 Corinthians 5:20—6:2 *Now is the time to be reconciled.*

Matthew 6:1–6, 16–18 *Pray, fast and give alms.*

The Spirit urges us into the desert discipline of the
lenten spring. For forty days we will strip away everything that separates us from God, beginning today, as
we are marked with a cross of ashes. Death and life in a
simple sign!

REFLECTION

The gospel passage for today begins by saying that Jesus told the listeners a parable. Jesus is actually telling them several two-line wisdom sayings that are more appropriately known as proverbs. But Luke does use the word "parable" to describe these sayings at other points in the gospel (4:23; 5:36), so that today's passage could have been introduced by saying that Jesus began to speak as if in parables.

Jesus does not often belittle other people or call people names, but in today's gospel Jesus calls those who are overly concerned with the flaws of others hypocrites. This term was generally considered to be derogatory. It comes from the world of Hellenistic drama and oratory where it meant "one who responds," or an actor. Jesus condemns people who act in a way that is not true to themselves. Jesus is encouraging his listeners to seek the gifts God gave them and to use those gifts to their fullest. Pretending to be something other than what one is, Jesus is telling us, is unworthy of his followers.

■ In what ways do you try to act like someone you are not? How can you take steps to recognize your own gifts and share them with others?

■ What gifts has God graced you with? How can you best express your gratitude to the Lord for these? How can you celebrate your gifts?

PRACTICE OF FAITH

MOTHER KATHARINE. When Katharine Drexel traveled in the west in the late 1800s, she was disturbed by the poverty that afflicted Native Americans. On a visit to Rome, Katharine asked Pope Leo XIII to send help. The pope replied, "My child, perhaps God wants to send you!" In 1891, with 13 other women, Katharine founded the Sisters of the Blessed Sacrament to work among native peoples in 16 states. When she learned that African Americans were not admitted to colleges in the South, she started Xavier University in New Orleans. Katharine died in 1955 at age 96. Pope John Paul II beatified her. We remember Blessed Katharine Drexel on Saturday, March 3. Blessed Katharine Drexel, inspire us to right the wrongs of racism.

PRACTICE OF HOPE

WE WILL BE CHANGED. There was a time when Nick did not know that someone named Jesus ever existed. He is the first to admit that during that time in his life, all he did was take from society. When I met him, he was in the Nebraska Correctional Youth Facility, serving one to seven years for burglary. I did not see a violent individual who didn't care about life, though. I saw someone who had used his time to get to know Jesus. Now he introduced other inmates to God. One of them, Michael, said every day was still a challenge for him, but he leaned on Nick's faith. Michael said he would like to be the person others could lean on after Nick's release. As for Nick, he hopes to be an evangelist. "I want to let Christ live through me. The work of God's hands—that's how I am now," he said.

PRACTICE OF CHARITY

OUR SPEECH. The reading from Sirach provides a remarkable reflection as we begin Lent this Wednesday. For the author of Sirach, one's speech reveals the orientation of one's heart; one who speaks maliciously can hardly be called virtuous. Jesus' words echo Sirach's: One's speech reveals an abundance of good, or evil, in the heart.

Fasting is one of the three customary ways to observe Lent. In addition to fasting from food, take stock of your own conversation in the coming days. Fast from words of anger: the curse hurled at another driver on the road, the sharp tone used with a spouse or child. Note the lack of charity in such words, and seek a better way to express your irritation or frustration. As with any lenten devotion, carry the practice into the Easter season and the rest of the year.

WEEKDAY READINGS (Mo) 17:19–27; (Tu) 35:1–12; (We) Ash Wednesday, see box; (Th) Deuteronomy 30:15–20; (Fr) Isaiah 58:1–9; (Sa) Isaiah 58:9–14

READING I *Exodus 34:29–35*

Moses came down from Mount Sinai. As he came down from the mountain with the two tablets of the covenant in his hand, Moses did not know that the skin of his face shone because he had been talking with God. When Aaron and all the Israelites saw Moses, the skin of his face was shining, and they were afraid to come near him. But Moses called to them; and Aaron and all the leaders of the congregation returned to him, and Moses spoke with them. Afterward all the Israelites came near, and he gave them in commandment all that the LORD had spoken with him on Mount Sinai. When Moses had finished speaking with them, he put a veil on his face; but whenever Moses went in before the LORD to speak with the LORD, he would take the veil off, until he came out; and when he came out, and told the Israelites what he had been commanded, the Israelites would see the face of Moses, that the skin of his face was shining; and Moses would put the veil on his face again, until he went in to speak with the LORD.

READING II *2 Corinthians 3:12—4:2*

Since, then, we have such a hope, we act with great boldness, not like Moses, who put a veil over his face to keep the people of Israel from gazing at the end of the glory that was being set aside. But their minds were hardened. Indeed, to this very day, when they hear the reading of the old covenant, that same veil is still there, since only in Christ is it set aside. Indeed, to this very day whenever Moses is read, a veil lies over their minds; but when one turns to the Lord, the veil is removed. Now the Lord is the Spirit, and where the Spirit of the Lord is, there is freedom. And all of us, with unveiled faces, seeing the glory of the Lord as though reflected in a mirror, are being transformed into the same image from one degree of glory to another; for this comes from the Lord, the Spirit.

Therefore, since it is by God's mercy that we are engaged in this ministry, we do not lose heart. We have renounced the shameful things that one hides; we refuse to practice cunning or to falsify God's word; but by the open statement of the truth we commend ourselves to the conscience of everyone in the sight of God.

GOSPEL *Luke 9:28–43*

Now about eight days after these sayings Jesus took with him Peter and John and James, and went up on the mountain to pray. And while he was praying,the appearance of his face changed, and his clothes became dazzling white. Suddenly they saw two men, Moses and Elijah, talking to Jesus. They appeared in glory and were speaking of his departure, which he was about to accomplish at Jerusalem. Now Peter and his companions were weighed down with sleep; but since they had stayed awake, they saw the glory of Jesus and the two men who stood with him. Just as the men were leaving him, Peter said to Jesus, "Master, it is good for us to be here; let us make three dwellings, one for you, one for Moses, and one for Elijah"—not knowing what he said. While he was saying this, a cloud came and overshadowed them; and they were terrified as they entered the cloud. Then from the cloud came a voice that said, "This is my Son, my Chosen; listen to him!" When the voice had spoken, Jesus was found alone. And they kept silent and in those days told no one any of the things they had seen.

On the next day, when they had come down from the mountain, a great crowd met Jesus. Just then a man from the crowd shouted, "Teacher, I beg you to look at my son; he is my only child. Suddenly a spirit seizes him, and all at once he shrieks. It convulses him until he foams at the mouth; it mauls him and will scarcely leave him. I begged your disciples to cast it out, but they could not." Jesus answered, "You faithless and perverse generation, how much longer must I be with you and bear with you? Bring your son here." While he was coming, the demon dashed him to the ground in convulsions. But Jesus rebuked the unclean spirit, healed the boy, and gave him back to his father. And all were astounded at the greatness of God.

REFLECTION

Place yourself in the position of the apostles in the gospel passage from Luke today. What sort of reaction would the transfiguration of Jesus stir up in your heart? Peter, John and James must have wondered who Jesus really was. The transfiguration could have been an answer. From the beginning of his gospel, Luke has been trying to tell the reader of the identity and significance of Jesus. Sometimes people need a miracle before they notice something important.

The answer to the question of Jesus' identity comes to us just as it came to the apostles at the transfiguration of the Lord. The answer comes not only through teaching and hearing, but through vision, experience and connection with other people of faith.

It is not only Jesus who was transformed. Jesus had been the divine Son of God from the beginning. Today's feast also celebrates the transformation of the apostles. Peter acclaims the goodness of the transfiguration and asks to mark the event by building three dwellings. Peter, James and John saw, heard and felt something outside the normal human experience. Despite their confusion, they will never be the same. The feast of the transfiguration is less about a change in Jesus and more about the change in the apostles.

We can insert ourselves into this story. The experience of apostles could happen to us during personal prayer or during a liturgy. An insight could arise that transforms us and takes our relationship with Jesus to a new level. Our celebration of the transfiguration of Jesus is also a time to open ourselves to the ever-present transforming power of the Lord.

■ **What experiences have been life-changing ones for you? How has your understanding of Christ changed because of these events?**

■ **How do you understand conversion? What role do you play in the conversion of your own life? Of the lives of others?**

PRACTICE OF FAITH

SEEING GLORY. Icons are paintings of Christ and the saints made by Greek, Russian and other Christians of the East. The icon allows the viewer to enter into the presence of the one portrayed. An iconographer's first icon is always an image of Christ's transfiguration, based on the gospel that we hear today. Find a book about icons this week. Do not look at the pictures as if they are ads on the side of a passing bus. Instead, contemplate one picture deeply. Set a timer for 15 minutes and gaze upon your chosen icon as though you were staring into the eyes of a lover. In a sense, you are!

PRACTICE OF HOPE

ON THE MOUNTAIN. People often refer to intense experiences as "mountaintop experiences." While I understood this concept intellectually, I never really got it until I started attending conventions of the National Association of Pastoral Musicians. These meetings bring thousands of cantors, composers, instrumentalists, liturgists and clergy together every two years. It is remarkable to hear so many people singing with their whole heart and soul, singing as if they really believe what they are singing. It also gives me hope to know that in an age when the news is full of shootings, violence, political wrangling and a million ways to become richer, faster and slimmer, people are seeking ways to work together. That is the only way true communion happens.

PRACTICE OF CHARITY

THE TRANSFIGURATION OF THE WORLD. Today's readings highlight the effect of God's glory on creation: Moses' face shone because of his encounter with God; Jesus' face and even his clothes were transformed. Yet this transformation is not for Moses or Jesus alone; all creation is destined to be transfigured by God's glory.

This Friday is the World Day of Prayer, which was begun by Church Women United, an ecumenical group that works for peace and justice. Each year, women from a different part of the world create a prayer service focusing on a social justice theme, from hunger to justice for women.

Participate in the observance of the World Day of Prayer in your parish or another local congregation. For more information, contact Church Women United, 1-800-CWU-5551; www.churchwomen.org. It is projects like this that can move the world toward complete transfiguration.

WEEKDAY READINGS (Mo) 17:19–27; (Tu) 35:1–12; (We) Ash Wednesday, see box page 54; (Th) Deuteronomy 30:15–20; (Fr) Isaiah 58:1–9; (Sa) Isaiah 58:9–14

LENT

Have mercy on me, O God!

Have mercy on me, O God,
according to your steadfast love;
according to your abundant mercy
blot out my transgressions.

Wash me thoroughly from my iniquity,
and cleanse me from my sin!
For I know my transgressions,
and my sin is ever before me.
Against you, you only, I have sinned,
and done that which is evil in your sight.

Let me hear with joy and gladness;
let the bones which you have broken rejoice.
Hide your face from my sins,
and blot out all my iniquities.

Create in me a clean heart, O God,
and put a new and right spirit within me.
Cast me not away from your presence,
and take not your holy spirit from me.

Deliver me from bloodshed,
    O God, God of my salvation,
and my tongue shall sing aloud
    of your deliverance.
O Lord, open my lips,
and my mouth shall show forth your praise.

—Psalm 51:1–4a, 8–11, 14–15

Like a gift we only want to want,
these forty days surround us once more
and you set about washing us, God.
Scrub and scour these stubborn ashes.
Separate what we are
from what we are not
and so bring on the lenten ordeal:
the prayer by day and night,
the fast that clears our sight,
the alms that set things right.
At the end, when we have lost again,
you alone make dry bones come together
and bruised bones dance
round the cross where sinners live
now and for ever.

—Prayer of the Season

READING I *Deuteronomy 26:1–11*

When you have come into the land that the LORD your God is giving you as an inheritance to possess, and you possess it, and settle in it, you shall take some of the first of all the fruit of the ground, which you harvest from the land that the LORD your God is giving you, and you shall put it in a basket and go to the place that the LORD your God will choose as the place where the name of God dwells. You shall go to the priest who is in office at that time, and say to him, "Today I declare to the LORD your God that I have come into the land that the LORD swore to our ancestors to give us."

When the priest takes the basket from your hand and sets it down before the altar of the LORD your God, you shall make this response before the LORD your God: "A wandering Aramean was my ancestor; he went down into Egypt and lived there as an alien, few in number, and there became a great nation, mighty and populous. When the Egyptians treated us harshly and afflicted us, by imposing hard labor on us, we cried to the LORD, the God of our ancestors; the LORD heard our voice and saw our affliction, our toil, and our oppression. The LORD brought us out of Egypt with a mighty hand and an outstretched arm, with a terrifying display of power, and with signs and wonders; and the LORD brought us into this place and gave us this land, a land flowing with milk and honey. So now I bring the first of the fruit of the ground that you, O LORD, have given me."

You shall set it down before the LORD your God and bow down before the LORD your God. Then you, together with the Levites and the aliens who reside among you, shall celebrate with all the bounty that the LORD your God has given to you and to your house.

[Roman Catholic: Deuteronomy 26:4–10]

READING II *Romans 10:8–13*

"The word is near you, on your lips and in your heart" (that is, the word of faith that we proclaim); because if you confess with your lips that Jesus is Lord and believe in your heart that God raised him from the dead, you will be saved. For one believes with the heart and so is justified, and one confesses with the mouth and so is saved. The scripture says, "No one who believes in the Lord will be put to shame." For there is no distinction between Jew and Greek; the same Lord is Lord of all and is generous to all who ask for help. For, "Everyone who calls on the name of the Lord shall be saved."

GOSPEL *Luke 4:1–13*

Jesus, full of the Holy Spirit, returned from the Jordan and was led by the Spirit in the wilderness, where for forty days he was tempted by the devil. He ate nothing at all during those days, and when they were over, he was famished. The devil said to him, "If you are the Son of God, command this stone to become a loaf of bread." Jesus answered the devil, "It is written, 'One does not live by bread alone.'"

Then the devil led Jesus up and showed him in an instant all the dominions of the world. And the devil said to him, "To you I will give their glory and all this authority; for it has been given over to me, and I give it to anyone I please. If you, then, will worship me, it will all be yours." Jesus answered the devil,

"It is written,
'Worship the Lord your God;
the Lord alone shall you serve.'"

Then the devil took Jesus to Jerusalem, and placed him on the pinnacle of the temple, saying to him, "If you are the Son of God, throw yourself down from here, for it is written,

'God will command the angels concerning you,
to protect you,' and
'On their hands they will bear you up,
so that you will not dash your foot
against a stone.'"

Jesus answered the devil, "It is said, 'Do not put the Lord your God to the test.'" Having finished every test, the devil departed from Jesus until an opportune time.

REFLECTION

Deuteronomy 6:4–5 proclaims: "Hear, O Israel: The Lord is our God, the Lord alone. You shall love the Lord your God with all your heart, and with all your soul, and with all your might." This passage, known as the *Shema* (from the Hebrew "to hear"), was the principal profession of faith for the Israelites, and continues to be so for Jews today. The practice of placing this passage in a special container and nailing it to the doorframe of the home points to the importance of this command. This, often referred to as the great commandment, is what the devil is challenging in the gospel passage for today.

If the greatest commandment is to love God with all one's heart and soul and might, then the greatest sin would be to break this command and not love God that way. Thus the devil hits Jesus hardest, and strikes at the most important aspect of Jewish religious life, by tempting Jesus to satisfy his hunger by turning stones into bread. The devil tempts Jesus to disavow the *Shema* and fill his heart with something other than God.

This and the other two temptations are resisted by Jesus, who answers with the word of God from the scriptures. In so doing, Jesus shows us that the word of God can indeed meet our hungers, breathe life into us, and strengthen and fortify us.

■ **What area of your life leads you into temptation? How can Christ serve as a source of strength against this temptation?**

■ **How do you love God with all your heart? Soul? Might?**

PRACTICE OF

FAITH

PRAY. FAST. GIVE ALMS. The practices of faith in Lent are basic training. In the gospel of Ash Wednesday, Matthew 6: 1–6, 16–21, the Lord Jesus lays out the spiritual calisthenics: Pray. Fast. Give alms, that is, share with the poor. Of course these are practices for other times of the year, too. But now especially, it's back to the basics. Pray every day. Go to Mass or prayer during the week, not just on Sunday. Fast, especially on Fridays. Give away stuff. You'll be surprised at how you begin to see things differently when you do.

PRACTICE OF

HOPE

SIGNS AND WONDERS. Today is a special day for the thousands of children and adults around the country who are hoping to be received into the Catholic church through baptism, confirmation and eucharist at the Easter Vigil. They will go to the cathedrals in their dioceses and proclaim their desire for these sacraments of initiation while their families and sponsors attest to their readiness. Their presence among us throughout the catechumenate—and in a special way during Lent—gives us an opportunity to renew our faith and to reclaim our hope in the resurrection. As they make their journey, these girls and boys, men and women, remind us how wonderful our gift of faith is. Even though Lent is a penitential season, it is hard not to rejoice with this new life all around us. Today we get a foretaste of Easter joy.

PRACTICE OF

CHARITY

A WANDERING ARAMEAN. All over the world, refugees are forced to flee due to war, extreme poverty, natural disasters or political oppression. Wars in the Balkans forced first Albanians, then Serbs, to flee their homes. The people of Africa, plagued by civil war in the Congo, Rwanda and Sierra Leone, as well as international conflict within Africa, have been forced to be constantly on the move. Central and South America have also seen great movements of people, due both to war and to lack of economic opportunity.

As people of faith, we are called to be in solidarity with these refugees on their journey. To learn more about refugees all over the world and to make a contribution, contact the International Rescue Committee, 122 E. 42nd St., New York NY 10168; 1-877-REFUGEE; www.intrescom.org.

WEEKDAY READINGS (Mo) Leviticus 19:1–2, 11–18; (Tu) Isaiah 55:10–11; (We) Jonah 3:1–10; (Th) Esther C:12, 14–16, 23–25; (Fr) Ezra 18:21–28; (Sa) Deuteronomy 26:16–19

READING I *Genesis 15:1–12, 17–18*

After these things the word of the LORD came to Abram in a vision, "Do not be afraid, Abram, I am your shield; your reward shall be very great." But Abram said, "O Lord GOD, what will you give me, for I continue childless, and the heir of my house is Eliezer of Damascus?" And Abram said, "You have given me no offspring, and so a slave born in my house is to be my heir." But the word of the LORD came to him, "This man shall not be your heir; no one but your very own issue shall be your heir." The LORD brought Abram outside and said, "Look toward heaven and count the stars, if you are able to count them." Then the LORD said to him, "So shall your descendants be." And Abram believed the LORD; and the LORD reckoned it to him as righteousness.

Then the LORD said to Abram, "I am the LORD who brought you from Ur of the Chaldeans, to give you this land to possess." But Abram said, "O Lord GOD, how am I to know that I shall possess it?" The LORD said to him, "Bring me a heifer three years old, a female goat three years old, a ram three years old, a turtledove, and a young pigeon." Abram brought the LORD all these and cut them in two, laying each half over against the other; but he did not cut the birds in two. And when birds of prey came down on the carcasses, Abram drove them away. As the sun was going down, a deep sleep fell upon Abram, and a deep and terrifying darkness descended upon him.

When the sun had gone down and it was dark, a smoking fire pot and a flaming torch passed between these pieces. On that day the LORD made a covenant with Abram, saying, "To your descendants I give this land, from the river of Egypt to the great river, the river Euphrates."

[*Roman Catholic: Genesis 15:5–12, 17–18*]

READING II *Philippians 3:17—4:1*

Brothers and sisters, join in imitating me, and observe those who live according to the example you have in us. For many live as enemies of the cross of Christ; I have often told you of them, and now I tell you even with tears. Their end is destruction; their god is the belly; and their glory is in their shame; their minds are set on earthly things. But our citizenship is in heaven, and it is from there that we are expecting a Savior, the Lord Jesus Christ. The Lord will transform the body of our humiliation that it may be conformed to the body of his glory, by the power that also enables him to make all things subject to himself.

Therefore, my brothers and sisters, whom I love and long for, my joy and crown, stand firm in the Lord in this way, my beloved.

GOSPEL *Luke 9:28–36*

Now about eight days after these sayings Jesus took with him Peter and John and James, and went up on the mountain to pray. And while he was praying, the appearance of his face changed, and his clothes became dazzling white. Suddenly they saw two men, Moses and Elijah, talking to Jesus. They appeared in glory and were speaking of his departure, which he was about to accomplish at Jerusalem. Now Peter and his companions were weighed down with sleep; but since they had stayed awake, they saw the glory of Jesus and the two men who stood with him. Just as the men were leaving him, Peter said to Jesus, "Master, it is good for us to be here; let us make three dwellings, one for you, one for Moses, and one for Elijah"—not knowing what he said. While he was saying this, a cloud came and overshadowed them; and they were terrified as they entered the cloud. Then from the cloud came a voice that said, "This is my Son, my Chosen; listen to him!" When the voice had spoken, Jesus was found alone. And they kept silent and in those days told no one any of the things they had seen.

[*Revised Common Lectionary: Luke 13:31–35*]

REFLECTION

The passage from Genesis unites material from two originally independent stories: The first is in verses 1–6 concerning Abram's promised descendants, and the second is from verses 7–20 about the promised land and the covenant ritual. This combination brings together three distinct yet related themes: the Lord's promise of Abram's descendants, the gift of the promised land, and the covenant between Abram and the Lord. Each of these themes tells us that God is part of human history.

The pastoral economy of Abram's time meant that many people devoted their lives to the care of livestock. In many ways, the animals themselves symbolized the life of the shepherd or farmer. To seal an agreement, people would cut an animal in half, set the halves a certain distance from one another, and walk between the halves and through the blood of the animal. In this ritual the animal symbolized the life of those making the promise. The ritual statement was that what had happened to the animal would happen to the one who broke the covenant.

Many of the belief systems of this time involved gods who were not particularly interested in daily human life. Other literature from this time describes gods battling and disrupting nature. Against this background, it is easy to see what an amazing event this Genesis reading relates: A god engaging in a constructive relationship with a human being, a god who makes covenant with a human being. Many of Abram's contemporaries would be shocked to learn of such a god. However, that is exactly what can be said of the God of Abram.

■ **How do you understand your own covenant relationship with God? How is this covenant expressed in your relationships with other people?**

■ **What rituals in your life express your relationship with God? How can you make these more a part of your daily life? In what ways can you share these with other people in your life?**

PRACTICE OF FAITH

FAST AND ABSTAIN. For centuries, Christians have fasted and abstained from certain foods during Lent. Wednesdays and Fridays were the traditional days for fasting (going without food, at least until after sunset, and then eating only a little). On the other days of Lent, Christian abstained from particular foods according to local custom. Eventually, giving up meat on Wednesdays and Fridays (and later just Fridays) replaced fasting. Maybe there were practical reasons for abstaining from meat in Lent: To have a fattened calf on Easter, you can't slaughter it too soon! Certainly there are spiritual reasons for fasting and abstaining: disciplining our appetites and putting off for a time gratification—all so that we better appreciate the goodness of our bodies, our food and our drink. Find meatless recipes to use daily or weekly. Fast on Fridays.

PRACTICE OF HOPE

COUNT THE STARS. Whenever I hear this phrase, I am reminded of a song from the musical "Les Miserables." In "Stars," Inspector Javert sings of his quest to find the fugitive Jean Valjean and return him to prison. Like Abram, Javert sees the stars as a covenant with God. But while Abram finds comfort in the stars as a reminder of God's goodness, Javert finds only a rigid standard of perfection that justifies his single-minded pursuit. Javert cannot bend, cannot accept the idea of redemption, and that is his downfall. I would rather look at the stars through Abram's eyes. To do that is to see a loving God who keeps his promises. What more can we ask?

PRACTICE OF CHARITY

NO OFFSPRING. Today's first reading records Abram's questioning God about an heir. Many people today can surely understand Abram's pain, as they too struggle with childlessness. Countless millions are spent each year on fertility treatments and *in vitro* fertilization, yet in the U.S. alone, thousands of children grow up without a permanent home. Some are considered too old to be "adoptable," and so spend their entire lives in foster care. In the rest of the world, many children have been left orphans by war or disease, especially in Africa, where AIDS and genocide have had a devastating effect. Consider adopting or opening your home to a foster child, or make a contribution to a local organization that offers aid to neglected and abused children.

WEEKDAY READINGS (Mo) Daniel 9:4–10; (Tu) Isaiah 1:10, 16–20; (We) Jeremiah 18:18–20; (Th) 17:5–10; (Fr) Genesis 37:3–4, 12–13, 17–28; (Sa) Micah 7:14–15, 18–20

READING I *Exodus 3:2, 4–7a, 13–15*

The angel of the LORD appeared to Moses in a flame of fire out of a bush; Moses looked, and the bush was blazing, yet it was not consumed. When the Lord saw that Moses had turned aside to see, God called to him out of the bush, "Moses, Moses!" And Moses said, "Here I am."

Then God said, "Come no closer! Remove the sandals from your feet, for the place on which you are standing is holy ground." God said further, "I am the God of your father, the God of Abraham, the God of Isaac, and the God of Jacob." And Moses hid his face, for he was afraid to look at God. Then the Lord said, "I have observed the misery of my people who are in Egypt; I have come down to deliver them from the Egyptians."

Moses said to God, "If I come to the Israelites and say to them, 'The God of your ancestors has sent me to you,' and they ask me, 'What is his name?' what shall I say to them?"

God said to Moses, "I AM WHO I AM." He said further, "Thus you shall say to the Israelites, 'I AM has sent me to you.'" God also said to Moses, "Thus you shall say to the Israelites, 'The LORD, the God of your ancestors, the God of Abraham, the God of Isaac, and the God of Jacob, has sent me to you': This is my name forever, and this my title for all generations."

[Complete Roman Catholic reading: Exodus 3:1–8, 13–15]
[Revised Common Lectionary: Isaiah 55:1–9]

READING II *1 Corinthians 10:1–6, 10–12*

I do not want you to be unaware, brothers and sisters, that our ancestors were all under the cloud, and all passed through the sea, and all were baptized into Moses in the cloud and in the sea, and all ate the same spiritual food, and all drank the same spiritual drink. For they drank from the spiritual rock that followed them, and the rock was Christ. Nevertheless, God was not pleased with most of them, and they were struck down in the wilderness.

Now these things occurred as examples for us, so that we might not desire evil as they did. And do not complain as some of them did, and were destroyed by the destroyer. These things happened to them to serve as an example, and they were written down to instruct us, on whom the ends of the ages have come. So if you think you are standing, watch out that you do not fall.

[Revised Common Lectionary: 1 Corinthians 10:1–13]

GOSPEL *Luke 13:1–9*

At that very time there were some present who told Jesus about the Galileans whose blood Pilate had mingled with their sacrifices. Jesus asked them, "Do you think that because these Galileans suffered in this way they were worse sinners than all other Galileans? No, I tell you; but unless you repent, you will all perish as they did. Or those eighteen who were killed when the tower of Siloam fell on them—do you think that they were worse offenders than all the others living in Jerusalem? No, I tell you; but unless you repent, you will all perish just as they did."

Then Jesus told this parable: "A man had a fig tree planted in his vineyard; and he came looking for fruit on it and found none. So he said to the gardener, 'See here! For three years I have come looking for fruit on this fig tree, and still I find none. Cut it down! Why should it be wasting the soil?' The gardener replied, 'Sir, let it alone for one more year, until I dig around it and put manure on it. If it bears fruit next year, well and good; but if not, you can cut it down.' "

Monday, March 19, 2001

JOSEPH, HUSBAND OF MARY

2 Samuel 7:4–5, 12–14, 16 *I will make David's throne endure.*

Romans 4:13, 16–18, 22 *He is father of us all.*

Matthew 1:16, 18–21, 24 *Joseph, Son of David, fear not!*

Near the beginning of spring, as the earth is about to awaken from its sleep, we tell the story of Joseph. In the Book of Genesis, Joseph is the "dreamer of dreams." In the Gospel of Matthew, Joseph dreams of the coming kingdom. Then he awakens to find himself the father of the king.

REFLECTION

The notion of repentance may be difficult for many contemporary Christians to understand, especially in light of the popularized stories of fire-and-brimstone preachers. Today's gospel offers some solid ways to approach reconciliation.

In the parable of the fig tree, Jesus is encouraging repentance. The man in the story was a property owner: He owned the fig tree and an orchard. If the man followed the direction of the Torah, the tree would have been growing already for nine years: three years of growth to maturity, three years when the fruit was not to be eaten (see Leviticus 19:23), and three years in which the owner had been expecting fruit from the tree. Jesus gives more care and one more year for the tree to give fruit. All this indicates that repentance is a process, not something completed in an instant. Jesus is encouraging those who hear this parable to understand the importance of nurturing their faith lives over time, with a view to growth and development throughout a lifetime, not just at isolated moments.

Another message of this parable comes out when we place ourselves alongside those who heard this parable for the first time from Jesus' mouth. Jesus' "vineyard parables" were usually aimed at the leadership of the nation, and Jesus' audience—mostly poorer people—would have understood that Jesus was taking their side against the leaders. In today's parable, the hearers would likely have interpreted the barren fig tree as a reference to then-current political or religious leaders. They also would have caught the word play between "let it alone" and "cut it down." In Aramaic, the word for forgiveness is the same as "let it alone." Some in Jesus' audience might have thought it would be a good idea to "cut down" their more unproductive leaders, but Jesus calls them to forgiveness and mercy. Even more important, he calls them to realize that despite people's inadequacies, at least some room—and some encouragement—must be provided for growth.

■ How do you understand the need for repentance in your own life? What are some ways you can participate in the process of repentance during this season of Lent?

■ How do you experience your faith journey? In what ways do you nurture your relationship with Christ?

PRACTICE OF FAITH

WINGS. Saint Augustine said, "Do you wish your prayer to fly toward God? Give it two wings, fasting and almsgiving." This is our lenten tradition! These practices are more effective when done together. Without fasting and almsgiving, our prayer may be mere words. Without prayer and fasting, our almsgiving is mere philanthropy. Without prayer and almsgiving, fasting is just dieting!

Try this: Put a container on your dining table. When you fast sit at the table for the time it would have taken you to eat. Reread last week's readings or read next week's. Figure out how much money you saved by not eating. Deposit that money in the container. Give it to the poor, either today or when your parish collects money at the end of Lent.

PRACTICE OF HOPE

HOLY GROUND. You wouldn't know it was there unless you were looking for it. A refuge from heartaches and illness, the healing garden occupies a small patch of land behind the Motherhouse of the Servants of Mary in Omaha. The wild flowers and grasses are beautiful, but what makes the place so attractive is a wonderful bronze sculpture of Jesus seated in the middle of the garden. Artist John Lajba has created a life-size image of Jesus that invites conversation and reflection. The sisters say they have seen people sitting by the sculpture, holding its hand and praying. Where is the holy ground in your life?

PRACTICE OF CHARITY

OSCAR ROMERO. This Saturday, March 24, is the 21st anniversary of the assassination of Archbishop Oscar Romero of El Salvador. This scholar-turned-prophet was a voice of hope for the poor in El Salvador. Because of his outspoken criticism of the economic system of his country that left so many in poverty, Romero was assassinated as he presided at Mass. Although not officially beatified, Romero has been acclaimed a martyr and saint because of his fearless stand for the cause of social justice. To commemorate his death, watch the movie *Romero*, available in most video stores. Let the archbishop's words and deeds challenge you to be a more active agent for justice in your own time and place.

WEEKDAY READINGS (Mo) Joseph, husband of Mary, see box; (Tu) Deuteronomy 3:25, 34–43; (We) 4:1, 5–9; (Th) Jeremiah 7:23–28; (Fr) Hosea 14:2–10; (Sa) 6:1–6

READING I *Exodus 17:2–7*

The people quarreled with Moses, and said, "Give us water to drink." Moses said to them, "Why do you quarrel with me? Why do you test the LORD?" But the people thirsted there for water; and the people complained against Moses and said, "Why did you bring us out of Egypt, to kill us and our children and livestock with thirst?"

So Moses cried out to the Lord, "What shall I do with this people? They are almost ready to stone me." The Lord said to Moses, "Go on ahead of the people, and take some of the elders of Israel with you; take in your hand the staff with which you struck the Nile, and go. I will be standing there in front of you on the rock at Horeb. Strike the rock, and water will come out of it, so that the people may drink."

Moses did so, in the sight of the elders of Israel. He called the place Massah and Meribah, because the Israelites quarreled and tested the Lord, saying, "Is the Lord among us or not?"

[Roman Catholic: Exodus 17:3–7]

[Revised Common Lectionary: Exodus 17:1–7]

READING II *Romans 5:1–2, 5–8*

Since we are justified by faith, we have peace with God through our Lord Jesus Christ, through whom we have obtained access to this grace in which we stand; and we boast in our hope of sharing the glory of God. And hope does not disappoint us, because God's love has been poured into our hearts through the Holy Spirit that has been given to us.

For while we were still weak, at the right time Christ died for the ungodly. Indeed, rarely will anyone die for a righteous person—though perhaps for a good person someone might actually dare to die. But it is proof of God's own love for us in that while we still were sinners Christ died for us.

[Revised Common Lectionary: Romans 5:1–11]

GOSPEL *John 4:5–15, 19–21, 24–26, 39, 40–42*

Jesus came to a Samaritan city called Sychar, near the plot of ground that Jacob had given to his son Joseph. Jacob's well was there, and Jesus, tired out by his journey, was sitting by the well. It was about noon.

A Samaritan woman came to draw water, and Jesus said to her, "Give me a drink." (His disciples had gone to the city to buy food.) The Samaritan woman said to him, "How is it that you, a Jewish man, ask a drink of me, a woman of Samaria?" (Jewish people do not share things in common with Samaritans.) Jesus answered her, "If you knew the gift of God, and who it is that is saying to you, 'Give me a drink,' you would have asked him, and he would have given you living water. The water that I will give will become in them a spring of water gushing up to eternal life." The woman said to Jesus, "Sir, give me this water, so that I may never be thirsty or have to keep coming here to draw water."

Jesus said to her, "Go, call your husband, and come back." The woman answered him, "I have no husband." Jesus said to her, "You are right in saying, 'I have no husband'; for you have had five husbands, and the one you have now is not your husband. What you have said is true!" The woman said to Jesus, "Sir, I see that you are a prophet. Our ancestors worshiped on this mountain, but you say that the place where people must worship is in Jerusalem."

Jesus said to her, "Woman, believe me, the hour is coming when you will worship the Father neither on this mountain nor in Jerusalem. God is spirit, and those who worship God must worship in spirit and truth." The woman said to him, "I know that Messiah is coming" (who is called Christ). "When he comes, he will proclaim all things to us." Jesus said to her, "Here I am, the one who is speaking to you."

Many Samaritans from that city believed in Jesus because of the woman's testimony. They asked him to stay with them; and Jesus stayed there two days. And many more believed because of his word. They said to the woman, "It is no longer because of what you said that we believe, for we have heard for ourselves, and we know that this is truly the Savior of the world."

[Complete reading: John 4:5–42]

REFLECTION

The first reading contrasts weak human nature with forgiving divine nature. The people blamed Moses for their own lack of hope and foresight. In their thirst for water, they lost a sense of the journey they had undertaken. The years they spent journeying in the desert were not simply a trip from point A to point B, but an important time of faith development. The people walked along their journey in order to foster their longing for their God. Their thirst for water, read as a symbol, suggests thirst for God, cleansing and rejuvenation. Even as the Israelites seek a deeper relationship with their God on their journey, their human nature leads them into frustration and anguish because they feel that they are getting nowhere as a people.

In answer to their complaints, God does the impossible, making water flow from a lifeless rock. This is not just a "nature miracle" that points to God's awesome power; this event expresses God's sustaining presence with the Israelites. The people, struggling in the journey of their lives, rediscover the God who cleanses them of the smudges of their quarrels and refreshes them for their journey.

The gospel passage also brings together a person on a journey of faith—the Samaritan woman—and the divine mercy of God, present in Jesus. The woman's journey unfolds throughout the story and evidences itself in the various titles she uses for Jesus. She first addresses him in a generic way: as "a Jewish man." Then she calls him "sir," and later "a prophet." Finally she recognizes Jesus as "Messiah" (see verse 29). These expressions show her deepening awareness of the identity of Jesus and mark her journey to the "promised land" of salvation. Just as the quarreling Israelites sought renewal in water, so does this woman. The renewal that both the Israelites and the woman receive comes in the form of a relationship with the God who satisfies the thirst of all who call out and approach in openness.

■ As people of God, we journey through life toward salvation. How is the journey going for you? What rest stops must you take along the way?

■ What titles do you give Christ? How do you name Christ? What do these names say about your relationship with Christ?

PRACTICE OF FAITH

DRAW WATER. About 70% of the earth's surface is covered by water. About 70% of the human body is water, too. Think of all the stories in the Bible that you know about water. Jot down a list in the margin, using short phrases to jog your memory: "Noah's ark," "crossing Jordan" and so on. What is God trying to tell us? Why do we use water to baptize? Scripture doesn't say, but one tradition says that the woman at the well with her water jug was named Photina, "the enlightened one." Thus water and enlightenment are joined in her story of her life-changing encounter with Christ.

Easter is coming. Find or make a beautiful container with a tight-fitting lid. Keep it empty in your place of prayer until Easter. Then take it to church, draw some water from the font and bring it home with you.

PRACTICE OF HOPE

LIVING WATER. Almost from the minute I met Rhonda, I knew that we would wind up at the Easter Vigil together. She started as an inquirer in the Rite of Christian Initiation of Adults in our parish when her son enrolled in school. She wanted to support him and strengthen her family by sharing the faith of her son and husband. As a member of the RCIA team (and later as her godparent), I took great joy in telling her about her upcoming baptism and teasing her about how long we were going to hold her under the water. Funny thing is, she didn't go into the water alone. Through her, all of us in that church experienced the living waters of baptism that night. Led by Rhonda, we chose to live in Christ again. We will never be the same for it.

PRACTICE OF CHARITY

NOTHING IN COMMON. The dialogue between Jesus and the person at the well should never have happened: Jesus was a Jew and male; not only was the person at the well a woman, she was a Samaritan, a heretic as far as the Jews were concerned. Yet the woman, with Jesus, overcame her fears and they reached over the boundaries their culture had taught.

Jesus and the woman have much to teach us. We are so often divided along ethnic, racial, socioeconomic and religious lines. As you observe Lent this year, identify a group of people, or a culture or religion you do not understand. Find some way, perhaps attending a church service or cultural event or even reading a book, to open your mind and broaden your understanding.

WEEKDAY READINGS (Mo) Joseph, Husband of Mary, see page 64; (Tu) Deuteronomy 3:25, 34–43; (We) 4:1, 5–9; (Th) Jeremiah 7:23–28; (Fr) Hosea 14:2–10; (Sa) 6:1–6

READING I *Joshua 5:9–12*

The LORD said to Joshua, "Today I have rolled away from you the disgrace of Egypt." And so that place is called Gilgal to this day. While the Israelites were camped in Gilgal they kept the passover in the evening on the fourteenth day of the month in the plains of Jericho. On the day after the passover, on that very day, they ate the produce of the land, unleavened cakes and parched grain. The manna ceased on the day they ate the produce of the land, and the Israelites no longer had manna; they ate the crops of the land of Canaan that year.

READING II *2 Corinthians 5:16–21*

From now on, therefore, we regard no one from a human point of view; even though we once knew Christ from a human point of view, we know him no longer in that way. So if anyone is in Christ, there is a new creation: everything old has passed away; see, everything has become new! All this is from God, who reconciled us through Christ to God, and has given us the ministry of reconciliation; that is, in Christ God was reconciling the world to God's own self, not counting their trespasses against them, and entrusting the message of reconciliation to us. So we are ambassadors for Christ, since God is appealing through us; we entreat you on behalf of Christ, be reconciled to God. For our sake God made Christ to be sin who knew no sin, so that in Christ we might become the righteousness of God.

[Roman Catholic: 2 Corinthians 5:17–21]

GOSPEL *Luke 15:1–3, 11–24*

Now all the tax collectors and sinners were coming near to listen to Jesus. And the Pharisees and the scribes were grumbling and saying, "This fellow welcomes sinners and eats with them."

So Jesus told them this parable: "There was a man who had two sons. The younger of them said to his father, 'Father, give me the share of the property that will belong to me.' So the father divided his property between them. A few days later the younger son gathered all he had and traveled to a distant country, and there he squandered his property in dissolute living. When he had spent everything, a severe famine took place throughout that country, and he began to be in need. So he went and hired himself out to one of the citizens of that country, who sent him to his fields to feed the pigs. He would gladly have filled himself with the pods that the pigs were eating; and no one gave him anything. But when he came to himself he said, 'How many of my father's hired hands have bread enough and to spare, but here I am dying of hunger! I will get up and go to my father, and I will say to him, "Father, I have sinned against heaven and before you; I am no longer worthy to be called your son; treat me like one of your hired hands." ' So he set off and went to his father. But while he was still far off, his father saw him and was filled with compassion; he ran and put his arms around him and kissed him. Then the son said to him, 'Father, I have sinned against heaven and before you; I am no longer worthy to be called your son.' But the father said to his slaves, 'Quickly, bring out a robe—the best one—and put it on him; put a ring on his finger and sandals on his feet. And get the fatted calf and kill it, and let us eat and celebrate; for this son of mine was dead and is alive again; he was lost and is found!' "

[Complete reading: Luke 15:1–3, 11–32]

Monday, March 26, 2001

ANNUNCIATION OF THE LORD

Isaiah 7:10–14 *A virgin will bear a child.*

Hebrews 10:4–10 *I come to do God's will.*

Luke 1:26–38 *Rejoice, O highly favored daughter!*

Because pregnancy outside of marriage was punishable by death, Mary's "yes" to the angel was an acceptance of death. But in this death, the risen Spirit conquers death. Mary's mortal body conceives the Immortal One. The paschal victory is won.

REFLECTION

The story of the prodigal son has always been considered a great story of God's forgiveness. And so it is. But it may also be thought of as a story of *God's* prodigality—God's foolish extravagance—and hence a story of God's priorities.

The behavior of the younger son of the parable is utterly reprehensible. He first insults his father by telling him that he wants what will come to him at his father's death. Basically, the son tells his father that he does not care whether his father is alive or dead. The son then offends his community by spending in a foreign land money that had been hard-earned by a Jew in Israel and meant to strengthen Israel. The son also insults his Jewish heritage by living with pigs, ritually unclean animals that no good Jew would even touch, let alone live with. He has, in effect, turned his back on his family, country and religious community.

But then, after spending all the money, he decides to return to his father who at least feeds his hired men decent food. And now the father behaves in a way his neighbors would call foolish. Without hearing a word of repentance from his son, the father runs to meet him. People of some dignity simply do not run, and one can almost hear the snickers of the people standing around as the father hikes up his robes and runs out to meet his wayward son. He then welcomes his son home with amazing extravagance—with a hug and a kiss, the finest of robes, a ring, shoes and a feast. And not a small private feast, for by ordering the slaughter of the fatted calf, the father clearly intends to invite the entire community. The father is inviting the whole village—by now probably convinced that he is a fool for his lavish response to his errant son—to join him in his prodigality, his reckless extravagance!

As the story ends, note that the father also acts "foolishly" in his dealing with his older son as well. The older son complains bitterly to his father, even lying about the younger son being involved with harlots. Despite such dishonorable behavior, the father responds with love, reassurance and an invitation to join the celebration.

■ **Can you identify with the younger son? When are the times in your life when God has behaved like the father in the story toward you? How can you celebrate this "foolishness" in your life?**

■ **In what ways can you imitate the extravagance of the father in your life? Who do you need to forgive?**

PRACTICE OF FAITH

MORNING AND EVENING. Christians have always prayed at sunrise and sunset. These pivotal points of the day remind us of God's power, of our own birth and death.

Try to be more aware of sunrise and sunset this week. Say these words from the church's morning prayer when you first see the light of day: "O Lord, open my lips / and my mouth shall declare your praise!" And pray this when the sun goes down: "O God, come to my assistance. / O Lord, make haste to help me!" If you live with another or with others, one can say the first part and the other(s) can complete the prayer.

PRACTICE OF HOPE

AMBASSADORS FOR CHRIST. The banners hanging over the exits of the Lutheran church in Decorah, Iowa, were simple yet powerful. "You are now entering your mission field," they reminded parishioners. It's not that these men and women were traveling anywhere far that weekend. They were just going out to their everyday lives, supported by the love of Christ and the hope of the resurrection. That love and hope are what they were being invited to share with the people they encountered at home, at school and at work. There is no doubt that there are those half a world away who need to hear the gospel, but so do our neighbors half a block away. All of us have the responsibility—and the privilege—of carrying Christ's message into a world that desperately needs to hear it.

PRACTICE OF CHARITY

PRODUCE OF THE LAND. The lenten practice of fasting keeps us mindful of food, and the texts of our tradition remind us of our reliance on God. Yet, in an age of high technology and genetic engineering, we are fast forgetting our dependence on the land, and subsequently on God, for our daily bread. Just 100 years ago, some 50% of U.S. citizens farmed; today, that number is less than 5%. Corporate agribusiness is quickly gobbling up the remaining family farms; the same is happening all over the world.

Read *A Calendar of Care* by James Schmitmeyer (available from LTP) to learn about the crisis in rural life. Consider buying organic or locally-grown produce, or participate in community-supported agriculture.

WEEKDAY READINGS (Mo) Annunciation of the Lord, see box; (Tu) Ezekiel 47:1–9, 12; (We) Isaiah 49:8–15; (Th) Exodus 32:7–14; (Fr) Wisdom 2:1, 12–22; (Sa) Jeremiah 11:18–20

READING I *1 Samuel 16:1, 5–7, 10–13*

The LORD said to Samuel, "I will send you to Jesse the Bethlehemite, for I have provided for myself a king among his sons." And Samuel sanctified Jesse and his sons and invited them to the sacrifice.

When they came, Samuel looked on Eliab and thought, "Surely the LORD's anointed is now before the LORD." But the LORD said to Samuel, "Do not look on his appearance or on the height of his stature, because I have rejected him; for the LORD does not see as mortals see; they look on the outward appearance, but the LORD looks on the heart." Jesse made seven of his sons pass before Samuel, and Samuel said to Jesse, "The LORD has not chosen any of these."

Samuel said to Jesse, "Are all your sons here?" And he said, "There remains yet the youngest, but he is keeping the sheep." And Samuel said to Jesse, "Send and bring him; for we will not sit down until he comes here." Jesse sent and brought him in. Now he was ruddy, and had beautiful eyes, and was handsome. The LORD said, "Rise and anoint him; for this is the one." Then Samuel took the horn of oil, and anointed him in the presence of his brothers; and the spirit of the LORD came mightily upon David from that day forward. Samuel then set out and went to Ramah.

[Revised Common Lectionary: 1 Samuel 16:1–13]

READING II *Ephesians 5:8–14*

Once you were darkness, but now in the Lord you are light. Live as children of light—for the fruit of the light is found in all that is good and right and true. Try to find out what is pleasing to the Lord. Take no part in the unfruitful works of darkness, but instead expose them. For it is shameful even to mention what such people do secretly; but everything exposed by the light becomes visible, for everything that becomes visible is light.

Therefore it says, "Sleeper, awake! Rise from the dead, and Christ will shine on you."

GOSPEL *John 9:1, 6–17, 34–38*

As Jesus walked along, he saw a man blind from birth. Jesus spat on the ground and made mud with the saliva and spread the mud on the man's eyes, saying to him, "Go, wash in the pool of Siloam" (which means Sent). Then he went and washed and came back able to see.

The neighbors and those who had seen him before as a beggar began to ask, "Is this not the man who used to sit and beg?" Some were saying, "It is he." Others were saying, "No, but it is someone like him." He kept saying, "I am the man." But they kept asking him, "Then how were your eyes opened?" He answered, "The man called Jesus made mud, spread it on my eyes, and said to me, 'Go to Siloam and wash.' Then I went and washed and received my sight." They said to him, "Where is he?" He said, "I do not know."

They brought to the Pharisees the man who had formerly been blind. Now it was a sabbath day when Jesus made the mud and opened his eyes. Then the Pharisees also began to ask him how he had received his sight. He said to them, "He put mud on my eyes. Then I washed, and now I see." Some of the Pharisees said, "This man is not from God, for he does not observe the sabbath." But others said, "How can a man who is a sinner perform such signs?" And they were divided. So they said again to the blind man, "What do you say about him? It was your eyes he opened." He said, "He is a prophet."

They answered him, "You were born entirely in sins, and are you trying to teach us?" And they drove him out.

Jesus heard that they had driven him out, and when he found him, he said, "Do you believe in the Son-of-Man?" He answered, "And who is he, sir? Tell me, so that I may believe in him." Jesus said to him, "You have seen him, and he is the one speaking with you." He said, "Lord, I believe." And he worshiped Jesus.

[Complete reading: John 9:1–41]

REFLECTION

Jesus' action of restoring the blind man's sight is a gift of grace, offered freely out of love. The gift that Jesus gives to the blind man includes his physical sight, and more: The man recognizes Jesus as a prophet and the Son of Man. He has received the gift of faith.

The blind man's experience is in contrast to those of his neighbors, the religious authorities, and the Pharisees. The neighbors, accustomed to seeing the blind man begging by the roadside, are confused. They do not trust what their eyes are telling them and cannot believe it is the same man. For the Pharisees, the healing of the blind man causes a different kind of confusion. Their notions of how a prophet or man of God acts are turned upside down. Because Jesus cured the blind man on the Sabbath, some of them consider Jesus a sinner; others, however, see it as a miracle and wonder how a sinner can perform such a miracle as this. Their focus on the rules and regulations prevents them from seeing the gift of God's love that Jesus' action manifests.

Through his preaching and ministry Jesus shone a light on "the unfruitful works of darkness" that were a part of the social, political and religious climate of his day. Jesus' words to the Samaritan woman that we heard last week, and his healing of the blind man in today's gospel point to what the light reveals. God's love is manifested and proclaimed by actions of forgiveness and healing.

We are moving ever closer to our celebration of the Easter Vigil, when all of the church will proclaim that Christ is our light. How is Christ our light? What darkness does Christ dispel? What blindness does Christ remove? These are questions that are as important for us today as they were for the first followers of Jesus.

■ **What social or political structures of our day are "in darkness"? If the light of the gospel were to shine on them, what would be different?**

■ **Look at the gospel readings for the third, fourth and fifth Sundays of Lent, Year A (pages 66, 70 and 74). Why do you think these readings are chosen for this time of the year?**

PRACTICE OF FAITH

NOW I SEE. Blindness is often used in the Bible as a metaphor for being unable to recognize God. This does not mean that blindness is a result of one's failings—the gospel makes it clear that this is not so. It is a metaphor, not a judgment on blind people! We fail to love because we don't see with our hearts.

After searching his soul about how he made his money—as a trader of African slaves—John Newton wrote the hymn *Amazing Grace:* "I once was blind, but now I see!" He repented, and worked strenuously to outlaw slavery.

Search your soul. Make a list of your blind spots. Review your list each night. Sing *Amazing Grace.*

PRACTICE OF HOPE

SLEEPER, AWAKE! There are so many ways of looking at things. Is the glass half empty or half full? Looking through the eyes of faith helps to bring things into focus. I am reminded of Ed, who had gone to church for years, but never had any real formation in the faith. He came into the catechumenate last year and blossomed before our eyes. He asked a lot of questions and did a lot of thinking, but it was obvious that Ed was seeing everything in a new way. This year he took a pay cut to teach in an inner-city Catholic school, where he helps young people to see the Christ he has come to know. He still jokingly complains about how cold the waters of baptism were, but he's happy to tell people how and why his life has changed.

PRACTICE OF CHARITY

BORN IN SIN. A recent Reuters news story reported that 44 percent of college students believed that serious illness is a "payback" for bad behavior. Often people are blamed for being homeless, women are blamed for being assaulted, people with HIV/AIDS are considered responsible for their infection, and alcoholism is thought to be a character flaw. On top of this, the politics of personal responsibility often results in legislation that cuts social programs and forces those already in need into more desperate situations.

Rather than indulge in false self-righteousness, look at others with compassion, seeing them as *persons* rather than AIDS victims or alcoholics or teenage mothers. Consider your own life and how luck, good and bad, has affected you and your situation in life.

WEEKDAY READINGS (Mo) Annunciation of the Lord, see page 68; (Tu) Ezekiel 47:1–9, 12; (We) Isaiah 49:8–15; (Th) Exodus 32:7–14; (Fr) Wisdom 2:1, 12–22; (Sa) Jeremiah 11:18–20

READING I   *Isaiah 43:16–21*

Thus says the LORD,
  who makes a way in the sea,
  a path in the mighty waters,
who brings out chariot and horse,
  army and warrior;
they lie down, they cannot rise,
  they are extinguished, quenched like a wick:
Do not remember the former things,
  or consider the things of old.
I am about to do a new thing;
  now it springs forth, do you not perceive it?
I will make a way in the wilderness
  and rivers in the desert.
The wild animals will honor me,
  the jackals and the ostriches;
for I give water in the wilderness,
  rivers in the desert,
to give drink to my chosen people,
  the people whom I formed for myself
so that they might declare my praise.

READING II   *Philippians 3:4–14*

If anyone else has reason to be confident in the flesh, I have more: circumcised on the eighth day, a member of the people of Israel, of the tribe of Benjamin, a Hebrew born of Hebrews; as to the law, a Pharisee; as to zeal, a persecutor of the church; as to righteousness under the law, blameless.

Yet whatever gains I had, these I have come to regard as loss because of Christ. More than that, I regard everything as loss because of the surpassing value of knowing Christ Jesus my Lord, for whose sake I have suffered the loss of all things, and I regard them as rubbish, in order that I may gain Christ and be found in him, not having a righteousness of my own that comes from the law, but one that comes through faith in Christ, the righteousness from God based on faith. I want to know Christ and the power of his resurrection and the sharing of his sufferings by becoming like him in his death, if somehow I may attain the resurrection from the dead.

Not that I have already obtained this or have already reached the goal but I press on to make it my own, because Christ Jesus has made me his own.

Beloved, I do not consider that I have made it my own but this one thing I do: forgetting what lies behind and straining forward to what lies ahead, I press on toward the goal for the prize of the heavenly call of God in Christ Jesus.

[Roman Catholic: Philippians 3:8–14]

GOSPEL   *John 8:1–11*

Jesus went to the Mount of Olives. Early in the morning he came again to the temple. All the people came to him and he sat down and began to teach them.

The scribes and the Pharisees brought a woman who had been caught in adultery; and making her stand before the people, they said to Jesus, "Teacher, this woman was caught in the very act of committing adultery. In the law, Moses commanded us to stone such women. Now what do you say?" They said this to test Jesus, so that they might have some charge to bring against him.

Jesus bent down and wrote with his finger on the ground. When the scribes and Pharisees kept on questioning him, Jesus straightened up and said to them, "Let anyone among you who is without sin be the first to throw a stone at her." And once again Jesus bent down and wrote on the ground. When the scribes and Pharisees heard what Jesus had said, they went away, one by one, beginning with the elders; and Jesus was left alone with the woman standing before him.

Jesus straightened up and said to her, "Woman, where are they? Has no one condemned you?" She said, "No one, sir." And Jesus said, "Neither do I condemn you. Go your way, and from now on do not sin again."

[Revised Common Lectionary: John 12:1–8]

REFLECTION

Isaiah writes a song of the desert. He quotes God as saying "I give water in the wilderness, rivers in the desert." The wilderness of the Middle East of Isaiah's time was an empty, lonely land, uncultivated, occupied mostly by nomads, not permanently settled. The earth there is dry marl, a loose and crumbly crust of sand, salt and clay. The heat during the day can be unbearable while the cold of night can be deadly.

The desert wilderness is a place of astonishing contrast: a place of intense heat and threatening cold; of relentless drought and violent flash floods; of nomads and cave dwellers. While the desert may be a forbidding place, it has been a place of salvation for the Hebrews. Despite its perilous contrasts, or perhaps in light of them, the wilderness is a place about which to sing. God fed and watered the chosen people there; a new covenant with God was born there. It is no wonder that Isaiah sings the salvation of God in the wilderness.

In the gospel reading, the woman who has been caught in adultery is in a different kind of wilderness. She is trapped, threatened by members of her community who want to see her killed, and isolated, with no one to defend her. Jesus is also trapped in a wilderness, trapped by those who bring the woman to him. If Jesus lets her go free, he will be charged with violating the law of Moses. If he insists that she be stoned, he will be inciting a violation of Roman law, as the Romans reserved capital punishment to themselves.

Jesus' response is to turn the focus away from the woman and onto the accusing crowd. Jesus challenges the scribes and Pharisees to examine their own hearts. His response—"Let the one without sin throw the first stone"—is like water in a wilderness of alienation and self-righteousness. As in the wilderness of Isaiah's song, here, too, renewal comes in the word of the Lord.

■ **What is the wilderness of your life? That place of extremes that seems to be without perspective, balance, life? How do you resolve a situation that at first glance can only have bad outcomes?**

■ **How do you experience the gift of water given to you by God to nourish your life? How do you express gratitude for this?**

PRACTICE OF FAITH

HE TAUGHT THEM. A fruitful practice is to imagine yourself in a gospel story, being attentive to your thoughts and feelings as you read the story. Read today's gospel passage slowly. Imagine that you are the woman. How do you feel? Imagine that you are one of the Pharisees. How do you feel? Imagine that you are the man caught in adultery, but not hauled out for public scrutiny. Imagine, too, that you are Jesus. What are your reactions in each case?

Christ can continue to teach us through the scriptures when we place ourselves in the story in this way. Make this kind of reflection a part of the time you spend with the Sunday readings.

PRACTICE OF HOPE

THROW A STONE. It is easy for us to distance ourselves from today's gospel. After all, we would never think of punishing people by throwing things at them. Or would we? Was it just the stones that would have hurt the woman caught in adultery? What about the looks of the people around her? What about their words?

In truth, all these things can do violence. In response, Pax Christi USA has developed a "Vow of Nonviolence." The national Catholic peace movement asks people to follow the example of Jesus "by accepting suffering rather than inflicting it; by persevering in nonviolence of tongue and heart; and by living conscientiously and simply so that I do not deprive others of the means to live." Change is possible. Peace can be created—one person at a time.

PRACTICE OF CHARITY

THEY MADE HER STAND THERE. The public humiliation of the woman caught in adultery by the "righteous" of her time is like the public finger-pointing in our own. So many people are publicly excoriated for what some perceive as sin. Our culture seems titillated by the "sins" of others, especially if it involves sex.

Yet Jesus seems to recognize the complexity of situations. Perhaps he wondered why the woman's accomplice was not dragged before him, since the two were "caught in the act." He certainly points out the hypocrisy of it all. During Lent, challenge yourself to recognize the complexity of others' lives. Allow yourself to recognize the deeper sinfulness of our society, which seeks the humiliation of others to satisfy our own sense of self-righteousness.

WEEKDAY READINGS (Mo) Deuteronomy 13:1–9, 15–17, 19–30, 33–62 or 13:41–62; (Tu) Numbers 21:4–9; (We) Deuteronomy 3:14–20, 91–92, 95; (Th) Genesis 17:3–9; (Fr) Jeremiah 20:10–13; (Sa) Ezra 37:21–28

READING I *Ezekiel 37:12–14*

Thus says the Lord GOD: I am going to open your graves, and bring you up from your graves, O my people; and I will bring you back to the land of Israel. And you shall know that I am the LORD, when I open your graves, and bring you up from your graves, O my people. I will put my spirit within you, and you shall live, and I will place you on your own soil; then you shall know that I, the LORD, have spoken and will act, says the LORD.
[*Revised Common Lectionary: Ezekiel 37:1–14*]

READING II *Romans 8:6–11*

To set the mind on the flesh is death, but to set the mind on the Spirit is life and peace. For this reason the mind that is set on the flesh is hostile to God; it doesn't submit to God's law—indeed it cannot, and those who are in the flesh cannot please God. But you are not in the flesh; you are in the Spirit, since the Spirit of God dwells in you. Anyone who does not have the Spirit of Christ does not belong to Christ. But if Christ is in you, though the body is dead because of sin, the Spirit is life because of righteousness. If the Spirit of the one who raised Jesus from the dead dwells in you, the one who raised Christ from the dead will give life to your mortal bodies also through this Spirit dwelling in you.
[*Roman Catholic: Romans 8:8–11*]

GOSPEL *John 11:3-7, 17, 20–27, 33–45*

Mary and Martha sent a message to Jesus, "Lord, he whom you love is ill." But when Jesus heard it, he said, "This illness does not lead to death; rather it is for God's glory, so that the Son of God may be glorified through it." Accordingly, though Jesus loved Martha and her sister and Lazarus, after having heard that Lazarus was ill, he stayed two days longer in the place where he was.

Then after this he said to the disciples, "Let us go to Judea again."

When Jesus arrived, he found that Lazarus had already been in the tomb four days.

When Martha heard that Jesus was coming, she went and met him, while Mary stayed at home. Martha said to Jesus, "Lord, if you had been here, my brother would not have died. But even now I know that whatever you ask from God, God will give you." Jesus said to her, "Your brother will rise again." Martha said to him, "I know that he will rise again in the resurrection on the last day." Jesus said to her, "I am the resurrection and the life. Those who believe in me, even though they die, will live, and everyone who lives and believes in me will never die. Do you believe this?" She said to him, "Yes, Lord, I believe that you are the Messiah, the Son of God, the one coming into the world."

Jesus was greatly disturbed in spirit and deeply moved. He said, "Where have you laid him?" They said to him, "Lord, come and see." Jesus began to weep. So the Judeans said, "See how he loved him!" But some of them said, "Could not the one who opened the eyes of the blind man have kept this man from dying?"

Then Jesus, again greatly disturbed, came to the tomb. It was a cave, and a stone was lying against it. Jesus said, "Take away the stone." Martha, the sister of the dead man, said to him, "Lord, already there is a stench because he has been dead four days." Jesus said to her, "Did I not tell you that if you believed, you would see the glory of God?"

So they took away the stone. And Jesus looked upward and said, "Father, I thank you for having heard me. I knew that you always hear me, but I have said this for the sake of the crowd standing here, so that they may believe that you sent me." When Jesus had said this, he cried with a loud voice, "Lazarus, come out!" The dead man came out, his hands and feet bound with strips of cloth, and his face wrapped in a cloth. Jesus said to them, "Unbind him, and let him go."

Many of the Judeans therefore, who had come with Mary and had seen what Jesus did, believed in him.
[*Complete reading: John 11:1–45*]

REFLECTION

We may have a difficult time understanding Ezekiel, who sees and hears strange things. The reading for today focuses on a bizarre image of a burial ground being opened and dry bones coming forth from it. At first glance this image is confusing, but in the context of Israel's history it carries a beautiful message of hope.

The Israelites had been carried away into captivity by the Babylonians. Their social, religious, political and economic life as a nation had been destroyed. There was no hope of a change, or a rescue. No hope, that is, until Ezeliel came on the scene. Ezekiel's response to God's call to prophecy brings the needed message of hope for a new life. The captive Israelites heard in this text a message of personal and social restoration. It is important to note that what Ezekiel prophesies is not a new life unconnected with what went before. In Ezekiel's prophecy, God will *restore* the people, not merely resuscitate them. This restoration means that they will be placed on their own land, filled with the spirit of the Lord, and they will live full lives based on the covenant with the Lord.

The gospel reading presents the same message. Jesus, Martha and Mary (and many others in Bethany) mourn the loss of Lazarus. Their mourning recalls the mourning of Israel during the exile. Just as God restored the Israelites in giving them back their land, their dignity, their spirit, so does God restore the life of Lazarus. The God that brought Israel out of exile continues, in Jesus, to restore to life those who believe.

It is important for us to note that neither the raising of Lazarus nor Israel's release from exile in Babylon was a mere resuscitation or an opportunity to just pick up where things left off. Both were restorations to a life based on covenant, to a life of purpose, a life of interdependence and truly valued relationships. In them, we see one way to begin to understand the meaning our faith gives to the resurrection of the dead.

■ **Who are prophets of hope in your life? In your world? How can you be a prophet of hope?**

■ **How has God touched you in your exile? How has God restored you?**

PRACTICE OF FAITH

UNBIND AND LET GO. Many people die—literally and figuratively—bound by our prejudices, shackled by structures that make a few people wealthy and many people poor, held immobile in tombs of despair when profits are more important than people. But God sides with the oppressed, raises them to life, and calls us to unbind them and let them go free. Take Jesus' command literally this week: Unbind a sweatshop worker by finding out where the clothes in your favorite store are made, and under what conditions. Then go to www.uniteunion.org and follow one of its suggestions. If you are baptized, celebrate the sacrament of reconciliation this week, and let the ministry of the church unbind your heart and set you free, too.

PRACTICE OF HOPE

UNTIE HIM. An old hymn celebrates "The Ties that Bind." When that describes the love of family, friends and God, it's wonderful. But there are other ties, ones that are less positive. We can be held fast by addictions, bad habits and sin, too. In order to break these bonds, we need the support of those around us.

I have often been humbled by the example of those who are going through the Rite of Christian Initiation of Adults. These men and women are fearless about looking at their lives and trying to discern what works, what doesn't and what will bring them closer to Jesus. That search never fails to enrich us and bring us closer together as the body of Christ. These are the ties that are meant to bind for a lifetime—and beyond.

PRACTICE OF CHARITY

RAISING THE DEAD. Just two years ago, stories of NATO's bombing of Serbia and Kosovo, of ethnic cleansing and accidental civilian casualties filled the news. Serbians first drove out and murdered ethnic Albanians in Kosovo; when they returned, Albanians did the same to Serbians, albeit on a smaller scale. Amid all this suffering, some, both Orthodox Serbian and Muslim Albanian, were trying to live together in peace. Among these, Mother Maharija, abbess of a Serbian Orthodox convent in Kosovo, sought to help all people in need.

Support the International Orthodox Christian Charities in its efforts to rebuild the Balkans and restore to life and right relationship its peoples: PO Box 630225, Baltimore MD 21263; 1-410-243-9820; www.iocc.org.

WEEKDAY READINGS (Mo) Deuteronomy 13:1–9, 15–17, 19–30, 33–62 or 13:41–62; (Tu) Numbers 21:4–9; (We) Deuteronomy 3:14–20, 91–92, 95; (Th) Genesis 17:3–9; (Fr) Jeremiah 20:10–13; (Sa) Ezra 37:21–28

READING I *Isaiah 50:4–7*

The Lord GOD has given me the tongue of a teacher,
that I may know how to sustain
the weary with a word.
Morning by morning the Lord GOD wakens—
wakens my ear to listen as those who are taught.
The Lord GOD has opened my ear,
and I was not rebellious,
I did not turn backward.
I gave my back to those who struck me,
and my cheeks to those who pulled out the beard;
I did not hide my face from insult and spitting.

The Lord GOD helps me;
therefore I have not been disgraced;
therefore I have set my face like flint,
and I know that I shall not be put to shame.
[Revised Common Lectionary: Isaiah 50:4–9a]

READING II *Philippians 2:6–11*

Although being in the form of God, Christ Jesus did not regard equality with God as something to be exploited, but relinquished it all, taking the form of a slave, being born in human likeness. And being found in human form, he humbled himself and became obedient to the point of death—even death on a cross.

Therefore God also highly exalted him and gave him the name that is above every name, so that at the name of Jesus every knee should bend, in heaven and on earth and under the earth, and every tongue should confess that Jesus Christ is Lord, to the glory of God, the Father.
[Revised Common Lectionary: Philippians 2:5–11]

GOSPEL *Luke 22:14—23:25, 32–56*

When the hour came, Jesus took his place at the table, and the apostles with him. He said to them, "I have eagerly desired to eat this Passover with you before I suffer; for I tell you, I will not eat it until it is fulfilled in the dominion of God." Then Jesus took a cup, and after giving thanks he said, "Take this and divide it among yourselves; for I tell you that from now on I will not drink of the fruit of the vine until the dominion of God comes." Then he took a loaf of bread, and when he had given thanks, he broke it and gave it to them, saying, "This is my body, which is given for you. Do this in remembrance of me." And Jesus did the same with the cup after supper, saying, "This cup that is poured out for you is the new covenant in my blood. But see, the one who betrays me is with me, and his hand is on the table. For the Son-of-Man is going as it has been determined, but woe to that one by whom he is betrayed!" Then they began to ask one another which one of them it could be who would do this.

A dispute also arose among them as to which one of them was to be regarded as the greatest. But Jesus said to them, "The rulers of the Gentiles are domineering; and those in authority over them are called benefactors. But not so with you; rather the greatest among you must become like the youngest, and the leader like one who serves. For who is greater, the one who is at the table or the one who serves? Is it not the one at the table? But I am among you as one who serves.

"You are those who have stood by me in my trials; and I confer on you, just as my Father has conferred on me, a dominion, so that you may eat and drink at my table in my dominion, and you will sit on thrones judging the twelve tribes of Israel.

"Simon, Simon, listen! Satan has demanded to sift all of you like wheat, but I have prayed for you that your own faith may not fail; and you, when once you have turned back, strengthen the community." And Simon Peter said to Jesus, "Lord, I am ready to go with you to prison and to death!" Jesus said, "I tell you, Peter, the cock will not crow this day, until you have denied three times that you know me." Jesus said to them, "When I sent you out without a purse, bag, or sandals, did you lack anything?" They said, "No, not a thing." He said to them, "But now, the one who has a purse must take it, and likewise a bag. And the one who has no sword must sell a cloak to buy one. For I tell you, this scripture must be fulfilled in me, 'And he was counted among the lawless'; and indeed what is written about me is being fulfilled." They said, "Lord, look, here are two swords." He replied, "It is enough."

Jesus came out and went, as was his custom, to the Mount of Olives; and the disciples followed him. When he reached the place, he said to them, "Pray that you may not come into the time of trial." Then he withdrew from them about a stone's throw, knelt down, and prayed, "Father, if you are willing, remove this cup from me; yet, not my will but yours be done." Then an angel from heaven appeared to Jesus and gave him strength. In his anguish Jesus prayed more earnestly, and his sweat became like great drops of blood falling down on the ground. When he got up from prayer, he came to the disciples and found them sleeping because of grief, and he said to them, "Why are you sleeping? Get up and pray that you may not come into the time of trial."

While Jesus was still speaking, suddenly a crowd came, and the one called Judas, one of the twelve, was leading them. Judas approached Jesus to kiss him; but Jesus said to him, "Judas, is it with a kiss that you are betraying the Son-of-Man?" When those who were around him saw what was coming, they asked, "Lord, should we strike with the sword?" Then one of them struck the slave of the high priest and cut off his right ear. But Jesus said, "No more of this!" And Jesus touched the slave's ear and healed him. Then Jesus said to the chief priests, the officers of the temple police, and the elders who had come for him, "Have you come out with swords and clubs as if I were a bandit? When I was with you day after day in the temple, you did not lay hands on me. But this is your hour, and the power of darkness!"

Then they seized Jesus and led him away, bringing him into the high priest's house. But Peter was following at a distance. When they had kindled a fire in the middle of the courtyard and sat down together, Peter sat among them. Then a servant, seeing Peter in the firelight, stared at him and said, "This man also was with him." But he denied it, saying, "Woman, I do not know him." A little later someone else, on seeing Peter, said, "You also are one of them." But Peter said, "Man, I am not!" Then about an hour later still another kept insisting, "Surely this man also was with Jesus; for he is a Galilean." But Peter said, "Man, I do not know what you are talking about!" At that moment, while he was still speaking, the cock crowed. The Lord turned and looked at Peter. Then Peter remembered the word of the Lord, who had said to him, "Before the cock crows today, you will deny me three times." And he went out and wept bitterly.

Now the men who were holding Jesus began to mock him and beat him; they also blindfolded him and kept asking him, "Prophesy! Who is it that struck you?" They kept heaping many other insults on him.

When day came, the assembly of the elders of the people, both chief priests and scribes, gathered together, and they brought Jesus to their council. They said, "If you are the Messiah, tell us." Jesus replied, "If I tell you, you will not believe; and if I question you, you will not answer. But from now on the Son-of-Man will be seated at the right hand of the power of God." All of them asked, "Are you, then, the Son of God?" Jesus said to them, "You say that I am." Then they said, "What further testimony do we need? We have heard it ourselves from his own lips!"

Then the assembly rose as a body and brought Jesus before Pilate. They began to accuse Jesus, saying, "We found this man perverting our nation, forbidding us to pay taxes to the emperor, and saying that he himself is the Messiah, a king." Then Pilate asked Jesus, "Are you the king of the Jews?" Jesus answered, "You say so." Then Pilate said to the chief priests and the crowds, "I find no basis for an accusation against this man." But they were insistent and said, "He stirs up the people by teaching throughout all Judea, from Galilee where he began even to this place."

When Pilate heard this, he asked whether the man was a Galilean. And when he learned that he was under Herod's jurisdiction, Pilate sent Jesus off to Herod, who was himself in Jerusalem at that time. When Herod saw Jesus, he was very glad, for he had been wanting to see him for a long time, because he had heard about Jesus and was hoping to see him perform some sign. Herod questioned him at some length, but Jesus gave him no answer. The chief priests and the scribes stood by, vehemently accusing him. Even Herod with his soldiers treated Jesus with contempt and mocked him; then he put an elegant robe on him, and sent him back to Pilate. That same day Herod and Pilate became friends with each other; before this they had been enemies.

Pilate then called together the chief priests, the leaders, and the people, and said to them, "You brought me this man as one who was perverting the people; and here I have examined him in your presence and have not found this man guilty of any of your charges against him. Neither has Herod, for he sent him back to us. Indeed, he has done nothing to deserve death. I will therefore have him flogged and release him."

Then they all shouted out together, "Away with this fellow! Release Barabbas for us!" (This was a man who had been put in prison for an insurrection that had taken place in the city, and for murder.) Pilate, wanting to release Jesus, addressed them again; but they kept shouting, "Crucify, crucify him!" A third time Pilate said to them, "Why, what evil has he done? I have found in him no ground for the sentence of death; I will therefore have him flogged and then release him." But they kept urgently demanding with loud shouts that Jesus should be crucified; and their voices prevailed. So Pilate gave his verdict that their demand should be granted. He released the man they asked for, the one who had been put in prison for insurrection and murder, and he handed Jesus over as they wished.

Two others also, who were criminals, were led away to be put to death with Jesus. When they came to the place that is called The Skull, they crucified Jesus there with the criminals, one on his right and one on his left. Then Jesus said, "Father, forgive them; for they do not know what they are doing." And they cast lots to divide his clothing. And the people stood by, watching; but the leaders scoffed at him, saying, "He saved others; let him save himself if he is the Messiah of God, the chosen one!" The soldiers also mocked him, coming up and offering him sour wine, and saying, "If you are the King of the Jews, save yourself!" There was also an inscription over him, "This is the King of the Jews."

One of the criminals who were hanged there kept deriding Jesus and saying, "Are you not the Messiah? Save yourself and us!" But the other rebuked him, saying, "Do you not fear God, since you are under the same sentence of condemnation? And we indeed have been condemned justly, for we are getting what we deserve for our deeds, but this man has done nothing wrong." Then he said, "Jesus, remember me when you come into your kingdom." He replied, "Truly I tell you, today you will be with me in Paradise."

It was now about noon, and darkness came over the whole land until three in the afternoon, while the sun's light failed; and the curtain of the temple was torn in two. Then Jesus, crying with a loud voice, said, "Father, into your hands I commend my spirit." Having said this, he breathed his last. When the centurion saw what had taken place, he praised God and said, "Certainly this man was innocent." And when all the crowds who had gathered there for this spectacle saw what had taken place, they returned home, beating their breasts. But all his acquaintances, including the women who had followed him from Galilee, stood at a distance, watching these things.

Now there was a good and righteous man named Joseph, who, though a member of the council, had not agreed to their plan and action. He came from the Jewish town of Arimathea, and he was waiting expectantly for the dominion of God. This man went to Pilate and asked for the body of Jesus. Then he took it down, wrapped it in a linen cloth, and laid it in a rock-hewn tomb where no one had ever been laid. It was the day of preparation, and the sabbath was beginning. The women who had come with Jesus from Galilee followed, and they saw the tomb and how his body was laid. Then they returned, and prepared spices and ointments.

[Complete reading: Luke 22:14—23:56]

REFLECTION

At the Passover meal — which Luke links with the "hour" — Jesus mentions a betrayer and the apostles ask *each other* who it might be. They do not ask Jesus (as they do in Matthew 26:22–25, Mark 14:17–20 and John 13:21–27), and thus effectively cut him out of the conversation. The apostles continue their own talk, arguing over their relative importance. Jesus joins the conversation to forewarn Simon of his coming denial and to speak of his own coming death; he is met with a lack of understanding. In the lonely prayer in the garden, Jesus finds the apostles sleeping, "because of grief." This section ends as Jesus is apprehended in the garden, gamely defended by one of the disciples. The journey of his ministry ends with Jesus' healing of the servant's ear.

The second phase of the journey, the "hour" of the power of darkness, begins with Peter's denial and with Jesus who "turned and looked at Peter" (the word used implies a piercing, straightforward look). Then Jesus is led to stand alone to face the mockery of the guards and the contempt and forked-tongue questions of the religious councillors, whose final question Jesus answers with an equivocation. He is then moved to face alone the sincere waffling of Pilate and the mockery and contempt of Herod, who is cheered on by the chief priests and scribes. Finally, Jesus stands alone as Pilate yields to the pressure of the crowd incited to action.

It is only during the final stage of his journey that some others attempt to side with Jesus: "A great number of the people," including women who express their grief, follow Jesus. As Jesus is stretched out on the cross, one criminal approaches in faith. And at the end, a member of the occupying army, a dissenting member of the religious council and the women from Galilee are the only ones who recognize Jesus. Luke, the master story-teller, has etched in bold colors the story of the prophet-savior, who came to proclaim the good news to the lowly — but completed his journey experiencing first-hand the depth of lowliness.

■ **Slowly read today's first reading, which has been used to describe Jesus' attitude in the face of suffering. When you see others who are suffering, how do you react? How do you attempt to understand what they may be going through?**

PRACTICE OF FAITH

PALMS. Why are we given palm tree leaves at church? Sure, we hear in the gospel about Christ's joyful entry into Jerusalem. But we're not just acting out some kind of amateur history pageant. When we accept the palm branch, hold it high, sing and walk with the church in procession, we are making a promise to follow Christ everywhere, from joy in Jerusalem to the cross on Calvary. The palm branches are blessed and sprinkled with baptism's holy water. We then take them home to be reminded to live as baptized people. Carry your palm home carefully — don't leave it behind as litter!

PRACTICE OF HOPE

WHO WOULD BELIEVE? As Rhonda's sponsor in the Rite of Christian Initiation of Adults, I heard many tough questions while she was preparing to enter the Catholic church. During Holy Week, she hit me with a couple of questions that still give me food for thought: "What's so good about Good Friday? It wasn't so good for Jesus, was it?" I had to admit that at first glance it was hard to see any good in such suffering. But Jesus' suffering freed us from sin and death forever. His death paved the way to eternal life — first for him and then for us through him. As we read the passion narrative, we read with hope. We know how the story really ends.

PRACTICE OF CHARITY

DEATH ON A CROSS. Unfortunately, our depictions of Jesus' crucifixion sometimes make it look more like a romanticized drama than the brutal execution it was. Crucifixion was the prescribed form of execution for slaves and non-Roman citizens; its cruelty was a sign to others of the same class to behave, lest the same thing happen to them.

Despite the fact that the person Christians acclaim as Savior was a victim of capital punishment, despite the fact that leaders such as John Paul II and the U.S. bishops have condemned it, capital punishment remains legal in the United States, one of the few industrialized nations that still practices it. Capital punishment is even (outrageously) given biblical warrant by some Christians. Such argumentation is not worthy of Christians, called to forgiveness seventy times seven times! Join the Friends Committee to Abolish the Death Penalty, 3721 Midvale Ave., Philadelphia PA 19129; 1-215-951-0330.

WEEKDAY READINGS (Mo) Isaiah 42:1–7; (Tu) 49:1–6; (We) 50:4–9

79

PASCHAL TRIDUUM

Holy is God! Holy and Strong! Holy immortal One, have mercy on us!

I am poured out like water,
and all my bones are out of joint;
my heart is like wax,
melted within my breast.

My tongue sticks to my jaws;
you lay me in the dust of death.
I can count all my bones.
They stare and gloat over me;
they divide my garments among them,
and cast lots for my clothing.

But you, O Lord, be not far away!
O my help, hasten to my aid!
Deliver my soul from the sword,
my life from the power of the dog!

I will tell of your name to my kindred;
in the midst of the congregation
    I will praise you.
All who fear the Lord, shout praise!
For God did not despise or abhor
the affliction of the afflicted,
nor hide from me,
but heard when I cried out.

The poor shall eat and be satisfied;
those who seek the Lord shall praise the Lord!
May your hearts live forever!
All the ends of the earth shall remember
and turn to the Lord.

—Psalm 22:14, 15bc, 17–20, 22–23a, 24, 26–27b

Holy God,
praise be yours for this tree of Paradise,
this tree that made Noah's saving Ark,
this tree whose branches embraced Jesus
and so shade and shelter us all.
Here may all the weary rest
these holy days,
hungry and thirsty for your word,
eating and drinking only your word
until, in the darkness between
Saturday and Sunday,
heaven and earth shall here be wed.
Then drowning waters shall be
waters of life
and the Savior's blood a banquet.
Holy God, praise be yours.

— Prayer of the Triduum

THE THREE DAYS

Holy Thursday brings the end to the Forty Days of Lent, which make up the season of anticipation of the great Three Days. Composed of prayer, almsgiving, fasting and the preparation of the catechumens for baptism, the season of Lent is now brought to a close and the Three Days begin as we approach the liturgy of Holy Thursday evening. As those to be initiated into the church have prepared themselves for their entrance into the fullness of life, so have we been awakening in our hearts, minds and bodies our own entrances into the life of Christ, experienced in the life of the church.

The Three Days, this Easter *Triduum* (Latin for "three days"), is the center, the core, of the entire year for Christians. These days mark the mystery around which our entire lives are played out. Adults in the community are invited to plan ahead so that the whole time from Thursday night until Easter Sunday is free of social engagements, free of entertainment and free of meals except for the simplest nourishment. We measure these days—indeed, our very salvation in the life of God—in step with the catechumens themselves; our own rebirths are revitalized as we participate in their initiation rites and as we have supported them along the way.

We are asked to fast on Good Friday and to continue fasting, if possible, all through Holy Saturday as strictly as we can so that we come to the Easter Vigil hungry and full of excitement, parched and longing to feel the sacred water of the font on our skin. Good Friday and Holy Saturday are days of paring down distractions so that we may be free for prayer and anticipation, for reflection, preparation and silence. The church is getting ready for the Great Night of the Easter Vigil.

As one who has been initiated into the church, as one whose life has been wedded to this community gathered at the table, you should anticipate the Triduum with concentration and vigor. With you, the whole church knows that our presence for the liturgies of the Triduum is not just an invitation.

Everyone is needed. We "pull out all the stops" for these days. As human persons, wedded to humanity by the joys and travails of life and grafted onto the body of the church by the sanctifying waters of baptism, we lead the new members into new life in this community of faith.

To this end, the Three Days are seen not as three liturgies distinct from one another but as one movement. These days have been connected intimately and liturgically from the early days of the Christian church. As a member of this community, you should be personally committed to preparing for and anticipating the Triduum and its culmination in the Vigil of the Great Night, Holy Saturday.

The church proclaims the direction of the Triduum by the opening antiphon of Holy Thursday, which comes from Paul's Letter to the Galatians (6:14). With this verse the church sets a spiritual environment into which we as committed Christians enter the Triduum:

> *We should glory in the cross of our Lord Jesus Christ, for he is our salvation, our life and resurrection; through him we are saved and made free.*

HOLY THURSDAY

On Thursday evening we enter into this Triduum together. Whether presider, baker, lector, preacher, wine maker, greeter, altar server, minister of the eucharist, decorator or person in the remote corner in the last pew of the church, we begin, as always, by hearkening to the word of God. These are the scriptures for the liturgy of Holy Thursday:

Exodus 12:1–8, 11–14
Ancient instructions for the meal of the Passover

1 Corinthians 11:23–26
Eat the bread and drink the cup until the return of the Lord

John 13:1–15
Jesus washes the feet of the disciples

Then we, like Jesus, do something strange: We wash feet. Jesus gave us this image of what the church is supposed to look like, feel like, act like. Our position—whether as washer or washed, servant or served—is a difficult one for us to take. Yet we learn from the discomfort, from the awkwardness.

Then we celebrate the eucharist. Because it is connected to the other liturgies of the Triduum on Good Friday and Holy Saturday night, the evening liturgy of Holy Thursday has no ending. Whether we stay to pray awhile or leave, we are now in the quiet, peace and glory of the Triduum.

GOOD FRIDAY
We gather quietly in community on Friday and again listen to the Word of God:

Isaiah 52:13—53:12
The servant of the Lord was crushed for our sins

Hebrews 4:14–16; 5:7–9
The Son of God learned obedience through his suffering

John 18:1—19:42
The passion of Jesus Christ

After the sermon, we pray at length for all the world's needs: for the church; for the pope, the clergy and all the baptized; for those preparing for initiation; for the unity of Christians; for Jews; for non–Christians; for atheists; for all in public office; and for those in special need.

Then there is another once-a-year event: The holy cross is held up in our midst and we come forward one by one to do reverence with a kiss, bow or genuflection. This communal reverence of an instrument of torture recalls the painful price, in the past and today, of salvation, the way in which our redemption is wrought, the stripes and humiliation of Jesus Christ that bring direction and life back to a humanity that is lost and dead. During the veneration of the cross, we sing not only of the sorrow but of the glory of the cross by which we have been saved.

Again, we bring to mind the words of Paul: "The cross of Jesus Christ . . . our salvation, our life and resurrection; through him we are saved and made free."

We continue in fasting and prayer and vigil, in rest and quiet, through Saturday. This Saturday for us is God's rest at the end of creation. It is Christ's repose in the tomb. It is Christ's visit with the dead.

EASTER VIGIL
Hungry now, pared down to basics, lightheaded from vigilance and full of excitement, we committed members of the church, the already baptized, gather in darkness and light a new fire. From this blaze we light a great candle that will make this night bright for us and will burn throughout the Easter season.

We hearken again to the Word of God with some of the most powerful narratives and proclamations of our tradition:

Genesis 1:1—2:2
Creation of the world

Genesis 22:1–18
The sacrifice of Isaac

Exodus 14:15—15:1
The Red Sea

Isaiah 54:5–14
You will not be afraid

Isaiah 55:1-11
Come, come to the water

Baruch 3:9–15, 32—4:4
The shining light

Ezekiel 36:16–28
The Lord says: I will sprinkle water

Romans 6:3–11
United with him in death

Mark 16:1–8
Jesus has been raised up

After the readings, we pray to all our saints to stand with us as we go to the font and bless the waters. The chosen of all times and all places attend to what is about to take place. The catechumens renounce evil, profess the faith of the church and are baptized and anointed.

All of us renew our baptism. For us these are the moments when death and life meet, when we reject evil and give our promises to God. All of this is in the communion of the church. So together we go to the table and celebrate the Easter eucharist.

EASTER

Christ is risen! Christ is truly risen!

O give thanks to the Lord, who is good;
whose steadfast love endures forever!
Let Israel say,
"God's steadfast love endures forever."

I was pushed hard, so that I was falling,
but the Lord helped me.
The Lord is my strength and my power;
the Lord has become my salvation.

I shall not die, but I shall live,
and recount the deeds of the Lord.
The Lord disciplined me severely,
but did not give me over to death.

Open to me the gates of righteousness,
that I may enter through them
and give thanks to the Lord.
The stone which the builders rejected
has become the cornerstone.
This is the Lord's doing;
it is marvelous in our eyes.

This is the day which the Lord has made;
let us rejoice and be glad in it.

—Psalm 118:1–2, 13–14, 17–19, 22–24

The heavens rumble alleluias,
earth dances to the tune
and the wail of the graves
itself becomes song.
All are singing with you, savior God,
at this wedding feast
for you have turned the world around,
inside out and upside down.
Now the homeless are at home
and the martyred embrace their assassins
and the rulers and bosses wonder
whose world this is after all.
After all, let us stand and sing
with the heavens and earth and the graves
and so proclaim that we live now only
in Christ who is Lord for ever and ever.

—Prayer of the Season

READING I *Acts 10:34–43*

Peter began to speak to the people: "I truly understand that God shows no partiality, but in every nation anyone who is God-fearing and does what is right is acceptable to God.

"You know the message God sent to the people of Israel, preaching peace by Jesus Christ—who is Lord of all. That message spread throughout Judea, beginning in Galilee after the baptism that John announced: how God anointed Jesus of Nazareth with the Holy Spirit and with power; how Jesus went about doing good and healing all who were oppressed by the devil, for God was with him. We are witnesses to all that he did both in Judea and in Jerusalem. They put him to death by hanging him on a tree; but God raised him on the third day and allowed him to appear, not to all the people but to us who were chosen by God as witnesses, and who ate and drank with him after he rose from the dead.

"Jesus commanded us to preach to the people and to testify that he is the one ordained by God as judge of the living and the dead. All the prophets testify about him that everyone who believes in him receives forgiveness of sins through his name."
[Roman Catholic: Acts 10:34, 37–43]

READING II *Colossians 3:1–4*

If you have been raised with Christ, seek the things that are above, where Christ is, seated at the right hand of God. Set your minds on things that are above, not on things that are on earth, for you have died, and your life is hidden with Christ in God. When Christ who is your life is revealed, then you also will be revealed with him in glory.
[Alternate Roman Catholic: 1 Corinthians 5:6–8]
[Revised Common Lectionary: 1 Corinthians 15:19–26 or Acts 10:34–43]

GOSPEL *John 20:1–18*

Early on the first day of the week, while it was still dark, Mary Magdalene came to the tomb and saw that the stone had been removed from the tomb. So she ran and went to Simon Peter and the other disciple, the one whom Jesus loved, and said to them, "They have taken the Lord out of the tomb, and we do not know where they have laid him."

Then Peter and the other disciple set out and went toward the tomb. The two were running together, but the other disciple outran Peter and reached the tomb first. He bent down to look in and saw the linen wrappings lying there, but he did not go in. Then Simon Peter came, following him, and went into the tomb. He saw the linen wrappings lying there, and the cloth that had been on Jesus' head, not lying with the linen wrappings but rolled up in a place by itself. Then the other disciple, who reached the tomb first, also went in, and he saw and believed; for as yet they did not understand the scripture, that Jesus must rise from the dead.

But Mary stood weeping outside the tomb. As she wept, she bent over to look into the tomb; and she saw two angels in white, sitting where the body of Jesus had been lying, one at the head and the other at the feet. They said to her, "Woman, why are you weeping?" She said to them, "They have taken away my Lord, and I do not know where they have laid him." When she had said this, she turned around and saw Jesus standing there, but she did not know that it was Jesus. Jesus said to her, "Woman, why are you weeping: Whom are you looking for?" Supposing him to be the gardener, she said to him, "Sir, if you have carried him away, tell me where you have laid him, and I will take him away." Jesus said to her, "Mary!" She turned and said to him in Hebrew, "Rabbouni!" (which means Teacher). Jesus said to her, "Do not hold on to me, because I have not yet ascended to the Father. But go to my brothers and say to them, 'I am ascending to my Father and your Father, to my God and your God.'"

Mary Magdalene went and announced to the disciples, "I have seen the Lord"; and she told them that Jesus had said these things to her.
[Roman Catholic: John 20:1–9; alternate Luke 24:1–12]

REFLECTION

A few years ago, during the Easter season, *Newsweek, Time* and other weekly magazines featured articles on the resurrection of Christ. These articles presented a wide array of views and understandings of the resurrection. It was amazing just how many diverse interpretations were represented. Such a diversity makes clear one fact: The resurrection is a mystery. And today's reading from the gospel of John offers the insight that the mystery of the resurrection can be explored, not only in the accounts of Jesus' post-resurrection appearances but also in the story of the empty tomb.

The Easter story in the gospel is something of a celebration of emptiness. Mary, Simon Peter and the other disciple are excited about finding an empty tomb; it is in this empty place that faith is born. John often employs irony in his gospel, and so it is in this story of the empty tomb. Nothing but sorrow should be associated with a tomb, and likely only despair and confusion when the known tomb of a loved one is found empty without explanation. Yet in this case it is a cause for cautious optimism. A new light is found, precisely in the empty tomb.

The stories from the empty tomb tradition serve several purposes, one of which is to remind the reader that faith in Christ comes through the process of one person sharing the community's story of faith—the gospel—with another. Faith is born in the telling of and the listening to the story. Today's gospel testifies that faith in the resurrection of Jesus grew from a few people sharing their experience of seeing nothing—an empty tomb—but believing in something—the bodily resurrection.

If faith in the resurrection is kept alive through the process of telling and hearing the story, then it is apparent that we, too, must tell others of the resurrection. Thus, the resurrection is not merely a past event but a continually proclaimed present reality.

■ **What empty tomb experiences have you had in your life? How have you found the resurrected Christ in those experiences?**

■ **When have you been at the foot of the cross? In the tomb? At the Last Supper?**

PRACTICE OF FAITH

EGGS. Legend has it that after seeing the risen Lord, Mary Magdalene went to preach to Pontius Pilate. Spying a bowl of hardboiled eggs on his table, Mary picked one up. It turned blood red. "This is how much Christ loves you," brave Mary said, "shedding his own blood when you condemned him."

"God raised him up," she explained, cracking the shell, exposing the glistening white of the egg. "And if you change your heart," she continued, breaking the egg and revealing its golden yolk, "your destiny, too, can be life in God forever."

Greek Christians color their eggs dark red. And in a few European cultures, you always eat Easter eggs with a friend. As a blessing, you crack your egg against your friend's egg and say "Christ is risen!" Your friend answers: "Christ is risen indeed!"

PRACTICE OF HOPE

SEEK WHAT IS ABOVE. Many people prefer Christmas, but Easter is my favorite holiday. I love the Easter Vigil, which brings Christ, our light, into our lives. I am awestruck by our salvation history, told in scripture and song. And I am moved to tears by those who stand in front of our community to profess their faith and receive the sacraments of initiation. As someone who was received into the church as an infant, I always envied those people who entered the church as adults. Someone spoke for me, but they speak for themselves. I confided this to a friend a few years ago and she gently reminded me that we do choose whether or not to follow Christ. It is a choice we proclaim with our lives. Easter gives us the hope we need to keep making that choice.

PRACTICE OF CHARITY

WE ARE WITNESSES. The celebration of Christ's resurrection is made even more joyous this year by the fact that all the world's Christians—Orthodox, Roman and Eastern Catholic, and Protestant—are celebrating the Pascha on the same day. Today can be not only a celebration of resurrection, but of Christian unity as well: In our great diversity, we are all witnesses to and servants of the same Christ. To learn more about the Eastern churches, read the U.S. bishops' statement *Eastern Catholics in the United States of America* (U.S. Catholic Conference, 3211 4th St. NE, Washington DC 20017-1194; 1-800-235-8722; www.nccbuscc.org). As part of your Easter celebration, today or later, attend one of the many ecumenical services often celebrated during the Easter season.

WEEKDAY READINGS (Mo) Acts 2:14, 22–32; (Tu) 2:36–41; (We) 3:1–10; (Th) 3:11–26; (Fr) 4:1–12; (Sa) 4:13–21

READING I *Acts 5:12–16*

Many signs and wonders were done among the people through the apostles. And the believers were all together in Solomon's Portico. None of the rest dared to join them, but the people held them in high esteem. Yet more than ever believers were added to the Lord, great numbers of both men and women, so that they even carried out the sick into the streets, and laid them on cots and mats, in order that Peter's shadow might fall on some of them as he came by. A great number of people would also gather from the towns around Jerusalem, bringing the sick and those tormented by unclean spirits, and they were all cured.

[Revised Common Lectionary: Acts 5:27–32]

READING II *Revelation 1:9–11, 12–13, 17–19*

I, John, your brother who share with you in Jesus the persecution and the kingdom and the patient endurance, was on the island called Patmos because of the word of God and the testimony of Jesus. I was in the spirit on the Lord's day, and I heard behind me a loud voice like a trumpet saying, "Write in a book what you see and send it to the seven churches." Then I turned to see whose voice it was that spoke to me, and on turning I saw seven golden lampstands, and in the midst of the lampstands I saw one like the Son-of-Man, clothed with a long robe and with a golden sash across his chest. When I saw him, I fell at his feet as though dead. But he placed his right hand on me, saying, "Do not be afraid; I am the first and the last, and the living one. I was dead, and see, I am alive forever and ever; and I have the keys of Death and of Hades. Now write what you have seen, what is, and what is to take place after this."

[Revised Common Lectionary: Revelation 1:4–8]

GOSPEL *John 20:19–31*

When it was evening on that day, the first day of the week, and the doors of the house where the disciples had met were locked for fear of the Judeans, Jesus came and stood among them and said, "Peace be with you." After he said this, he showed them his hands and his side. Then the disciples rejoiced when they saw the Lord. Jesus said to them again, "Peace be with you. As the Father has sent me, so I send you." When he had said this, he breathed on them and said to them, "Receive the Holy Spirit. If you forgive the sins of any, they are forgiven them; if you retain the sins of any, they are retained."

But Thomas (who was called the Twin), one of the twelve, was not with them when Jesus came. So the other disciples told him, "We have seen the Lord." But he said to them, "Unless I see the mark of the nails in his hands, and put my finger in the mark of the nails and my hand in his side, I will not believe."

A week later his disciples were again in the house, and Thomas was with them. Although the doors were shut, Jesus came and stood among them and said, "Peace be with you." Then he said to Thomas, "Put your finger here and see my hands. Reach out your hand and put it in my side. Do not doubt but believe." Thomas said to Jesus, "My Lord and my God!" Jesus said to him, "Have you believed because you have seen me? Blessed are those who have not seen and yet have come to believe."

Now Jesus did many other signs in the presence of his disciples, which are not written in this book. But these are written so that you may come to believe that Jesus is the Messiah, the Son of God, and that through believing you may have life in his name.

R E F L E C T I O N

If you had been a reporter at the beginning of the first century simply trying to record the events of Jesus' life, you would have had your hands full. If you were intent on providing more than a mere chronicle of events, and wanted to produce a testimony of faith that would be relevant to a particular community, your task would have been even larger. For one thing, you would have had to take into consideration the needs and concerns of your audience.

John took on this monumental task in his gospel. He considered the concerns of the young church that was his audience: the doubt and skepticism of the first generation of people who had not actually seen Jesus with their own eyes. These people were wondering if they could put their faith in someone they had not seen. To meet their objections, John emphasizes the bodily resurrection of Jesus.

It is a shame that for all of history the disciple Thomas will always be remembered as "the doubter." In reality he behaves as any of us might well have. He serves as a sympathetic model for John's community. In earlier stories, Thomas consistently behaved boldly. He needs to experience the risen Christ, and is not afraid to say so. He boldly states his needs, willing to question in order to grow. When Thomas comes face to face with Christ, that is enough. Thomas boldly proclaims his faith in Christ on the spot, without even touching Christ. Thomas' proclamation of faith is born out of his bold questioning.

The first words said by Jesus in this passage are a greeting of peace. It is a wish for "right relationship" (the literal meaning of *shalom*), one that resonates despite the turmoil of the disciples. The fledgling Christian community is called to foster right relations with Christ and with each other. In a post-resurrection world, Christians will need to draw strength and courage from relationship with each other and from each other's testimonies of the reality of the risen Christ.

■ **What have been some of the doubts you have experienced in your life? How did you deal with them?**

■ **Is it acceptable for you to question your faith? Can you have peace in your heart and still bring questions to mind? How do you balance our God-given desire for knowledge with our call to faith?**

PRACTICE OF FAITH

PEACE. The first gift that the risen Lord gives to us is peace, a deep and abiding assurance that love is stronger than violence and death. As baptized people, we are commissioned by Christ to share this peace with others. In our celebration of the eucharist and in daily prayer, we share the sign of peace. This is not a sociable interruption, but a ritual act that gives God glory, and changes us.

When you share the sign of peace, look into the other person's eyes. Clasp—don't shake—hands. Or embrace. See in each other the risen Lord breathing peace. Say clearly, "Christ's peace be with you."

PRACTICE OF HOPE

DO NOT BE AFRAID. Computers have revolutionized the way we think and operate. One of the many positive things they have brought to easy reach is Bible research. A friend recently took me through a program developed by Ligouri Publications that allowed us to search the Bible by word or phrase. We found 393 verses with the word "fear," but we found "love" 518 times and "hope" 174 times—more than enough to dispel "fear." If that weren't enough, the scriptures advised us to "be not afraid" 81 times. We didn't look up the word "trust." We decided that was one word that made all the other words and phrases possible.

The U. S. bishops have included the New American Bible on their website. Daily readings are also available there. Visit www.nccbuscc.org.

PRACTICE OF CHARITY

THE MARK OF THE NAILS. We must never forget that the Risen One still carries the marks of his execution in his body. We are constantly reminded that death is still a powerful force, even while our world is on its way to resurrection. Last Friday's second anniversary of the massacre at Columbine High School is just such a reminder. The killing of 16 people by two high school students, and their own suicides, shocked the United States and the world. The massacre highlighted once again the glorification of violence in popular culture, the accessibility of guns in the U. S. and the estrangement of many teenagers in our society. Consider supporting the efforts of Handgun Control, Inc., a group that lobbies for greater federal gun control 1225 Eye Street, NW, Suite 1100, Washington DC 20005; 1–202–898–0792; www.handguncontrol.org. More importantly, find ways to reach out to troubled kids in your own area.

WEEKDAY READINGS (Mo) 4:23–31; (Tu) 4:32–37; (We) 1 Peter 5:5–14; (Th) Acts 5:27–33; (Fr) 5:34–42; (Sa) 6:1–7

READING I   *Acts 5:27–32, 40–41*

When the temple police had brought the apostles, they had them stand before the council. The high priest questioned them, saying, "We gave you strict orders not to teach in this name, yet here you have filled Jerusalem with your teaching and you are determined to bring this man's blood on us." But Peter and the apostles answered, "We must obey God rather than any human authority. The God of our ancestors raised up Jesus, whom you had killed by hanging him on a tree. God exalted this Jesus to be Leader and Savior at God's right hand, to give repentance to Israel and forgiveness of sins. And we are witnesses to these things, and so is the Holy Spirit who has been given to those who obey God."

Then the council ordered the apostles not to speak in the name of Jesus, and let them go. As they left the council, they rejoiced that they were considered worthy to suffer dishonor for the sake of the name.
[Revised Common Lectionary: Acts 9:1–6 (7–20)]

READING II   *Revelation 5:11–14*

Then I looked, and I heard the voice of many angels surrounding the throne and the living creatures and the elders; they numbered myriads of myriads and thousands of thousands, singing with full voice, "Worthy is the Lamb that was slaughtered to receive power and wealth and wisdom and might and honor and glory and blessing!" Then I heard every creature in heaven and on earth and under the earth and in the sea, and all that is in them, singing, "To the one seated on the throne and to the Lamb be blessing and honor and glory and might forever and ever!" And the four living creatures said, "Amen!" And the elders fell down and worshiped.

GOSPEL   *John 21:1–14*

Jesus showed himself again to the disciples by the Sea of Tiberias; and he showed himself in this way. Gathered there together were Simon Peter, Thomas called the Twin, Nathanael of Cana in Galilee, the sons of Zebedee, and two others of his disciples. Simon Peter said to them, "I am going fishing." They said to him, "We will go with you." They went out and got into the boat, but that night they caught nothing.

Just after daybreak, Jesus stood on the beach; but the disciples did not know that it was Jesus. Jesus said to them, "Children, you have no fish, have you?" They answered him, "No." He said to them, "Cast the net to the right side of the boat, and you will find some." So they cast it, and now they were not able to haul it in because there were so many fish. That disciple whom Jesus loved said to Peter, "It is the Lord!" When Simon Peter heard that it was the Lord, he put on some clothes, for he was naked, and jumped into the sea. But the other disciples came in the boat, dragging the net full of fish, for they were not far from the land, only about a hundred yards off.

When they had gone ashore, they saw a charcoal fire there, with fish on it, and bread. Jesus said to them, "Bring some of the fish that you have just caught." So Simon Peter went aboard and hauled the net ashore, full of large fish, a hundred fifty-three of them; and though there were so many, the net was not torn. Jesus said to them, "Come and have breakfast." Now none of the disciples dared to ask him, "Who are you?" because they knew it was the Lord. Jesus came and took the bread and gave it to them, and did the same with the fish. This was now the third time that Jesus appeared to the disciples after he was raised from the dead.
[Complete reading: John 21:1–19]

REFLECTION

What a character Peter turns out to be! In this selection from Acts of the Apostles, Peter boldly teaches in the name of Jesus and proclaims that it is better to "obey God than any human authority." What is amazing is that the high priest had ordered the apostles not to speak in the name of Jesus. Peter's behavior now is quite different from when he denied even knowing Jesus earlier in the gospel. How did this character development take place? How could Peter have overcome his earlier weakness when he denied his friend and Lord so that he now confidently faces the council and professes his faith in Jesus?

Peter had struggled with his call to discipleship from the beginning and his faith always seemed variable. He first admitted his sinfulness, but followed Jesus nonetheless. He later went on to proclaim that Jesus is the Christ, the son of the living God. Later, however, his discipleship seems to hit a low point as Jesus calls him Satan when Peter fails to understand Jesus' teaching. But the lowest point for Peter comes with his threefold denial of Jesus before the crucifixion.

All of Peter's struggles and triumphs lead to the story we read today in the passage from the gospel of John. The story culminates with Peter being called upon to feed Jesus' sheep. In an unexpected move, Jesus invites the man who had misunderstood him, questioned him, and even denied him to care for the lives of others. In commissioning Peter, Jesus chose someone who was not perfect; Jesus chose someone who struggled with and grew in faith. Jesus chose someone who had clearly engaged in the long process of coming to understand what it means to be a human being and a person of faith. Peter's struggle led to a faith that was built on bedrock.

■ **In what ways do you struggle with your humanity? How are you like Peter in your struggle?**

■ **Have you questioned your faith in Christ? How so? In what ways did Christ affirm and guide you in your questioning?**

PRACTICE OF FAITH

PHILIP AND JAMES. Thursday, May 3, is the feast of the apostles Philip and James. Philip perhaps is best known for his invitation to his friend Nathanael to "come and see" this person called Jesus. After having decided to follow Jesus, Philip could not help but share his discovery with his friend.

Philip stands as a good example of the practice of faith for us today. His interest in Jesus was piqued; he found the Lord's message irresistible, and he had to share his experience with another. Week after week we spend time with the word of God in study and in prayer. Follow Philip's example and invite someone, just one other person, to "come and see" this person of Jesus, present in your prayer group, church or home.

PRACTICE OF HOPE

CAST THE NET. Fishing can be an iffy proposition. You go out onto the water with great hope and sometimes luck favors you. I've also heard many stories about "the one that got away."

For a long time, it looked like Andy was one who got away when Jesus cast his net. He lived hard and fast, and he admitted to me that he had "walked on the dark side." There was a lot of sweetness in my friend, and he tried to change. A lifetime of bad habits finally caught up with him, however. High blood pressure and kidney failure put him into the hospital and, eventually, a coma. According to his brother, Andy's last word was "Jesus." Andy tried to run, but Jesus never gave up on him.

PRACTICE OF CHARITY

FOR THE SAKE OF THE NAME. It might be easy for us to forget that, in some parts of the world, proclaiming the gospel is done under the threat of death. The killing of religious leaders in Guatemala, East Timor and China highlight the fact that, even as we celebrate resurrection, the forces of death continue their battle against life. From Europe to Africa, various minority religious groups are persecuted by governments who find their religions threatening or subversive.

In its declaration on religious liberty *Dignitatis humanae,* the Second Vatican Council declared that "the right of the human person to religious freedom must be given such recognition in the constitutional order of society as will make it a civil right" (#2). Support the efforts of Christian Solidarity International, which promotes religious freedom for all the world's people, CSI-USA, 3334 East Coast Highway, Corona del Mar CA 92625; www.csi-int.ch.

WEEKDAY READINGS (Mo) 6:8–15; (Tu) Acts 7:51–8:1; (We) 8:1–8; (Th) 1 Corinthians 15:1–8; (Fr) Acts 9:1–20; (Sa) 9:31–42

READING I *Acts 13:14, 43–52*

Paul and Barnabas went on from Perga and came to Antioch in Pisidia. And on the sabbath day they went into the synagogue and sat down.

When the meeting of the synagogue broke up, many Jews and devout converts to Judaism followed Paul and Barnabas, who spoke to them and urged them to continue in the grace of God.

The next sabbath almost the whole city gathered to hear the word of the Lord. But when the Jewish officials saw the crowds, they were filled with jealousy; and blaspheming, they contradicted what was spoken by Paul. Then both Paul and Barnabas spoke out boldly, saying, "It was necessary that the word of God should be spoken first to you. Since you reject it and judge yourselves to be unworthy of eternal life, we are now turning to the Gentiles. For so the Lord has commanded us, saying,

'I have set you to be a light for the Gentiles,
so that you may bring salvation to the ends
of the earth.'"

When the Gentiles heard this, they were glad and praised the word of the Lord; and as many as had been destined for eternal life became believers. Thus the word of the Lord spread throughout the region. But the officials incited the devout women of high standing and the leading men of the city, and stirred up persecution against Paul and Barnabas, and drove them out of their region. So they shook the dust off their feet in protest against them, and went to Iconium. And the disciples were filled with joy and with the Holy Spirit.

[Revised Common Lectionary: Acts 9:36–43]

READING II *Revelation 7:9–17*

After this I looked, and there was a great multitude that no one could count, from every nation, from all tribes and peoples and languages, standing before the throne and before the Lamb, robed in white, with palm branches in their hands. They cried out in a loud voice, saying, "Salvation belongs to our God who is seated on the throne, and to the Lamb!"

And all the angels stood around the throne and around the elders and the four living creatures, and they fell on their faces before the throne and worshiped God, singing, "Amen! Blessing and glory and wisdom and thanksgiving and honor and power and might be to our God forever and ever! Amen."

Then one of the elders addressed me, saying, "Who are these, robed in white, and where have they come from?" I said to him, "Sir, you are the one that knows." Then he said to me, "These are they who have come out of the great ordeal; they have washed their robes and made them white in the blood of the Lamb. For this reason they are before the throne of God, and worship God day and night within the temple, and the one who is seated on the throne will shelter them. They will hunger no more, and thirst no more; the sun will not strike them, nor any scorching heat; for the Lamb at the center of the throne will be their shepherd, and will guide them to springs of the water of life, and God will wipe away every tear from their eyes."

[Roman Catholic: Revelation 7:9, 14–17]

GOSPEL *John 10:22–30*

At that time the festival of the Dedication took place in Jerusalem. It was winter, and Jesus was walking in the temple, in the portico of Solomon. So the Judeans gathered around him and said to him, "How long will you keep us in suspense? If you are the Messiah, tell us plainly." Jesus answered, "I have told you, and you do not believe. The works that I do in my Father's name testify to me; but you do not believe, because you do not belong to my sheep. My sheep hear my voice. I know them, and they follow me. I give them eternal life, and they will never perish. No one will snatch them out of my hand. What my Father has given me is greater than all else, and no one can snatch it out of the Father's hand. The Father and I are one."

[Roman Catholic: John 10:27–30]

REFLECTION

According to some scholars, today's gospel reading is misplaced within the gospel of John because it is not with the rest of the "shepherd discourse," which appears at verses 1–18 of this chapter. However, other scholars contend that the passage is not misplaced, since it conforms to a pattern that John often uses in his writing. John often returns to a theme already presented and developings it a step further. The earlier "shepherd discourse" used parables of a gate, while this passage focuses on the relationship between the shepherd and the sheep.

In the ancient Mediterranean world, sheep often symbolized honor. This connection of sheep and honor probably came about since sheep do not cry out when they are shorn or are in life-threatening danger (see Isaiah 53:7). This was seen as an example of how an honorable person should behave in adversity.

It is also interesting to note that in the centuries before the birth of Jesus, shepherds were considered quite honorable people. Herding sheep was seen as a noble profession. David, the great king, was a shepherd in his youth, and other kings were praised as shepherds of their people. Psalm 23 describes God as a shepherd.

By Jesus' time, however, shepherds were seen in a different light. Shepherds were scorned as unclean, living outside among animals. They were often unable to spend much time at home with their families because they were constantly in the fields guarding their animals.

Jesus may be seen as a shepherd from both perspectives. In one sense, he is a great and honorable king who leads with strength and love. In another sense, his life is like that of an itinerant, homeless vagabond, regarded with contempt and disdain by the established. In either way, when Jesus tells us he has sheep, he is giving his followers a place of honor and a pledge of loyal support. A good shepherd would die to protect the sheep.

■ **How does Christ honor you? How do you place your trust in Christ, your shepherd?**

■ **What metaphors do you often use for God? Why have you chosen the ones you have? What do they say to you about our God?**

PRACTICE OF FAITH

ROBED IN LOVE. The fact that we have "play clothes" and "power suits" acknowledges that what we wear affects how we understand ourselves. At baptism, each of us was given something to wear. The baby's gown or the adult's alb is a sign that baptism makes us new creations in Christ. Our calling is to join the throng in the Book of Revelation who stand before God's throne dressed in robes washed in Christ's blood. Copy Colossians 3:12, 14 on a piece of paper and hang it on your closet door: "As God's chosen ones, holy and beloved, clothe yourself with compassion, kindness, humility, meekness and patience. Above all, clothe yourself in love."

PRACTICE OF HOPE

INSTRUMENT OF SALVATION. A prison movie is not my idea of a good time. That's why I put off seeing *The Shawshank Redemption* for so long. Big mistake. Its themes of friendship and endurance rightly place it on one cable channel's list of new classics.

The movie is not always easy to watch. The relationships that develop between the characters, however, make it clear that they rely on each other for their very survival—body and soul. The key is hope. While one inmate, Red, sees this virtue as dangerous, another reminds him that "hope is a good thing, maybe the best of things, and no good thing ever dies." These words become a saving grace for Red after his parole. They allow him to live again.

PRACTICE OF CHARITY

SHEL SILVERSTEIN. May 11 marks the anniversary of the death of Shel Silverstein, a poet and author who wrote unique poetry and stories for children. His ability to write poetry in the language of children brought many to love poetry. His 1964 story "The Giving Tree," about a boy and the tree who loved him, is still loved by children and adults alike. To commemorate a man who brought so many children to love reading, buy a child in your life a book, or bring him or her to the local public library. Support the local Reading Is Fundamental program, which provides schoolchildren with free books. These small acts of charity can encourage greater literacy, as well as a lifetime of reading and love of books.

WEEKDAY READINGS (Mo) 11:1–18; (Tu) 11:19–26; (We) 12:24—13:5; (Th) 13:13–25; (Fr) 13:26–33; (Sa) 13:44–52

READING I *Acts 14:21–27*

Paul and Barnabas returned to Lystra, then on to Iconium and Antioch. There they strengthened the souls of the disciples and encouraged them to continue in the faith, saying, "It is through many persecutions that we must enter the kingdom of God." And after they had appointed elders for them in each church, with prayer and fasting they entrusted them to the Lord in whom they had come to believe.

Then they passed through Pisidia and came to Pamphylia. When they had spoken the word in Perga, they went down to Attalia. From there they sailed back to Antioch, where they had been commended to the grace of God for the work that they had completed. When they arrived, they called the church together and related all that God had done with them, and how he had opened a door of faith for the Gentiles.

[Revised Common Lectionary: Acts 11:1–8]

READING II *Revelation 21:1–6*

I saw a new heaven and a new earth; for the first heaven and the first earth had passed away, and the sea was no more. And I saw the holy city, the new Jerusalem, coming down out of heaven from God, prepared as a bride adorned for her husband. And I heard a loud voice from the throne saying, "See, the home of God is among mortals. God will dwell with them as their God; they will be God's people, and that very God will be with them, and will wipe every tear from their eyes. Death will be no more; mourning and crying and pain will be no more, for the first things have passed away."

And the one who was seated on the throne said, "See, I am making all things new," and also said, "Write this, for these words are trustworthy and true." Then the one seated on the throne said to me, "It is done! I am the Alpha and the Omega, the beginning and the end. To the thirsty I will give water as a gift from the spring of the water of life."

[Roman Catholic: Revelation 21:1–5]

GOSPEL *John 13:31–35*

When Judas had gone out, Jesus said, "Now the Son-of-Man has been glorified, and God has been glorified in him. If God has been glorified in him, God will also glorify him in God's own self and will glorify him at once. Little children, I am with you only a little longer. You will look for me; and as I said to the Judeans so now I say to you, 'Where I am going, you cannot come.' I give you a new commandment, that you love one another. Just as I have loved you, you also should love one another. By this everyone will know that you are my disciples, if you have love for one another."

REFLECTION

An "inclusion" is a literary device that frames a passage or section of writing. There is something of an inclusion framing the entire Bible, and we are introduced to it in today's reading from Revelation.

In the first lines of the Bible, in the book of Genesis, there is a dark abyss, in Hebrew *tohum vobahu*. These words are similar in meaning to the words for "monster" or "evil," are are paired with the word for "water." God must create an orderly world out of the "monstrous water." How? Genesis tells us that a wind from God blows across this water. The Hebrew word for wind, *ruah,* also means "breath" or "spirit." In other words, God breathes out and the wind blows the water away so that creation will be safe from drowning in the monstrous sea. Scripture never mentions an end to God's breathing out. God's breath continues to blow the water aside to keep the earth safe. If God were ever to stop breathing upon creation, the world would be in danger.

Today's reading from the book of Revelation, the last book of the Bible, tells us that the threat of the monstrous sea flooding the earth is now gone forever. Revelation states there is "a new heaven and new earth"; and that "the sea was no more." Because of the salvation accomplished in Christ and the dawning of the kingdom of God, peace can now reign. Humanity can have hope in the future. God's saving action has ended the threat to all creation.

The passage from the gospel of John places the saving action of God in the appropriate context—love. Deuteronomy 6:4 records the greatest of commandments —love God. Jesus now gives a new commandment to his followers—love one another. This command fulfills, or completes, the command to love God. There are no limits on the love we should have. This new command is the culmination of Jesus' farewell address and serves as the guiding principle for the life of the community. The "monstrous sea" will truly be no more when the human race can put away guns, bombs, war, resentments and prejudice. The sea will truly be no more when we give ourselves to this new commandment.

■ **How do you experience God's breath or spirit blowing to keep you safe from harm? How do you share that spirit with others?**

■ **How do you express this new command without limitations?**

PRACTICE OF FAITH

WATER OF LIFE. If you have not done so yet, take a container to church and bring home some water from the baptismal font. At home, place the water in your best bowl, and give it a place of honor—set apart on your dining table or your dresser. Put a nice placemat underneath it. Each morning when you wake up, dip your fingers in the water and trace the sign of the cross on yourself. Sing "Alleluia!", or say "Springs of water, bless the Lord! Give God glory and praise forever!" Keep the bowl of baptism's water at least until Pentecost—June 3. As it evaporates, add more water with a prayer of thanksgiving.

PRACTICE OF HOPE

THEY CALLED THE CHURCH TOGETHER. An agreement between the Catholic church and the Lutheran church on the eve of the new millennium offers a glimmer of hope for Christian unity. Catholics and Lutherans now share a common understanding of justification for the first time in nearly 500 years. In a joint declaration, church leaders acknowledged: "By grace alone, in faith in Christ's saving work and not by any merit on our part, we are accepted by God and receive the Holy Spirit, who renews our hearts while equipping and calling us to good works." Much work remains to be done, but this step toward reconciliation and healing offers us a glimpse of the "new heaven and new earth" envisioned by John.

PRACTICE OF CHARITY

A NEW EARTH. Christian faith has long held that all of creation will be redeemed. The natural world, along with humanity, shares in the resurrection.

But, just as humanity is not yet redeemed and still suffers, the natural world suffers under the burden of industrial pollutants. Despite efforts to reduce emissions, acid rain continues to plague the Adirondacks of upstate New York and the Great Smoky Mountains in Tennessee, destroying plant life and making streams and lakes inhospitable to fish and other wildlife. Even the vistas of the Grand Canyon are becoming obscured due to emissions from cars and industry.

Charity to the environment begins at home. Use less electricity; carpool or take public transportation. For tips on environmentally responsible choices, visit www.oneearth.org; or order the *Yearning for Balance Action Kit,* a guide to reducing consumption, from the Center for a New American Dream; 877-68-DREAM; www.newdream.org.

WEEKDAY READINGS (Mo) 1:15–17, 20–26; (Tu) 14:19–28; (We) 15:1–6; (Th) 15:7–21; (Fr) 15:22–31; (Sa) 16:1–10

READING I *Acts 15:22ab, 23a, 24–25, 27–29*

The apostles and the elders, with the consent of the whole church, decided to choose men from among their members and to send them to Antioch with Paul and Barnabas, with the following letter: "Since we have heard that certain persons who have gone out from us, though with no instructions from us, have said things to disturb you and have unsettled your minds, we have decided unanimously to choose representatives and send them to you, along with our beloved Barnabas and Paul.

"We have therefore sent Judas and Silas, who themselves will tell you the same things by word of mouth. For it has seemed good to the Holy Spirit and to us to impose on you no further burden than these essentials: that you abstain from what has been sacrificed to idols, and from blood and from what is strangled and from fornication. If you keep yourselves from these, you will do well. Farewell."
[Revised Common Lectionary: Acts 16:9–15]
[Complete Roman Catholic: Acts 15:1–2, 22–29]

READING II *Revelation 21:10, 22–27*

And in the spirit the angel carried me away to a great, high mountain and showed me the holy city Jerusalem coming down out of heaven from God. I saw no temple in the city, for its temple is the Lord God the Almighty and the Lamb. And the city has no need of sun or moon to shine on it, for the glory of God is its light, and its lamp is the Lamb. The nations will walk by its light, and the rulers of the earth will bring their glory into it. Its gates will never be shut by day—and there will be no night there. People will bring into it the glory and the honor of the nations. But nothing unclean will enter it, nor anyone who practices abomination or falsehood, but only those who are written in the Lamb's book of life.
[Roman Catholic: Revelation 21:10–14, 22–23]
[Complete Revised Common Lectionary: Revelation 21:10, 22—22:5]

GOSPEL *John 14:23–29*

Jesus said,"Those who love me will keep my word, and my Father will love them, and we will come to them and make our home with them. Whoever does not love me does not keep my words; and the word that you hear is not mine, but is from the Father who sent me.

"I have said these things to you while I am still with you. But the Advocate, the Holy Spirit, whom the Father will send in my name, will teach you everything, and remind you of all that I have said to you. Peace I leave with you; my peace I give to you. I do not give to you as the world gives. Do not let your hearts be troubled, and do not let them be afraid. You heard me say to you, 'I am going away, and I am coming to you.' If you loved me, you would rejoice that I am going to the Father, because the Father is greater than I. And now I have told you this before it occurs, so that when it does occur, you may believe."
[Revised Common Lectionary alternate: John 5:1–9]

Thursday, May 24, 2001

ASCENSION OF THE LORD

Acts 1:1–11 *Why stand staring at the skies?*

Ephesians 1:17–23 *The fullness of Christ has filled the universe.*

Luke 24:46–53 *You are witnesses of all this.*

On this fortieth day of Easter, we are told to stop gazing at the clouds and to start spreading the good news. The resurrection of Christ didn't end with the Lord Jesus. All creation is ascending into glory. All the universe is becoming divine.

Note: In many dioceses, the Ascension of the Lord is transferred to Sunday, May 27.

REFLECTION

"Word." That was the response I got from a teenager recently when I said something he considered to be the truth. The Hebrew term *dabar* is most often translated as "word" in English. Like most words, *dabar* has numerous meanings depending on context. It can mean "word," "stuff," "essence," "reality" or even "presence." This multivalent term is used to describe God's presence coming upon Jeremiah (Jeremiah 1:4), and Ezekiel uses the word many times in his prophetic book to name his experiences of the "stuff" or the "essence" of God.

This Hebrew term *dabar* is translated in the Greek of the New Testament with the familiar *logos*. This Greek word carries many of the same connotations as *dabar*. Thus, "the word was with God and the word was God" from the prologue of the gospel of John (1:1) is an expression of the identity of Jesus. And to say that the word lived among us (John 1:14) means that the essence or reality of God has dwelled among humanity.

My teenaged acquaintance's use of "word" to mean "truth" was accurate. In today's gospel reading Jesus tells us that his word will never pass away. The one constant in the life of the world will be the truth of God's steadfast presence. This teaching was of great comfort to the members of John's community, who had seen the Roman armies ransack Jerusalem and leave the Temple in ruins in the year 70. Not only was a beautiful structure that was part of Jerusalem's history destroyed, but so was the symbol of God's presence with the people. Surely many people felt that their connection with God had been severed in some way. But Jesus states that his word will not pass away, but will continue to be spoken through the "paraclete" or advocate, the Holy Spirit. This Spirit will allow the word of Christ—the presence of the Father—to make its home among us always.

■ How do you hear the word?

■ How do you speak the word? How do you live as a paraclete, as an advocate?

PRACTICE OF FAITH

LAMB LAMP. The paschal candle is a sign of the Risen Christ, the Lamb who is the light of the City of God. At the Easter Vigil, we take the light from the paschal candle to a smaller candle of our own: We are called to spread the light of the Lamb. When we die, the paschal candle burns brightly near our coffin, leading us to the New Jerusalem. Buy or make a beautiful sturdy pillar candle. Keep it near your bowl of baptism's holy water. Light it when you pray. When you strike the match, sing or say "Christ our Light! Thanks be to God."

PRACTICE OF HOPE

PEACE OF MIND. Columbine. The name still calls up grief, anger and disbelief, even though it has been some time since two young gunmen took the lives of 12 of their classmates and a teacher before killing themselves at the Colorado high school. Instead of allowing themselves to be mired in hatred, the families of those who were killed and injured are seeking HOPE—Healing of People Everywhere. The goal of HOPE Columbine is to have a new library ready to open when classes start this fall. Plans call for the existing library, the focal point of the massacre, to be remodeled into an atrium. Organizers see this as an opportunity to bring people together in a constructive healing project.

PRACTICE OF CHARITY

PEACE I LEAVE YOU. The gift of Christ's peace is a gift desperately craved by many of the world's people. Yet the United States has been an agent of armed conflict over the past decade. According to the U.S. Arms Control and Disarmament Agency, the United States sold or gave away some $190 billion dollars worth of military weaponry to a startling number of nations, including combatants such as Pakistan and India, and Turkey and Greece. Is this what agents of Christ's peace are called to do? Write your representatives and demand a change in this destructive policy; U.S. House of Representatives, Washington DC 20515; U.S. Senate, Washington, DC 20510.

WEEKDAY READINGS (Mo) 16:11–15; (Tu) 16:22–34; (We) 17:15, 22—18:1; (Th) Ascension of the Lord, see box; (Fr) Acts 18:9–18; (Sa) 18:23–28

READING I   *Acts 7:55–60*

Standing before the high priest and the council, Stephen, filled with the Holy Spirit, gazed into heaven and saw the glory of God and Jesus standing at the right hand of God. "Look," he said, "I see the heavens opened and the Son of Man standing at the right hand of God!" But they covered their ears, and with a loud shout all rushed together against him. Then they dragged him out of the city and began to stone him; and the witnesses laid their coats at the feet of a young man named Saul. While they were stoning Stephen, he prayed, "Lord Jesus, receive my spirit." Then he knelt down and cried out in a loud voice, "Lord, do not hold this sin against them." When he had said this, he died.

[Revised Common Lectionary: Acts 16:16–34]

READING II   *Revelation 22:12–14, 16–17, 20–21*

"See, I am coming soon; my reward is with me, to repay according to everyone's work. I am the Alpha and the Omega, the first and the last, the beginning and the end."

Blessed are those who wash their robes, so that they will have the right to the tree of life and may enter the city by the gates. "It is I, Jesus, who sent my angel to you with this testimony for the churches. I am the root and the descendant of David, the bright morning star." The Spirit and the bride say, "Come." And let everyone who hears say, "Come." And let everyone who is thirsty come. Let anyone who wishes take the water of life as a gift.

The one who testifies to these things says, "Surely I am coming soon." Amen. Come, Lord Jesus! The grace of the Lord Jesus be with all the saints. Amen.

GOSPEL   *John 17:20–26*

Jesus prayed: "I ask not only on behalf of these, but also on behalf of those who will believe in me through their word, that they may all be one. As you, Father, are in me and I am in you, may they also be in us, so that the world may believe that you have sent me. The glory that you have given me I have given them, so that they may be one, as we are one, I in them and you in me, that they may become completely one, so that the world may know that you have sent me and have loved them even as you have loved me. Father, I desire that those also, whom you have given me, may be with me where I am, to see my glory, which you have given me because you loved me before the foundation of the world.

"Righteous Father, the world does not know you, but I know you; and these know that you have sent me. I made your name known to them, and I will make it known, so that the love with which you have loved me may be in them, and I in them."

Saturday night through Sunday dawn,
June 2–3, 2001

PENTECOST VIGIL

Genesis 11:1–19 *At Babel the Lord confused their speech.*
  or

Exodus 19:3–8,16–20 *Fire and wind descended on Sinai.*
  or

Ezekiel 37:1–14 *O spirit, breathe on the dead!*
  or

Joel 3:1–5 *On the Day of the Lord I will impart my own spirit.*

Romans 8:22–27 *We have the Spirit as first fruits.*

John 7:37–39 *Let the thirsty come to drink of living waters.*

We end Eastertime the way we began it, with a nighttime vigil, poring over the scriptures. We keep watch on Mount Sinai, where we meet God face to face and receive the life-giving Spirit. Our paschal journey, begun so long ago in ashes, is finished in fire.

REFLECTION

The reign of God is now present here on earth, but will be fulfilled only in the world yet to come. We can look to Jesus for clues about how God's reign will take hold in our midst and what some it will look like. In the reading today from the gospel of John, Jesus prays for the unity of all who believe in him. In his words and in his deeds, Jesus spent himself inviting diverse people to unite in a community of faith. Ultimately, Jesus sought to gather around a common table all who would join him. He intended to invite all believers to a royal banquet, one that will inaugurate the reign of God here on earth.

Jesus' teaching, actions and prayer tell us that at least one component of the reign of God present here and now on earth is the unity of all who profess faith in Jesus Christ. The reign of God is not revealed in isolation or exclusion, but in inclusivity and bonds of community.

The story of the martyrdom of Stephen in the Acts of the Apostles dramatically points to the reign of God yet to come. Stephen sees the future reign of God as the ultimate destiny of human life, and thus sees no need to hide his love of God. Stephen is willing to give his life to enter the heavens where Christ stands at the right hand of God. Stephen realizes what Jesus had said in his prayer that all might be united with the Father in glory.

The prayer of Jesus that we overhear in the gospel becomes our prayer, especially at our community celebrations of the Mass. The eucharistic banquet we share is an experience of the reign of God present in our midst. The example of Stephen also points us toward the future reign of God, where in the fullness of time, all creation shall be united with God in glory.

■ **What are the communities of faith to which you belong? How is the love of Jesus expressed in your involvement with others?**

■ **How do you celebrate the reign of God now present on earth? What do you think the future reign of God will be like? What leads you to think the way you do?**

PRACTICE OF FAITH

TREE OF LIFE. It was a tree—the one in the center of the garden whose fruit God told our first parents not to eat—that estranged us from one another in the first place. And it is a tree—the executioner's cruel gibbet, the cross—that ultimately reconciles us. Not from the beginning, yet from early on, Christians have used the cross as sign of salvation. In the third century, Christians would sometimes etch a cross on the eastern wall of their home, as a reminder to pray toward the east, the place where the sun rises. If you don't have a cross hanging in a prominent place in your home, find or make a worthy one. Hang it in a good place and decorate it with fresh flowers this week.

PRACTICE OF HOPE

WE ARE ONE. Families can be fractious. Simply sharing a name with someone does not mean you will think or act or believe alike. We who call ourselves Catholic are the same sort of family. We belong to the same church; we just have different ways of showing it. An initiative spearheaded by the late Cardinal Joseph Bernardin seeks to restore charity to the dialogue that began after the Second Vatican Council. The vision for his Catholic Common Ground Project is a church "centered on faith in Jesus, marked by accountability to the living Catholic tradition and ruled by a renewed spirit of civility, dialogue, generosity, and broad and serious consultation." The discussion he began five years ago continues and it must. Bernardin was right. We have to be able to extend this hope to each other, before we can offer it to anyone else.

PRACTICE OF CHARITY

MEMORIAL DAY. This Monday, we keep our annual observance of Memorial Day. Begun in 1868, three years after the end of the U.S. Civil War, Memorial Day is an opportunity to pray for reconciliation and an end to war. This is especially important because of the increasing involvement of children in wars around the world. The United Nations estimates that over the past decade, two million children have been killed by armed conflict, one million orphaned, six million seriously injured, and some twelve million left homeless. The Vietnam Veterans of America Foundation has programs in El Salvador, Vietnam, Angola and Cambodia to help children disabled due to war; 2001 South St. NW, 7th Floor, Washington DC 20009; 1-202-483-9222; vvaf.org.

WEEKDAY READINGS (Mo) 19:1–8; (Tu) 20:17–27; (We) 20: 28–38; (Th) Zephaniah 3:14–18 or Romans 12:9–16; (Fr) Acts 25:13–21; (Sa) 28:16–20, 30–31

READING I *Acts 2:1–11*

When the day of Pentecost had come, they were all together in one place. And suddenly from heaven there came a sound like the rush of a violent wind, and it filled the entire house where they were sitting. Divided tongues, as of fire, appeared among them, and a tongue rested on each of them. All of them were filled with the Holy Spirit and began to speak in other languages, as the Spirit gave them ability.

Now there were devout Jews from every nation under heaven living in Jerusalem. And at this sound the crowd gathered and was bewildered, because each one heard them speaking in the native language of each. Amazed and astonished, they asked, "Are not all these who are speaking Galileans? And how is it that we hear, each of us, in our own native language? Parthians, Medes, Elamites, and residents of Mesopotamia, Judea and Cappadocia, Pontus and Asia, Phrygia and Pamphylia, Egypt and the parts of Libya belonging to Cyrene, and visitors from Rome, both Jewish-born and proselytes, Cretans and Arabs—in our own languages we hear them speaking about God's deeds of power."

[Revised Common Lectionary: Acts 2:1–21 or Genesis 11:1–9]

READING II *Romans 8:8–17*

Those who are in the flesh cannot please God. But you are not in the flesh; you are in the Spirit, since the Spirit of God dwells in you. Anyone who does not have the Spirit of Christ does not belong to Christ. But if Christ is in you, though the body is dead because of sin, the Spirit is life because of righteousness. If the Spirit of the one who raised Jesus from the dead dwells in you, the one who raised Christ from the dead will give life to your mortal bodies also through this Spirit dwelling in you.

So then, brothers and sisters, we are debtors, not to the flesh, to live according to the flesh—for if you live according to the flesh, you will die; but if by the Spirit you put to death the deeds of the body, you will live. For all who are led by the Spirit of God are children of God.

For you did not receive a spirit of slavery to fall back into fear, but you have received a spirit of adoption. When we cry, "Abba! Father!" it is that very Spirit bearing witness with our spirit that we are children of God, and if children, then heirs, heirs of God and joint heirs with Christ—if, in fact, we suffer with Christ so that we may also be glorified with Christ.

[Roman Catholic alternate: 1 Corinthians 12:3–7, 12–13]

GOSPEL *John 14:15–16, 23–26*

Jesus said, "If you love me, you will keep my commandments. And I will ask the Father, who will give you another Advocate, to be with you forever.

"Those who love me will keep my word, and my Father will love them, and we will come to them and make our home with them. Whoever does not love me does not keep my words; and the word that you hear is not mine, but is from the Father who sent me.

"I have said these things to you while I am still with you. But the Advocate, the Holy Spirit, whom the Father will send in my name, will teach you everything, and remind you of all that I have said to you."

[Roman Catholic alternate: John 20:19–23]

[Revised Common Lectionary: John 14:8–17 (25–27)]

REFLECTION

The story of the disciples who locked themselves behind closed doors out of fear would have struck a chord with the Christians of the late first century who, like their predecessors in the faith, found themselves living in fear. And the words of Jesus likely had the same transforming power for both groups. Jesus comes among the disciples and offers peace, *shalom.*

The Hebrew notion of peace meant more than an absence of violence or distress. It also meant more than simple toleration. The *shalom* of Jesus means the establishment of right relationships among human beings. Jesus' peace looks beyond a mere cessation of hostilities to the achievement of balance, justice and mutual respect. The peace that Jesus brings is a peace that fosters mutual support and strength. For both the disciples hiding behind locked doors and the Christians of the late first century, this gift of peace was exactly what was needed to lead them out into the world.

Jesus' action of breathing on the disciples is a further sign that the community of believers is to put aside fear. At first glance, it may seem like an odd gesture. But there is a precedent here. In the beginning, God breathed on the waters to begin the work of creation (Genesis 1:2). Here, Jesus breathes on his followers to establish them as a new creation and to send them out to create a world of right relationships.

The reading from the Acts of the Apostles follows in this understanding and gives concrete form to Jesus' words. Pentecost itself is an act of new creation. The Spirit of Pentecost comes like a breath, a powerfully strong breath, and reorders relationships; those who were estranged are united in a shared language of the Spirit. The Christian community is given the confidence to grow and share testimony with all peoples about the powerful deeds of God.

■ **In what ways do you participate in the new creation introduced by Jesus? How do you share this new creation with others?**

■ **How can you cultivate right relationships with others?**

PRACTICE OF FAITH

RUSH OF WIND. A sign of the Holy Spirit is a rush of wind, or a gentle breeze, God's breath moving over the waters, breathed into the noses of the clay man and clay woman on the river bank (see Genesis 2). As our 50 days of Easter come to an end, celebrate the presence of God in wind and in breath. Hang up a set of wind chimes (if they won't disturb the neighbors!). When you hear them, stop and say "Come, Holy Spirit!" Play a kazoo, a harmonica, a penny whistle or pan pipes; even if you don't know how, blow into them until you get a pleasing sound. Fly a kite. Daydream as you watch a weathervane move to and fro. Pray: "Come, Holy Spirit!"

PRACTICE OF HOPE

MIGHTY ACTS. We elect our lawmakers and they act in our name, but somehow government often seems to be a force unto itself. It is easy for an individual to feel helpless to effect any change at all. That's where community organizing comes in. Church congregations around the country have joined hands to remind members of their role as citizens. One group, Omaha Together One Community (OTOC), started in 1993 by addressing community policing, juvenile justice and health issues. Now 35 congregations strong, OTOC continues to be a voice for the people who aren't being heard. This hasn't always won them friends, but organizers say it is only natural for faith-based communities to lead this kind of constructive dialogue.

PRACTICE OF CHARITY

FROM EVERY NATION. Pentecost is a good opportunity to become more aware of the needs of the church throughout the world. Many communities lack the ministers and financial resources to fulfill their mission of proclaiming the Good News and building up God's reign of justice. Some parishes partner with a faith community in another part of the world, or even in their own locale, lending support and receiving in return the gifts of another community of faith. Participate in your own community's partnering program. If your parish is not currently involved in such an effort, begin the process yourself, or contribute to the efforts of some other group involved in this mission.

WEEKDAY READINGS (Mo) Tobit 1:1, 3; 2:1–8; (Tu) 2:9–14; (We) 3:1–11, 16–17; (Th) 6:10–11; 7:1, 9–17; 8:4–9; (Fr) 11:5–17; (Sa) 12:1, 5–15, 20

SUMMER ORDINARY TIME

Give us care like yours for this earth.

Praise is due to you,
O God in Zion.

You visit the earth and water it,
you greatly enrich it;
the river of God is full of water.
You provide its grain,
for so you have prepared it.

You water its furrows abundantly,
settling its ridges,
softening it with showers,
and blessing its growth.
You crown the year with your bounty.

The hills gird themselves with joy,
the meadows clothe themselves with flocks,
the valleys deck themselves with grain,
they shout and sing together for joy.

—Psalm 65:1a, 9–11a, 12b–13

God who called each day's creation good,
all we have for our food
and shelter and clothing
are the crust and air, the light and water
    of this planet.
Give us care like yours for this earth:
to share its bounty
with generations to come
and with all alike in this generation,
to savor its beauty and respect its power,
to heal what greed and war and foolishness
have done to your earth and to us.
Bring us finally to give thanks,
always and everywhere.

—Prayer of the Season

READING I *Proverbs 8:1–4, 22–31*

Does not Wisdom call,
    and does not Understanding raise her voice?
On the heights, beside the way,
    at the crossroads she takes her stand;
beside the gates in front of the town,
    at the entrance of the portals she cries out:
"To you, O people, I call,
    and my cry is to all that live.

"The LORD created me at the beginning of creation,
    the first of the LORD's acts of long ago.
Ages ago I was set up,
    at the first, before the beginning of the earth.
When there were no depths I was brought forth,
    when there were no springs abounding
        with water.
Before the mountains had been shaped,
    before the hills, I was brought forth—
when the LORD had not yet made earth and fields,
    or the world's first bits of soil.
I was there when the LORD established the heavens,
    and drew a circle on the face of the deep,
and made firm the skies above,
    and established the fountains of the deep,
and assigned to the sea its limit,
    so that the waters might not transgress the
        LORD's command,
when the foundations of the earth were marked out,
    then I was beside the LORD, like a master worker;
and I was daily the LORD's delight,
    rejoicing before the LORD always,
rejoicing in the LORD's inhabited world
    and delighting in the human race."
[Roman Catholic: Proverbs 8:22–31]

READING II *Romans 5:1–5*

Therefore, since we are justified by faith, we have peace with God through our Lord Jesus Christ, through whom we have obtained access to this grace in which we stand; and we boast in our hope of sharing the glory of God. And not only that, but we also boast in our sufferings, knowing that suffering produces endurance, and endurance produces character, and character produces hope, and hope does not disappoint us, because God's love has been poured into our hearts through the Holy Spirit that has been given to us.

GOSPEL *John 16:12–15*

"I still have many things to say to you, but you cannot bear them now. When the Spirit of truth comes, you will be guided into all the truth; for the Spirit will not speak out of the Spirit's own authority, but will speak whatever the Spirit hears, and will declare to you the things that are to come. The Spirit will glorify me, taking what is mine and declaring it to you. All that the Father has is mine. For this reason I said that the Spirit will take what is mine and declare it to you."

REFLECTION

The doctrine of the Trinity is not spelled out explicitly in the scriptures but it is fair to say that it is implied in many places. The gospel for today is one of these. The passage tells us that Jesus is the complete revelation of the Father, and that the Spirit will carry this revelation to future generations. The Spirit will not bring anything new, but will help people to understand Jesus Christ.

One could spend years grappling with the mystery of the Trinity. But some things are foundational. The mystery of the Trinity does not mean that God is somehow divided, or that there are multiples of God. Notice that Christians are baptized into the name (notice, *singular* "name") of the Father and of the Son and of the Holy Spirit. Our God is one. As a seventh-century council of the church put it: "The Father is what the Son is, the Son what the Father is, the Father and the Son what the Spirit is, that is, by nature one God."

The mystery of the Trinity tells us about a relationship of activity. We see this in today's gospel where Father, Son and Spirit take on diverse activities toward a common goal. The unity of the Trinity is not diminished by this diversity of action, which is in accord with the very identity of God as made known by Jesus in today's gospel.

Our understanding of the Trinity can rightly encourage us in our efforts to live according to the gospel. Patterning ourselves on the example of the Trinity, we can appreciate our diversity and cultivate the gifts that we each uniquely possess. We should take joy in our talents, our own particular insights and our styles of prayer and relating to God. Our differences as members of the community of faith may rightly be celebrated as a way to acclaim our belief in a triune God.

■ **How does the Spirit unveil Christ in your experiences? How can you participate in the Spirit's activity of revealing Christ?**

■ **In what ways do you celebrate unity and diversity in your life?**

PRACTICE OF FAITH

FATHER, SON AND HOLY SPIRIT. This is the name into which we are baptized. All Christian communities follow Christ's command literally, and baptize new believers "in the name of the Father and of the Son and of the Holy Spirit." Here is an ancient blessing from the Celtic church (from lands that are now Ireland and northwest France) that you can pray as you wash your face.

The three palmfuls of the Sacred Three
To preserve me from every envy or evil eye:
The palmful of the Father of life;
The palmful of the Christ of love;
The palmful of the Spirit of peace,
The God of threefold love.

PRACTICE OF HOPE

DAY BY DAY. Integrating our faith into everyday life takes effort. Thanks to the Collaborative Ministry Office of Creighton University, help is just a few mouse-clicks away. The office has developed a 34-week online retreat complete with tips on how to get started, reflections by Jesuit Father Larry Gillick, readings and prayers. It requires only a little time each day, and the staff reminds us that even a small change in our pattern is an opening that allows God to work in us. "Be open and trust in a God who is not outdone in generosity," they say. To get started, go to www.creighton.edu and click on "Online Ministries."

PRACTICE OF CHARITY

DELIGHTING IN THE HUMAN RACE. Divine Wisdom is often portrayed, as in today's first reading, teaching human beings and delighting in them as God's creations.

God indeed delights in humanity, and the diversity of human cultures can itself teach us something about God's gloriously diverse creative activity. We, too, should delight in the cultures of other human beings as an act of praise to God.

In many places, summer is a time of cultural festivals: Irish, Italian, African American, the many cultures of the Caribbean and Latin America. Take advantage of these occasions; they are opportunities for all of us to learn more about each other and come to appreciate the diversity of humankind. Only then will we be able to live the communion of the Trinity that we celebrate today.

WEEKDAY READINGS (Mo) Acts 11:21–26; 13:1–3; (Tu) 2 Corinthians 1:18–22; (We) 3:4–11; (Th) 3:15—4:1, 3–6; (Fr) 4:7–15; (Sa) 5:14–21

READING I   *Genesis 14:18–20*

When Abram heard that his nephew, Lot, had been taken captive, he led forth his trained men, and routed the abductors. After Abram's return King Melchizedek of Salem brought out bread and wine; he was priest of God Most High. He blessed Abram and said,

> "Blessed be Abram by God Most High,
> maker of heaven and earth;
> and blessed be God Most High,
> who has delivered your enemies
>   into your hand!"

And Abram gave him one tenth of everything.

READING II   *1 Corinthians 11:23–26*

For I received from the Lord what I also handed on to you, that the Lord Jesus on the night when he was betrayed took a loaf of bread, and when he had given thanks, he broke it and said, "This is my body that is for you. Do this in remembrance of me." In the same way he took the cup also, after supper, saying, "This cup is the new covenant in my blood. Do this, as often as you drink it, in remembrance of me." For as often as you eat this bread and drink the cup, you proclaim the Lord's death until he comes.

GOSPEL   *Luke 9:11–17*

Jesus spoke to the crowds about the kingdom of God, and healed those who needed to be cured. The day was drawing to a close, and the twelve came to him and said, "Send the crowd away, so that they may go into the surrounding villages and country-side, to lodge and get provisions; for we are here in a deserted place." But Jesus said to them, "You give them something to eat." They said, "We have no more than five loaves and two fish—unless we are to go and buy food for all these people." For there were about five thousand men. And Jesus said to his disciples, "Make the people sit down in groups of about fifty each." They did so and made them all sit down. And taking the five loaves and the two fish, he looked up to heaven, and blessed and broke them, and gave them to the disciples to set before the crowd. And all ate and were filled. What was left over was gathered up, twelve baskets of broken pieces.

Friday, June 22, 2001

SACRED HEART OF JESUS

Ezekiel 34:11–16   *I myself will pasture my sheep and give them rest.*

Romans 5:5–11   *The love of God has been poured out in our hearts.*

Luke 15:3–7   *Rejoice with me because I have found my lost sheep.*

This is an echo of Good Friday, a reminder that every Friday is kept with renewed efforts to understand and to share the compassion of God. If Christ lives in our hearts, we bear the love of God in our own bodies.

REFLECTION

There is much to learn from Luke's description of the feeding of the multitude, especially as it relates to our feast of the Body and Blood of Christ. In the first part of verse 11 (not a part of today's reading) Jesus welcomes the crowd that had followed him. This sets a tone of hospitality from the outset, one that continues throughout the event that follows. It is first seen in Jesus giving the crowd the gift of his speech and his healing, and it continues with the feeding of the crowd.

When Jesus tells the apostles to give the crowd something to eat, they grumble their dissatisfaction (almost resentment) at what they consider a suggestion that they buy food for all present. But Jesus proves through his actions that providing money (at least, without anything more) is not what he means by hospitality and is not what is needed to fill the people; it is the power of the Lord that will feed them. Jesus' prayer, blessing and provision of abundant food point to the power and true character of divine hospitality.

In addition to showing the nature of Christian hospitality, Jesus also exemplifies the attitude of hospitality. As a general rule, it was a servant's job to serve food to others; a person in any position of authority would never serve at table. Nor would the host of the meal. But Jesus, the ultimate authority and the host of this gathering, takes on the role of a servant by providing the meal for the crowd. Hospitality in Jesus' understanding involves the actions of one who acts as servant to others.

These attitudes of Jesus are passed on to the disciples as they are instructed to make the people sit, and to set the food before them. This demonstration of hospitable service by Jesus and his invitation to his disciples to participate in it foreshadow Jesus' act of service at the Last Supper where he washes his disciples' feet. This foreshadowing is an important connection to the table of the Last Supper at which Jesus nourishes his disciples with his body and blood. The message is unambiguous: Those who would follow Christ are to lead lives of hospitable service that meets the real needs of others. In so doing we share with others the food that truly satisfies and nourishes, the presence of Christ that dwells in each of us.

■ **In what ways do you share the presence of Christ that dwells inside you? How do you share Christian hospitality with others?**

PRACTICE OF FAITH

PRAYER AT MEALS. It is an instinct to give God thanks before eating and drinking. For those of us who are baptized, our ultimate table prayer is the eucharistic prayer of the Mass. To be true to that prayer, to which we weekly sing our assent, our "Amen!", we must keep the habit of praying before meals at home. A simple sign of the cross before eating can be a blessing. Or we can use these words: "Bless us, O Lord, and these your gifts, which we are about to receive from your bounty, through Christ our Lord. Amen."

PRACTICE OF HOPE

THEY ALL ATE. Some have suggested that in today's gospel so many people were able to feast on so little because everyone shared what they had. That same idea is what makes the Souper Bowl a success each year. A faith initiative started by a South Carolina youth group in 1990, the collection is taken by young people in congregations around the country on or near Super Bowl Sunday. The requested amount: $1. Some collect canned goods as well. Each church decides where its contributions will go. Soup kitchens, food banks and the missions have all benefited from the effort, according to national organizers. For more information, visit www.souperbowl.com.

PRACTICE OF CHARITY

UNTIL THEY HAD ENOUGH. Today's gospel should remind us that the bread and wine we share are more than a ritual banquet: The eucharist has everything to do with the meals we share and the just distribution of food for all people. The feeding of five thousand people at no cost to them should tell us something about God's abundance: It is meant for all people, and it's free.

The coupling of this reading with the feast of the Body and Blood of Christ prevents us from overly spiritualizing the real presence of Christ in the eucharist. Among other things, our eucharistic celebration is a model for what is supposed to be happening in the world: Every person should have a just share of the produce of the earth; no person should ever go hungry; all of God's children have a right to food.

Find an organization, such as Catholic Relief Services (PO Box 1790, Baltimore MD 21203–7090; 1–800–736–3467; www.catholicrelief.org), that supports self-sustaining agriculture throughout the world. In these ways, we can truly live the eucharist we celebrate.

WEEKDAY READINGS (Mo) 2 Corinthians 6:1–10; (Tu) 8:1–9; (We) 9:6–11; (Th) 11:1–11; (Fr) Sacred Heart, see box; (Sa) 2 Corinthians 12:1–10

READING I *2 Samuel 11:26—12:3a, 4–7a, 9ab, 13–15*

When the wife of Uriah heard that her husband was dead, she made lamentation for him. When the mourning was over, David sent and brought her to his house, and she became his wife, and bore him a son.

But the thing that David had done displeased the LORD, and the LORD sent Nathan to David. Nathan came to him, and said to him, "There were two men in a certain city, the one rich and the other poor. The rich man had very many flocks and herds; but the poor man had nothing but one little ewe lamb, which he had bought. Now there came a traveler to the rich man, and he was loath to take one of his own flock or herd to prepare for the wayfarer who had come to him, but he took the poor man's lamb, and prepared that for the guest who had come to him."

Then David's anger was greatly kindled against the man. He said to Nathan, "As the LORD lives, the man who has done this deserves to die; he shall restore the lamb fourfold, because he did this thing, and because he had no pity."

Nathan said to David, "You are the man! Thus says the LORD, the God of Israel: I anointed you king over Israel, and I rescued you from the hand of Saul. Why have you despised the word of the LORD, to do what is evil in the LORD'S sight? You have struck down Uriah the Hittite with the sword, and have taken his wife to be your wife."

David said to Nathan, "I have sinned against the LORD." Nathan said to David, "Now the LORD has put away your sin; Nevertheless, because by this deed you have utterly scorned the LORD, the child that is born to you shall die." Then Nathan went to his house.

The LORD struck the child that Uriah's wife bore to David, and it became very ill.

[Complete reading: 2 Samuel 11:26—12:10, 13–15]

READING II *Galatians 2:15–16a, 19–20*

We ourselves are Jews by birth and not Gentile sinners; yet we know that a person is justified not by the works of the law but through faith in Jesus Christ. For through the law I died to the law, so that I might live to God. I have been crucified with Christ; and it is no longer I who live, but it is Christ who lives in me. And the life I now live in the flesh I live by faith in the Son of God, who loved me and gave himself for me.

[Complete reading: Galatians 2:15–21]

GOSPEL *Luke 7:36–50*

One of the Pharisees asked Jesus to eat with him, and Jesus went into the Pharisee's house and took his place at the table. And a woman in the city, who was a sinner, having learned that he was eating in the Pharisee's house, brought an alabaster jar of ointment. She stood behind Jesus at his feet, weeping, and began to bathe his feet with her tears and to dry them with her hair. Then she continued kissing his feet and anointing them with the ointment. Now when the Pharisee who had invited Jesus saw it, he said to himself, "If this man were a prophet, he would have known who and what kind of woman this is who is touching him—that she is a sinner."

Jesus spoke up and said to him, "Simon, I have something to say to you." "Teacher," he replied, "speak." "A certain creditor had two debtors; one owed five hundred denarii, and the other fifty. When they could not pay, the creditor canceled the debts for both of them. Now which of them will love the creditor more?" Simon answered, "I suppose the one for whom the creditor canceled the greater debt." And Jesus said to him, "You have judged rightly." Then turning toward the woman, he said to Simon, "Do you see this woman? I entered your house; you gave me no water for my feet, but she has bathed my feet with her tears and dried them with her hair. You gave me no kiss, but from the time I came in she has not stopped kissing my feet. You did not anoint my head with oil, but she has anointed my feet with ointment. Therefore, I tell you, her sins, which were many, have been forgiven; hence she has shown great love. But the one to whom little is forgiven, loves little." Then Jesus said to the woman, "Your sins are forgiven." But those who were at the table with him began to say among themselves, "Who is this who even forgives sins?" And Jesus said to the woman, "Your faith has saved you; go in peace."

[Complete reading: Luke 7:36—8:3]

R E F L E C T I O N

When the woman came to Jesus and used her tears to wash his feet, one image that comes to mind is that she was pouring out the tears of sorrow and pain that she had been saving her entire life. Although Luke does not bring this image into his description, the thought is nonetheless a powerful one. This woman, shunned as a sinner by the community and religious leaders, was able to place all of her sorrows at the feet of Jesus. And Jesus accepts her, forgives her sin and prepares a way for her to re-enter the life of a community, the community of faith.

Luke's description of the encounter between Jesus and the woman differs from the descriptions of the same event in the other gospels (see Matthew 26:6ff; Mark 14:3ff; John 12:1ff). Luke brings his own concerns to the story and makes several points. Throughout his gospel, Luke writes of forgiveness as a hallmark of Christian life. This is the first time in the gospel that faith, forgiveness and salvation are joined, but it will not be the last (see 8:12, 48; 17:19; 18:42). In Luke, salvation comes in response to expressed faith.

One of the most pervasive of Luke's themes is Jesus' care for the poor. In line with this theme, Luke does not have Jesus repeat the statement Matthew and Mark record, "The poor you always have with you." Instead, Jesus responds to the woman's bold acts of hospitality by forgiving her sins and wishing her peace. This wish of peace is another common theme in Luke, representing a desire for the establishment of right relationships within the community. Jesus rebukes the Pharisee for his lack of hospitality and for his unhealthy relationship with God and the rest of the community.

■ **How can you pour out your sorrows to Christ? What are the sorrows that you would like to give over to Christ? What are some of the tears of joy that you could share?**

■ **What do you make of the concern for the poor that Luke emphasizes in his gospel? Just what does such a concern mean for Christians today?**

PRACTICE OF FAITH

SOME WOMEN. The gospel of Luke records the names of more women disciples of Jesus than the other gospels do. But even Luke fails to record the name of the woman who anoints Jesus' feet. In Mark's version of this same story, Jesus says that because of the care she has shown, this woman will be remembered forever, but even that gospel does not tell us her name! (See Mark 14:1–9.) Go through this book and mark all the names of female followers of Jesus that are mentioned. Then in the margins of this page, write the names of all the women and girls you know who have washed the feet of Christ by caring for the poor. Remember their names.

PRACTICE OF HOPE

CANCELED THE DEBTS. The last year has been filled with calls for creditors to forgive all or part of the debts owed to them. Does this sound like too grand a gesture for ordinary people? One couple in my parish didn't think so. They decided to celebrate Jubilee Year 2000 by forgiving their daughter's school debt. It was a sacrifice for them, but love can bear a little sacrifice.

The Jubilee Year may be over, but there is no statute of limitation on faith and hope. There are debts you can forgive even now. And don't forget the debts that have nothing to do with money.

PRACTICE OF CHARITY

WOMEN AND POVERTY. Today's readings present two troubling depictions of women. Bathsheba is considered little more than property to be won; the woman in the gospel has long been assumed to be a prostitute, although the text in no way indicates this.

Such is the condition of many women in the world today. A combination of poverty and sexism prevents many from ever achieving self-sufficiency. One strategy, known as micro-credit, has shown great success in bringing very poor women to prosperity. Community banks grant very small loans to very poor women to start small businesses that provide them and their children with income. There are many not-for-profit organizations that employ this strategy, liberating millions of women all over the world from dependence and poverty. For more information, contact the Trickle Up Program, 121 W. 27th St., Suite 504, New York, NY 10001; 1-212-362-7958; www.trickleup.org.

WEEKDAY READINGS (Mo) 2 Corinthians 6:1–10; (Tu) 8:1–9; (We) 9:6–11; (Th) 11:1–11; (Fr) Sacred Heart; see page 106; (Sa) 2 Corinthians 12:1–10

READING I *Isaiah 49:1, 3–6b*

Listen to me, O coastlands,
    pay attention, you peoples from far away!
The LORD called me before I was born,
    and while I was in my mother's womb
      God named me.

And the LORD said to me, "You are my servant,
    Israel, in whom I will be glorified."
But I said, "I have labored in vain,
    I have spent my strength for nothing and vanity;
yet surely my cause is with the LORD,
    and my reward with my God."

And now the LORD says,
    who formed me as a servant from the womb,
to bring Jacob back to God,
    and that Israel might be gathered to the LORD,
for I am honored in the sight of the LORD,
    and my God has become my strength—
the LORD says,
"I will give you as a light to the nations,
    that my salvation may reach to the end
      of the earth."

[Complete reading: Isaiah 49:1–6]

READING II *Acts 13:22–26*

"When he was removed, God made David their king. In testifying about him God said, 'I have found David, son of Jesse, to be a man after my heart, who will carry out all my wishes.' Of this man's posterity God has brought to Israel a Savior, Jesus, as God promised; before his coming John had already proclaimed a baptism of repentance to all the people of Israel. And as John was finishing his work, he said, 'What do you suppose that I am? I am not he. No, but one is coming after me; I am not worthy to untie the thong of the sandals on his feet.'

"My brothers, you descendants of Abraham's family, and others who fear God, to us the message of this salvation has been sent."

GOSPEL *Luke 1:57–66, 80*

Now the time came for Elizabeth to give birth, and she bore a son. Her neighbors and relatives heard that the Lord had shown great mercy to her, and they rejoiced with her.

On the eighth day they came to circumcise the child, and they were going to name him Zechariah after his father. But his mother said, "No; he is to be called John." They said to her, "None of your relatives has this name." Then they began motioning to his father to find out what name he wanted to give him. He asked for a writing tablet and wrote, "His name is John." And all of them were amazed. Immediately his mouth was opened and his tongue freed, and he began to speak, praising God. Fear came over all their neighbors, and all these things were talked about throughout the entire hill country of Judea. All who heard them pondered them and said, "What then will this child become?" For, indeed, the hand of the Lord was with him.

The child grew and became strong in spirit, and he was in the wilderness until the day he appeared publicly to Israel.

Friday, June 29, 2001

PETER AND PAUL, APOSTLES

VIGIL

Acts 3:1–10 *Peter cried, "Look at us!"*

Galatians 1:11–20 *God chose to reveal Christ to me.*

John 21:15–19 *Simon Peter, do you love me?*

DAY

Acts 12:1–11 *The chains dropped from Peter's wrists.*

2 Timothy 4:6–8, 17–18 *I have kept the faith.*

Matthew 16:13–19 *I entrust to you the keys of the kingdom.*

Today we keep a festival in honor of the two apostles who began the harvest of God's reign. They preached from Jerusalem to Rome, keeping the Easter commandment to bring the good news to the ends of the earth.

REFLECTION

In today's gospel narrative of the birth of John the Baptist, Luke tells a story of liberation from social constrictions. The story of the birth of John tells of the new life that comes of acting in accord with the will of God.

Elizabeth was an elderly woman who had had no children. In her society, her childlessness would have been considered a punishment by God, and therefore she would have been held in low esteem. But God discounts the judgment of Elizabeth's social group and blesses her with a child in her old age. By making her the mother of a great prophet, the Lord releases Elizabeth from the scorn her village would have placed upon her.

Upon the birth of a son, the cultural expectation would have been that he would be given some form of the father's name. However, the pressure to follow the custom is overcome, first by Elizabeth and then by Zechariah. Elizabeth takes the lead in this important decision, which is yet another challenge to cultural expectations. The name given, John, has deeper significance than just defying the neighbors' expectations. Choosing a name that comes from outside the "priestly" tradition indicates that the line of priests is broken to make way for the new high priest, Jesus Christ.

Elizabeth and Zechariah choose over and over to follow the call of the Lord as it comes to them through the angel Gabriel, and not to follow the customs of their society. But while they ignore human norms, they keep the religious law that their child be circumcised on the eighth day. In telling of the circumcision of John, Luke is commenting on more than the loyalty of Elizabeth and Zechariah to the word of God. The circumcision makes clear that John is part of the covenant that Israel shares with the Lord. This is an important point for Luke to make to the members of his predominantly Gentile audience. They needed to understand the roots of the Christian movement. It was important for the new religion to remain connected with Judaism.

■ What social norms might you need to break in order to follow Christ more effectively? What would be the reaction of friends and family if you abandoned some of these norms?

■ Do you feel free to praise God in your life? What do you need to do to show your faith in the Lord more freely?

PRACTICE OF FAITH

LIGHT TO THE NATIONS. Before the precision of modern measuring tools, June 24 was thought to be the longest day of the year—the day after which sunlight gradually decreases until, the ancients thought, December 25. (We now know that June 21 is the longest day and that December 21 is the shortest.) So of course the birth of the great forerunner of the Lord was celebrated on this brightest day of summer. John the Baptist is a beacon, calling for all to turn to Christ and live. It is a custom to celebrate this night with bonfires—a good excuse to sit around a campfire or fireplace tonight and give thanks to God.

PRACTICE OF HOPE

THE LORD HAS SPOKEN. The billboard that loomed over the busy street corner in Pittsburgh was simple, but everyone stopped to read it: "Don't make me come down there. God." Most people chuckled. Some rolled their eyes and walked on. Either way, it made an impact. Billboards like this have popped up all over the country. Created by the Smith Agency, an advertising company in Fort Lauderdale, the billboard campaign was sponsored by an anonymous donor who wanted to remind people that God can help. From the commotion these signs have caused, it seems clear that people are eager to hear God's voice. While God speaks to us all the time, we don't always recognize the messengers—or the message. God always finds a way.

PRACTICE OF CHARITY

I AM SENDING MY MESSENGER. John the Baptist, in addition to "preparing the way" for Jesus, was a teacher in his own right. Even before Jesus's ministry, Luke tells us, "John proclaimed the good news to the people" (3:18).

It is perhaps easier for us to let great prophets live in the past, to believe that the age of prophecy is over.

Without a doubt, however, great prophets are alive and well in our own day. Nelson Mandela, Desmond Tutu and the Dalai Lama are still living; Dorothy Day, Thomas Merton, Mother Teresa and Dr. Martin Luther King, Jr., have preceded us to the heavenly banquet already. Their writings can be guides for us as we seek to be prophetic voices in our own time and place. Find a good biography or collection of writings by a prophet you admire. Let that person's example guide you to greater acts of charity and justice.

WEEKDAY READINGS (Mo) Genesis 12:1–9; (Tu) 13:2, 5–18; (We) 15:1–12, 17–18; (Th) 16:1–12, 15–16; (Fr) Peter and Paul, see box; (Sa) Genesis 18:1–15

READING I   *Isaiah 65:1–2, 7b, 8–9*

I was ready to be sought out by those
    who did not ask,
    to be found by those who did not seek me.
I said, "Here I am, here I am,"
    to a nation that did not call on my name.
I held out my hands all day long
    to a rebellious people,
who walk in a way that is not good,
    following their own devices.
I will measure into their laps
    full payment for their actions.

Thus says the LORD:
As the wine is found in the cluster,
    and they say, "Do not destroy it,
    for there is a blessing in it,"
so I will do for my servants' sake,
    and not destroy them all.
I will bring forth descendants from Jacob,
    and from Judah inheritors of my mountains;
my chosen shall inherit it,
    and my servants shall settle there.
[Complete reading: Isaiah 65:1–9]

READING II   *Galatians 3:23–29*

Now before faith came, we were imprisoned and guarded under the law until faith would be revealed. Therefore the law was our disciplinarian until Christ came, so that we might be justified by faith. But now that faith has come, we are no longer subject to a disciplinarian, for in Christ Jesus you are all children of God through faith. As many of you as were baptized into Christ have clothed yourselves with Christ. There is no longer Jew or Greek, there is no longer slave or free, there is no longer male and female; for all of you are one in Christ Jesus. And if you belong to Christ, then you are Abraham's offspring, heirs according to the promise.

GOSPEL   *Luke 8:26–39*

Then Jesus and his disciples arrived at the country of the Gerasenes, which is opposite Galilee. As Jesus stepped out on land, a man of the city who had demons met him. For a long time he had worn no clothes, and he did not live in a house but in the tombs. When he saw Jesus, he fell down before him and shouted at the top of his voice, "What have you to do with me, Jesus, Son of the Most High God? I beg you, do not torment me"—for Jesus had commanded the unclean spirit to come out of the man. (For many times it had seized him; he was kept under guard and bound with chains and shackles, but he would break the bonds and be driven by the demon into the wilds.) Jesus then asked him, "What is your name?" He said, "Legion"; for many demons had entered him. The demons begged Jesus not to order them to go back into the abyss.

Now there on the hillside a large herd of swine was feeding; and the demons begged Jesus to let them enter these. So Jesus gave them permission. Then the demons came out of the man and entered the swine, and the herd rushed down the steep bank into the lake and was drowned.

When the swineherds saw what had happened, they ran off and told it in the city and in the country. Then people came out to see what had happened, and when they came to Jesus, they found the man from whom the demons had gone sitting at the feet of Jesus, clothed and in his right mind. And they were afraid. Those who had seen it told them how the one who had been possessed by demons had been healed. Then all the people of the surrounding country of the Gerasenes asked Jesus to leave them; for they were seized with great fear. So he got into the boat and returned. The man from whom the demons had gone begged that he might be with him; but Jesus sent him away, saying, "Return to your home, and declare how much God has done for you." So the man went away, proclaiming throughout the city how much Jesus had done for him.

REFLECTION

The story in today's gospel might strike us as strange, even frightening in its images. There is a naked homeless man, a cemetery, demons, chains and shackles, ranting and raving, an abyss and a herd of possessed, drowned swine. In addition, the title often given to this piece—the story of the Gerasene demoniac—frames it as an unbelievable tale of the bizarre, the supernatural. At first reading we may only be able to think of it as just another story about Jesus' supernatural power.

But if we look at the way Luke describes the situation of the man before and after his encounter with Jesus, our understanding deepens. We see a man who "had demons" (v. 27) become someone "in his right mind" (v. 35); someone who "had worn no clothes" (v. 27) become "clothed" (v. 35); someone who "did not live in a house" (v. 27) - lived "in the tombs" (v. 27) and the "wilds" (v. 29) now moving "throughout the city" (v. 39). This is more than just a tale of Jesus' supernatural power over demons. It is a witness to Jesus' desire and strength to restore to wholeness all who believe in the word of God, and testimony that new life in the Lord means life within a community

Luke crafted his version of this story (see Mark 5:1–20 for another version) to speak to his Gentile readers of the nature of Christian life: It is a life lived within the human community. Luke might also be making a point about the nature of Christian community. Jesus brought a Gerasene—who comes from a land that is "opposite Galilee"—out of isolation and into community life, but he left him where he found him, that is, "opposite Galilee." He felt no need to make the restored disciple abandon his own community to search elsewhere for Christian community life. As Jesus did for the Gerasene, Luke might well have been saying to his Gentile readers, the risen Christ continues to do, gathering those considered outsiders into communities of faith wherever they might be.

■ **In what areas of your life are you without clothes, or in the tombs, or in the wilds? Where do you need to be restored to wholeness, to human community?**

■ **How can your community of faith encourage your growth? What would you ask of your community in this regard?**

PRACTICE OF FAITH

DECLARE HOW MUCH. After Jesus cures the man with demons, he gives him a commission: "Return to your home, and declare how much God has done for you." It can be difficult sharing news about what God has done for us. We are often afraid of sounding like fanatics, so we try to live our lives in quiet gratitude. But Jesus' command echoes in our ears. Once healed, we are commissioned to be witnesses and to share that healing power with others. Try this: Before praying at dinner, go around the table and have each member of the family or household say one thing that God has done this day. Give thanks for these things as well as for the food.

PRACTICE OF HOPE

I WILL NOT KEEP SILENT. Is it easier to turn a blind eye to injustices around you, or to continue speaking out until something is done? As I reflect on the readings for this Sunday, I am reminded of Dr. Martin Luther King, Jr., who almost certainly faced this question as he spoke out for civil rights. He was criticized for being impatient. His motives were questioned. In his *Letter from the Birmingham Jail,* King said he was satisfied to be considered an extremist. His model was Jesus, whom he called an extremist for love. "Will we be extremists for hate or will we be extremists for love?" he wrote. King concluded that the world was "in dire need of creative extremists."

PRACTICE OF CHARITY

DEMONS. Commentators have often suggested that the demoniac of today's gospel may have been a person with mental illness. In our time as in Jesus' time, mental illness is a difficult issue. Many people simply do not understand depression or schizophrenia, and don't know what to do if someone they love seems to be contemplating suicide. According to 1997 statistics, suicide was the eighth leading cause of death in the U.S., claiming some 30,000 lives; 500,000 were treated for suicide attempts. Teenagers are at high risk, especially teens who are questioning their sexual orientation, who attempt suicide at 3.4 times the rate as their heterosexual peers. White men over 65 account for the largest number of suicides. For more information about suicide prevention, contact the American Foundation for Suicide Prevention, 120 Wall St., 22nd Floor, New York NY 10005; 1-888-333-AFSP; www.afsp.org.

WEEKDAY READINGS (Mo) Genesis 12:1–9; (Tu) 13:2, 5–18; (We) 15:1–12, 17–18; (Th) 16:1–12, 15–16; (Fr) Peter and Paul, apostles, see page 110; (Sa) Genesis 18:1–15

READING I *1 Kings 19:15–16, 19–21*

Then the LORD said to Elijah, "Go, return on your way to the wilderness of Damascus; when you arrive, you shall anoint Hazael as king over Aram. Also you shall anoint Jehu son of Nimshi as king over Israel; and you shall anoint Elisha son of Shaphat of Abel-meholah as prophet in your place."

So Elijah set out from there, and found Elisha son of Shaphat, who was plowing. There were twelve yoke of oxen ahead of him, and he was with the twelfth. Elijah passed by him and threw his mantle over Elisha. He left the oxen, ran after Elijah, and said, "Let me kiss my father and my mother, and then I will follow you." Then Elijah said to him, "Go back again; for what have I done to you?" Elisha returned from following Elijah, took the yoke of oxen, and slaughtered them; using the equipment from the oxen, he boiled their flesh, and gave it to the people, and they ate. Then Elisha set out and followed Elijah, and became his servant.

READING II *Galatians 5:1, 13–18*

For freedom Christ has set us free. Stand firm, therefore, and do not submit again to a yoke of slavery.

For you were called to freedom, brothers and sisters; only do not use your freedom as an opportunity for self-indulgence, but through love become slaves to one another. For the whole law is summed up in a single commandment, "You shall love your neighbor as yourself." If, however, you bite and devour one another, take care that you are not consumed by one another.

Live by the Spirit, I say, and do not gratify the desires of the flesh. For what the flesh desires is opposed to the Spirit, and what the Spirit desires is opposed to the flesh; for these are opposed to each other, to prevent you from doing what you want. But if you are led by the Spirit, you are not subject to the law.

[Revised Common Lectionary: Galatians 5:1, 13–25]

GOSPEL *Luke 9:51–62*

When the days drew near for Jesus to be taken up, he set his face to go to Jerusalem. And he sent messengers ahead of him. On their way they entered a village of the Samaritans to make ready for him; but the people did not receive him, because his face was set toward Jerusalem. When his disciples James and John saw it, they said, "Lord, do you want us to command fire to come down from heaven and consume them?" But Jesus turned and rebuked them. Then they went on to another village.

As they were going along the road, someone said to Jesus, "I will follow you wherever you go." And Jesus said to him, "Foxes have holes, and birds of the air have nests; but the Son-of-Man has nowhere to lay his head." To another Jesus said, "Follow me." But he said, "Lord, first let me go and bury my father." But Jesus replied, "Let the dead bury their own dead; but as for you, go and proclaim the dominion of God." Another said, "I will follow you, Lord; but let me first say farewell to those at my home." Jesus replied, "No one who puts a hand to the plow and looks back is fit for the dominion of God."

REFLECTION

In some ways, the gospel of Luke is like a travelogue of Jesus' journey to Jerusalem. In today's reading Jesus "sets his face to go to Jerusalem," but this is just one moment in a larger context where all that Jesus does takes place on the way to Jerusalem. Commentators suggest that Luke used this Jerusalem-oriented travelogue to create a sense of longing for Jerusalem in his predominantly non-Palestinian Gentile audience. They would not have been very familiar with sacredness of Jerusalem in Jewish life. It was the home of the Temple and its Holy of Holies where the Ark of the Covenant was kept. It was also King David's capital. Jerusalem was an important point of reference and source of identity for the Jewish people with whom the Gentile converts to Christianity would be interacting, and Luke wanted these Gentiles to feel connected to it.

It is interesting that the second volume of Luke's work, the Acts of the Apostles, focuses on the movement of the first Christians away from Jerusalem. This travelogue tells the stories of the early disciples taking the gospel to the other regions of the Mediterranean through their teaching, preaching and healing. Acts stands, in part, for the proposition that Christ cannot be limited to one place or time but is accessible at all times, to anyone, at any place.

Along the way to Jerusalem, Jesus runs into his disciples' prejudice toward the Samaritans. There had been a long history of tension between the Israelites and the Samaritans, and it might have been easy for Jesus to sympathize with James and John in their feelings toward the Samaritans. Their desire to call down fire is reminiscent of 2 Kings 1:10, where Elijah commands fire to fall upon his enemies. Jesus' response is clear; he rebukes them and continues on his journey.

The life of the church and of each Christian involves a journey patterned after Jesus' journey toward Jerusalem. This implies a certain lack of attachment to routine, a certain understanding of the itinerant nature of discipleship. But as the example of the early Christians shows, the journey is what focuses us on our mission and forms us into a community of believers.

■ **Describe your journey toward the new Jerusalem. What sort of images do you have of your faith journey? Who are some of the people who journey with you?**

PRACTICE OF FAITH

HAND TO PLOW. Often it seems that all of our efforts to help others, to be holy, come to naught. The line at the soup kitchen never ends. When we think we've made a dent in racism, another black child is beaten or another Latino worker passed over for promotion. Some people see the quest for fairness as some evil "radical feminist" plot. Even in the church, lots of people who once put their hands to the plow have stopped, and are longing for some imaginary past when things were perfect. Redouble your efforts this week. If you serve one night a month at the homeless shelter, try two this month. If you've fallen out of the practice of daily prayer, start again.

PRACTICE OF HOPE

PATH TO LIFE. We make a mistake when we think of children as the leaders of tomorrow: There are so many who lead by example right now. One of these is Nicholas Breach of Camp Hill, PA. When he found out that he had a terminal brain-stem tumor, he could have concentrated on his own needs. It would have been only natural to do so. Instead he thought of others. He decided to donate his organs. "I wanted to give up hope," he told the Associated Press, "but now I can help other people." He did more than give help, however. His generous contribution—and the contribution of other organ donors around the country—gives hope and life to people in despair. We are humbled in the presence of such grace.

PRACTICE OF CHARITY

JESUS REBUKED THEM. This Thursday, July 4, the United States' celebration of independence and freedom, is also the anniversary of the three-day, two-state shooting spree of Benjamin Smith, a white supremacist from Illinois. His violence resulted in the deaths of two people, Ricky Byrdsong, an African American and former Northwestern University basketball coach, and Won Joon Yoon, a graduate student of Korean descent in Bloomington, Illinois. Among the wounded were Orthodox Jews and other Asian Americans and African Americans. Most disturbing was Smith's religious justification for his white supremacist views.

Too often, people of faith only speak out against racism and anti-Semitism when it is too late. Get involved in your own parish's efforts to combat the many forms of prejudice; if your parish is not actively involved in the fight against hatred, ask why not.

WEEKDAY READINGS (Mo) Genesis 18:16–33; (Tu) Ephesians 2:19–22; (We) Genesis 21:5; 8–20; (Th) 22:1–19; (Fr) 23:1–4, 19; 24:1–8, 62–67; (Sa) 27:1–5, 15–29

READING I *Isaiah 66:10–14*

Rejoice with Jerusalem, and be glad for the city,
    all you who love her;
rejoice with Jerusalem in joy,
    all you who mourn over her—
that you may nurse and be satisfied
    from her consoling breast;
that you may drink deeply with delight
    from her glorious bosom.
For thus says the LORD:
I will extend prosperity to Jerusalem like a river,
    and the wealth of the nations
        like an overflowing stream;
and you shall nurse and be carried on her arm,
    and dandled on her knees.
As a mother comforts her child,
    so I will comfort you;
    you shall be comforted in Jerusalem.
You shall see, and your heart shall rejoice;
    your bodies shall flourish like the grass;
and it shall be known that my hand is with
        my servants,
    and my indignation is against my enemies.

READING II *Galatians 6:14–18*

May I never boast of anything except the cross of
our Lord Jesus Christ, by which the world has been
crucified to me, and I to the world. For neither circumcision nor uncircumcision is anything; but a
new creation is everything! As for those who will
follow this rule—peace be upon them, and mercy,
and upon the Israel of God.

From now on, let no one make trouble for me; for
I carry the marks of Jesus branded on my body.

May the grace of our Lord Jesus Christ be with
your spirit, brothers and sisters. Amen.

[Revised Common Lectionary: Galatians 6:(1–6), 7–16]

GOSPEL *Luke 10:1–12, 16–20*

After this the Lord appointed seventy others and
sent them on ahead of him in pairs to every town
and place where he himself intended to go. Jesus
said to them, "The harvest is plentiful, but the laborers are few; therefore ask the Lord of the harvest to
send out laborers for the harvesting. Go on your
way. See, I am sending you out like lambs into the
midst of wolves. Carry no purse, no bag, no sandals;
and greet no one on the road. Whatever house you
enter, first say, 'Peace to this house!' And if anyone is
there who shares in peace, your peace will rest on
that person; but if not, it will return to you. Remain
in the same house, eating and drinking whatever
they provide, for the laborer deserves to be paid. Do
not move about from house to house. Whenever you
enter a town and its people welcome you, eat what
is set before you; cure the sick who are there, and
say to them, 'The dominion of God has come near to
you.' But whenever you enter a town and they do
not welcome you, go out into its streets and say,
'Even the dust of your town that clings to our feet,
we wipe off in protest against you. Yet know this:
the dominion of God has come near.' I tell you, on
that day it will be more tolerable for Sodom than for
that town."

"Whoever listens to you listens to me, and whoever rejects you rejects me, and whoever rejects me
rejects the one who sent me."

The seventy returned with joy, saying, "Lord, in
your name even the demons submit to us!" Jesus
said to them, "I watched Satan fall from heaven like
a flash of lightning. See, I have given you authority
to tread on snakes and scorpions, and over all the
power of the enemy; and nothing will hurt you.
Nevertheless, do not rejoice at this, that the spirits
submit to you, but rejoice that your names are written in heaven."

[Roman Catholic: Luke 10:1–12, 17–20]

REFLECTION

For Jesus' original audience, the image of the harvest was a vivid one. Most lived in an agrarian society and understood the images of planting and growing that Jesus often used. This particular reference provides a picture of a harvest ready to be gathered. Those sent out to gather it in must work hard but will see bountiful results. There is an urgency here. Those of Jesus' time knew that unharvested grain would quickly rot in the field. For Jesus, harvesters are needed immediately. For "the dominion of God has come near."

Yet the task is not without danger. Jesus sends out his disciples as "lambs into the midst of wolves." Those who share Jesus' ministry will be opposed, even hunted down. Jesus' admonitions about what to carry on the journey are not some moral code for the disciples but rather an encouragement to be practical, travel lightly and be careful.

The disciples are commissioned to preach the gospel and to cast out demons. By casting out demons, Jesus shows his power, and by passing this same power to his disciples, Jesus elevates them to his position. When the disciples exercise the authority Jesus gave them, they are actually putting all evil under the authority of Jesus, recognizing Jesus as one who can control evil. This power of Jesus shows not only his authority over creation but his divinity, which is its source.

A further point in this passage centers around the plans for lodging. Jesus' instructions imply that the seventy were to rely on the hospitality of others. In fact, this may be aimed at the community Luke is writing for, a community that recognized that hospitality is to be provided to itinerant preachers in return for their service. This is a strong message to both ancient and modern readers. Discipleship requires hospitality to visitors because they may be God's messengers.

■ **What are some demons in your life? How can you invite Christ to give you authority over them?**

■ **Has Christ commissioned you? If so, how? How can you open yourself up to hear the call to go gather the harvest?**

PRACTICE OF FAITH

BE GLAD FOR THE CITY. In the late 1800s, people all over the world began migrating from rural communities to cities, creating huge metropolitan areas. Beginning in the 1950s, people (at least in the United States and Canada) began leaving the cities for the suburbs. Often, cities are left with great needs but shrinking abilities to provide them. Yet cities are living treasuries of our history. The Bible begins in a garden—Eden—but ends in a city—the New Jerusalem. Get to know your city, and look within it for signs of the City of God. This week, take a field trip. Visit your cathedral. Go downtown. Stop in any churches that you pass by.

PRACTICE OF HOPE

MARKS OF JESUS. We often wear the cross. I'm not talking about jewelry (although many witness this way), but about the sign of the cross that we trace on ourselves in prayer. It is so familiar that I think we sometimes take it for granted. That's what makes the Rite of Acceptance so powerful in the RCIA. The cross is an integral symbol in this rite, which moves inquirers into the catechumenate. They are asked to accept the cross with all the hope and responsibility it represents. Then they receive the sign of the cross on their forehead, eyes, ears, mouth, shoulders, hands and feet. It is a moving experience for candidates, catechumens, sponsors and the assembly. It reminds us all that we belong to Christ.

PRACTICE OF CHARITY

KATERI TEKAWITHA. In the Roman Catholic church, this Saturday is the memorial of Kateri Tekawitha, a seventeenth-century Native American of the Mohawk nation. Her beatification in 1980 was another celebration of the great diversity of the people of God.

Her people, however, have suffered greatly at the hands of Christians. The brutal forced resettlement of many eastern tribes and the nineteenth-century "Indian Wars" against many western tribes can hardly be called anything but genocide. Great numbers of Native Americans continue to live in poverty today, their cultures practically destroyed by white "civilization." Their condition today cries out for justice and action by Christian people. Join the Native American Rights Fund, an organization that defends the legal rights of Native American tribes: 1506 Broadway, Boulder CO 80302; 1-303-447-8760; www.narf.org.

WEEKDAY READINGS (Mo) Genesis 28:10–22; (Tu) 32:23–33; (We) 41:55–57; 42:5–7, 17–24; (Th) 44:18–21, 23–29; 45:1–5; (Fr) 46:1–7, 28–30; (Sa) 49:29–32; 50:15–26

READING I *Deuteronomy 30:9–14*

The LORD your God will make you abundantly prosperous in all your undertakings, in the fruit of your body, in the fruit of your livestock, and in the fruit of your soil. For the LORD will again take delight in prospering you, delighting in you as in your ancestors, when you obey the LORD your God by observing the commandments and decrees of the LORD that are written in this book of the law, because you turn to the LORD your God with all your heart and with all your soul.

Surely, this commandment that I am commanding you today is not too hard for you, nor is it too far away. It is not in heaven, that you should say, "Who will go up to heaven for us, and get it for us so that we may hear it and observe it?" Neither is it beyond the sea, that you should say, "Who will cross to the other side of the sea for us, and get it for us so that we may hear it and observe it?" No, the word is very near to you; it is in your mouth and in your heart for you to observe.

[Roman Catholic: Deuteronomy 30:10–14]

READING II *Colossians 1:15–20*

Christ is the image of the invisible God, the firstborn of all creation; for in Christ all things in heaven and on earth were created, things visible and invisible, whether thrones or dominions or rulers or powers— all things have been created through him and for him. Christ himself is before all things, and in him all things hold together. Christ is the head of the body, the church; Christ is the beginning, the first-born from the dead, so that he might come to have first place in everything. For in Christ all the fullness of God was pleased to dwell, and through Christ God was pleased to reconcile to himself all things, whether on earth or in heaven, by making peace through the blood of his cross.

[Revised Common Lectionary: Colossians 1:1–14]

GOSPEL *Luke 10:25–37*

Just then a lawyer stood up to test Jesus. "Teacher," he said, "what must I do to inherit eternal life?" Jesus said to him, "What is written in the law? What do you read there?" He answered, "You shall love the Lord your God with all your heart, and with all your soul, and with all your strength, and with all your mind; and your neighbor as yourself." And Jesus said to him, "You have given the right answer; do this, and you will live."

But wanting to justify himself, the lawyer asked Jesus, "And who is my neighbor?" Jesus replied, "A man was going down from Jerusalem to Jericho, and fell into the hands of robbers, who stripped him, beat him, and went away, leaving him half dead. Now by chance a priest was going down that road; and when he saw him, he passed by on the other side. So likewise a Levite, when he came to the place and saw him, passed by on the other side. But a Samaritan while traveling came near him; and when the Samaritan saw him, he was moved with pity. He went to him and bandaged his wounds, having poured oil and wine on them. Then he put him on his own animal, brought him to an inn, and took care of him. The next day the Samaritan took out two denarii, gave them to the innkeeper, and said, 'Take care of him; and when I come back, I will repay you whatever more you spend.'

"Which of these three, do you think, was a neighbor to the man who fell into the hands of the robbers?" The lawyer said, "The one who showed him mercy." Jesus said to him, "Go and do likewise."

REFLECTION

In first-century Palestinian Judaism, a "neighbor" was defined as a fellow Israelite. Leviticus 19:18 defines "neighbor" as "any of your people." By making a Samaritan the example of a good neighbor, Jesus explodes the boundaries of who is one's neighbor.

The roots of the animosity between the Israelites and the Samaritans go back to a time some 700 years before Jesus' day, when Assyria defeated the northern kingdom of Israel (Samaria). The Israelite elite were deported and other people were settled on their land. The Israelites who remained eventually intermarried with the foreigners and thus became "unclean," as were their descendants. When the people of Judah returned to their land after the Babylonian exile, they refused to reunite with the Samaritans. The Samaritans had offered to work with the returning Judeans to rebuild the Temple, but the offer was rejected. As a result, the Samaritans established their own temple on Mount Gerizim. By the time of Jesus, the Romans had exacerbated the conflict by building a temple to Caesar Augustus in Samaria, thus showing favor to Samaria over Judea.

With this history, it would have been a tremendous shock for Jesus' listeners to hear that there could be a "good Samaritan." Jesus' use of the Samaritan may have been even more shocking to his listeners than we know; there is evidence of a similar rabbinic parable in which the good neighbor is an Israelite layperson rather than a Samaritan. If the lawyer knew the parable, he probably would have expected the good neighbor to be a fellow Israelite. Instead, Jesus inserts an Israelite enemy into an otherwise ordinary parable.

This story's challenge is not directed at Israelite listeners alone, but to their Samaritan enemies as well—or any enemies for that matter. Most people in Luke's audience—regardless of their backgound—would have known of the animosity between the Samaritans and the Judeans. Thus, the message would almost certainly be seen to apply to other conflicts between members of different races, nations or religious groups.

■ **Who do you consider a "Samaritan" ? How can you reconcile yourself to that person or group of people?**

■ **In what ways do you identify with the characters in the story? At what times have you been the lawyer, the priest, the Levite, the Samaritan, or the innkeeper?**

PRACTICE OF FAITH

BARTOLOME. On Tuesday, the Lutheran calendar commemorates a Roman Catholic priest, Bartolomé de Las Casas. Bartolomé was born in Seville in 1474. He came to the West Indies in 1502 to manage the family estates. But when he saw how the native peoples were oppressed, he joined the Dominicans and was the first priest ordained in the Americas. Many at that time believed that Native Americans and Africans were "savages": The only way to "save" them was to discipline them with hard work and European culture. Bartolomé argued that the native peoples were human beings deserving respect. At the age of 70 he became bishop of Chiapas, Mexico.

PRACTICE OF HOPE

MOVED WITH PITY. We pass by people in need every day. In doorways, on subway platforms, on street corners, even on farms, they offer us opportunities to help. I confess that I don't always know what to do. The need seems too great for one person to make any difference at all. But Sal Dimiceli proves that it can be done. He established "The Time is Now," an organization that donates to dozens of charities. Thanks to him, people have mattresses and pillows, coats and shoes, food and safe housing. Now Dimiceli is working to rally the Christian community to the cause. "God would not turn a deaf ear to them and neither should we," he said.

PRACTICE OF CHARITY

ONE WHO SHOWED MERCY. Jesus constantly criticized religion without action, ritual without justice. Today's story is a challenge to think about the root of charity: compassion. Charity is only Christian when it is rooted in the recognition that we are united with those in need; our well-being, our very salvation, is at stake in their particular condition. Christian charity recognizes that in Christ, God has become one with humankind. It is impossible to look at human beings the same way again. Love of God and love of neighbor are forever tied together. As a result, acts of charity, or better, of justice, are an intrinsic, indispensable part of being a follower of Jesus.

WEEKDAY READINGS (Mo) Exodus 1:8–14, 22; (Tu) 2:1–15; (We) 3:1–6, 9–12; (Th) 3:13–20; (Fr) 11:10—12:14; (Sa) 12:37–42

READING I *Genesis 18:1–10*

The LORD appeared to Abraham by the oaks of Mamre, as he sat at the entrance of his tent in the heat of the day. Abraham looked up and saw three men standing near him. When he saw them, he ran from the tent entrance to meet them, and bowed down to the ground. He said, "My lord, if I find favor with you, do not pass by your servant. Let a little water be brought, and wash your feet, and rest yourselves under the tree. Let me bring a little bread, that you may refresh yourselves, and after that you may pass on—since you have come to your servant." So they said, "Do as you have said." And Abraham hastened into the tent to Sarah, and said, "Make ready quickly three measures of choice flour, knead it, and make cakes." Abraham ran to the herd, and took a calf, tender and good, and gave it to the servant, who hastened to prepare it. Then he took curds and milk and the calf that he had prepared, and set it before them; and he stood by them under the tree while they ate.

They said to him, "Where is your wife Sarah?" And he said, "There, in the tent." Then one said, "I will surely return to you in due season, and your wife Sarah shall have a son."

READING II *Colossians 1:24–28*

I am now rejoicing in my sufferings for your sake, and in my flesh I am completing what is lacking in Christ's afflictions for the sake of his body, that is, the church. I became its servant according to God's commission that was given to me for you, to make the word of God fully known, the mystery that has been hidden throughout the ages and generations but has now been revealed to the saints. To them God chose to make known how great among the Gentiles are the riches of the glory of this mystery, which is Christ in you, the hope of glory. It is Christ whom we proclaim, warning everyone and teaching everyone in all wisdom, so that we may present everyone mature in Christ.

[Revised Common Lectionary: Colossians 1:15–28]

GOSPEL *Luke 10:38–42*

Now as Jesus and his disciples went on their way, he entered a certain village, where a woman named Martha welcomed him into her home. She had a sister named Mary, who sat at the Lord's feet and listened to what he was saying. But Martha was distracted by her many tasks; so she came to Jesus and asked, "Lord, do you not care that my sister has left me to do all the work by myself? Tell her then to help me." But the Lord answered her, "Martha, Martha, you are worried and distracted by many things; there is need of only one thing. Mary has chosen the better part, which will not be taken away from her."

REFLECTION

Hospitality in the ancient world, especially hospitality to strangers, was a religious act. Exhortations to hospitality are prominent in the Hebrew scriptures. This is rooted in Israel's nomadic past and experience of exile; the Israelites often had to rely on the hospitality of others to survive. One role of women in the ancient world was to offer hospitality through domestic service. This hospitality symbolized a sacred pledge of security and care.

The gospel reading approaches hospitality from two different angles. Martha's hospitality and her concern for her sister's lack of contribution to it reflect what she believes to be the teaching of her faith tradition. Her sister Mary sits at the feet of Jesus in the position of a student, something women typically did not do, thus violating the cultural norms that impel Martha to domestic service. By responding as he does, Jesus affirms Mary's behavior. Jesus' response would have come as a shock because of Mary's violation of her cultural role.

At first glance this story could appear to be a simple argument between two sisters, but it is a witness to diversity in ministry. The story highlights both active ministry—serving at table, seeing to the needs of others—and contemplative ministry—simply being attentively present to the Lord. Both ministries are authentic responses to Jesus. In this instance, Jesus legitimates a faith response that had not yet been recognized as appropriate for a woman.

■ **Do you identify more with Mary or Martha? Is it easier for you to attentively listen, or do your prefer to be active in your ministry, seeing to the physical needs and comforts of others?**

■ **When have you received hospitality from another? When have you been hospitable to others? How was Christ present in these moments?**

PRACTICE OF FAITH

UNDER THE OAKS. When Abraham and Sarah showed hospitality to three strangers who came out of the desert by the oaks of Mamre, they quickly realized that they were entertaining God! This scene is captured famously by the Russian Orthodox monk Andrei Rublev, who painted an icon (holy picture) of the scene around the year 1411. He named his icon "Trinity," because Christians often see the three visitors as messengers of Father, Son and Holy Spirit. Look in an art book this week for a picture of this famous icon. If you can find a reproduction in an art store, hang it near your door or in your kitchen as a reminder to show hospitality.

PRACTICE OF HOPE

REFRESH YOURSELVES. It is important to remember that even Jesus paused from time to time to relax, talk with his friends and think. *HOPE* magazine offers a way to reflect, lift the spirit and gather information at the same time. The home page for this publication says its primary mission is to help people "become part of the solution." *HOPE's* web site includes editorials, forums, book reviews and an area devoted to socially responsible investing. The "marketplace" offers information on organizations that promote peace and justice. *HOPE* is published quarterly. Look for *HOPE* online at www.hopemag.com or call 207-359-4651.

PRACTICE OF CHARITY

MARTHA, MARTHA. A friend of mine once told me that every time she hears today's gospel passage, she gets mad at Jesus. "Martha was only trying to make sure everyone was comfortable, and Jesus goes and hurts her feelings." But when this story is read in conjunction with today's first reading, and Martha is placed alongside Abraham, she serves as a model of hospitality for us.

In this day and age, it is difficult to open one's home to strangers. Yet there are many opportunities to offer hospitality to those in need. One terrific opportunity is the Ronald McDonald House, which provides housing and hospitality to the families of sick children. Volunteer at your local Ronald McDonald House (write to One Kroc Drive, Oak Brook IL 60523; www.rmhc.com), or participate in a similar ministry at a hospital in your area. May we all one day be gently chided by the Lord for being too hospitable!

WEEKDAY READINGS (Mo) Exodus 14:5–18; (Tu) 14:21—15:1; (We) 2 Corinthians 4:7–15; (Th) Exodus 19:1–2, 9–11, 16–20; (Fr) 20:1–17; (Sa) 24:3–8

READING I *Genesis 18:20–32*

The LORD said, "How great is the outcry against Sodom and Gomorrah and how very grave their sin! I must go down and see whether they have done altogether according to the outcry that has come to me; and if not, I will know."

So the men turned from there, and went toward Sodom, while Abraham remained standing before the LORD. Then Abraham came near and said, "Will you indeed sweep away the righteous with the wicked? Suppose there are fifty righteous within the city; will you then sweep away the place and not forgive it for the fifty righteous who are in it? Far be it from you to do such a thing, to slay the righteous with the wicked, so that the righteous fare as the wicked! Far be that from you! Shall not the Judge of all the earth do what is just?" And the LORD said, "If I find at Sodom fifty righteous in the city, I will forgive the whole place for their sake." Abraham answered, "Let me take it upon myself to speak to the LORD, I who am but dust and ashes. Suppose five of the fifty righteous are lacking? Will you destroy the whole city for lack of five?" And the LORD said, "I will not destroy it if I find forty-five there." Again he spoke to the LORD, "Suppose forty are found there." The LORD answered, "For the sake of forty I will not do it." Then Abraham said, "Oh, do not let the LORD be angry if I speak. Suppose thirty are found there." The LORD answered, "I will not do it, if I find thirty there." He said, "Let me take it upon myself to speak to the LORD. Suppose twenty are found there." The LORD answered, "For the sake of twenty I will not destroy it." Then Abraham said, "Oh, do not let the LORD be angry if I speak just once more. Suppose ten are found there."

The LORD answered, "For the sake of ten I will not destroy it."

READING II *Colossians 2:12–14*

When you were buried with Christ in baptism, you were also raised with him through faith in the power of God, who raised him from the dead. And when you were dead in trespasses and the uncircumcision of your flesh, God made you alive together with Christ, having forgiven us all our trespasses, erasing the record that stood against us with its legal demands. God set this aside, nailing it to the cross.
[Revised Common Lectionary: Colossians 2:6–15 (16–19)]

GOSPEL *Luke 11:1–13*

Jesus was praying in a certain place, and after he had finished, one of his disciples said to him, "Lord, teach us to pray, as John taught his disciples." Jesus said to them, "When you pray, say:

Father, hallowed be your name.
Let your dominion come.
Give us each day our daily bread.
And forgive us our sins,
for we ourselves forgive
everyone indebted to us.
And do not bring us to the time of trial."

And Jesus said to them, "Suppose one of you has a friend, and you go to that friend at midnight and say, 'Friend, lend me three loaves of bread; for a friend of mine has arrived, and I have nothing to set out.' And the friend answers from within, 'Do not bother me; the door has already been locked, and my children are with me in bed; I cannot get up and give you anything.' I tell you, even though the friend will not get up and provide anything because of the friendship, at least because of the neighbor's persistence the friend will get up and provide whatever is needed.

"So I say to you, Ask, and it will be given you; search, and you will find; knock, and the door will be opened for you. For everyone who asks receives, and everyone who searches finds, and for everyone who knocks, the door will be opened. Is there anyone among you who, if your child asks for a fish, will give a snake instead of a fish? Or if the child asks for an egg, will give a scorpion? If you then, who are evil, know how to give good gifts to your children, how much more will the heavenly Father give the Holy Spirit to those who ask!"

REFLECTION

The gospel reading echoes the Genesis reading's emphasis on persistent and bold prayer. The Lord's Prayer has become a sign of Christian unity. It is the hallmark of the kind of prayer Christians are called to. The Lukan account of this prayer is a shorter version of what most Christians know as the Lord's Prayer, which combines words from Matthew's account and Luke's.

The most striking aspect of the prayer for the first-century listener would have been the bold naming of the all-powerful Lord of life as "father," or in Aramaic, *abba*. Although this word is typically understood as "daddy," its use carries a deeper meaning. The word implies utmost respect and reverence for the one addressed as *abba*. It is an address used for one with authority, the head of a household, for example.

In ancient Near Eastern society, the father of the household was a very significant figure. The Hebrew people of this period did not believe in an afterlife. One "lived" after death through one's children, and children owed a debt of gratitude and respect to their fathers. The term *abba* reflects the ancient religion's duties of children to parent.

The Hebrew scriptures make clear that the honor a child is to give a parent is a matter of law (see Exodus 20:12; Leviticus 19:3). One addressed as *abba,* then, truly deserves respect in the Jewish tradition. This is not to say that *abba* does not also convey an intimate, familiar and loving "daddy" image. Indeed, the word combines both respect and familiarity.

Jesus' use of the image of father for relationship with God expresses both aspects conveyed by the term *abba:* deep respect and gratitude, as well as intimacy, familiarity and trust. It is from this basic relationship of child to parent that the petitions of the Lord's Prayer flow.

■ **How can you best pray the Lord's Prayer? What images besides fatherhood can you bring to your understanding of God as you read the scriptures?**

■ **How is your prayer these days? How might you pray better or more intentionally? What forms of prayer have you tried? What other forms would you like to experience? How can you learn more about the prayer life of the church?**

PRACTICE OF FAITH

ASK. Asking is perhaps the form of prayer that we are most familiar with: "Dear God, please help/give . . ." This is called prayer of *petition.* Asking for what we need in prayer is basic: Give us this day our daily bread. But as baptized people, we do not only ask for ourselves. We always pray too for others, especially those who do not pray, do not know how to pray, or for whatever reason cannot or will not pray. When we pray on behalf of others, it is called prayer of *intercession,* a petition that has a wide reach. At evening or at bedtime, when you ask for what you need, remember others who are in need as well. Include them too in your prayer.

PRACTICE OF HOPE

LOAVES OF BREAD. There are few things more comforting than the smell of fresh bread. It seems to put right whatever is wrong. It makes a house a home. At St. Pius X Parish in Omaha, bread helps to make the church a spiritual home for newcomers. One of the parish's many outreaches, the bread and baked goods ministry welcomes new members face to face. The bread, a simple symbol of life and hospitality, literally opens the door to parish life and new friendships. This sense of community is essential to a true eucharistic celebration, in which bread draws us even closer together as the Body of Christ.

It can be daunting to move to a new city or a new neighborhood, but parishioners at St. Pius X are doing what they can to make the transition a little easier.

PRACTICE OF CHARITY

THE POWER OF PRAYER. Many of the problems of the world seem out of our control: What can we do about AIDS and war in Africa? How can we feed the starving people of North Korea? How can a just God permit so much human suffering? How can human beings permit so much human suffering?

In light of these seemingly solution-less problems, prayer is perhaps the only consistent act of charity we can manage. Jesus himself promises that the voices of God's people united in prayer will bring a divine response. Perhaps praying makes us more mindful of the ways we can contribute to the world's redemption; perhaps it reminds us how dependent we are on God. Whatever its effect, it is our duty as baptized children of God to pray always for the sake of the world.

WEEKDAY READINGS (Mo) Exodus 32:15–24, 30–34; (Tu) 33:7–11;34:5–9, 28; (We) 34:29–35; (Th) 40:16–21, 34–38; (Fr) Leviticus 23:1, 4–11, 15–16, 27, 34–37; (Sa) 25:1, 8–17

READING I *Ecclesiastes 1:2, 12–14; 2:18–23*

Vanity of vanities, says the Teacher,
vanity of vanities! All is vanity.

I, the Teacher, when king over Israel in Jerusalem, applied my mind to seek and to search out by wisdom all that is done under heaven; it is an unhappy business that God has given to human beings to be busy with. I saw all the deeds that are done under the sun; and see, all is vanity and a chasing after wind.

I hated all my toil in which I had toiled under the sun, seeing that I must leave it to those who come after me—and who knows whether they will be wise or foolish? Yet they will be master of all for which I toiled and used my wisdom under the sun. This also is vanity. So I turned and gave my heart up to despair concerning all the toil of my labors under the sun, because sometimes one who has toiled with wisdom and knowledge and skill must leave all to be enjoyed by another who did not toil for it. This also is vanity and a great evil. What do mortals get from all the toil and strain with which they toil under the sun? For all their days are full of pain, and their work is a vexation; even at night their minds do not rest. This also is vanity.

[Roman Catholic: Ecclesiastes 1:2; 2:21–23]

READING II *Colossians 3:1–11*

So if you have been raised with Christ, seek the things that are above, where Christ is, seated at the right hand of God. Set your minds on things that are above, not on things that are on earth, for you have died, and your life is hidden with Christ in God. When Christ who is your life is revealed, then you also will be revealed with him in glory.

Put to death, therefore, whatever in you is earthly: fornication, impurity, passion, evil desire, and greed (which is idolatry). On account of these the wrath of God is coming on those who are disobedient. These are the ways you also once followed, when you were living that life. But now you must get rid of all such things—anger, wrath, malice, slander, and abusive language from your mouth.

Do not lie to one another, seeing that you have stripped off the old self with its practices and have clothed yourselves with the new self, which is being renewed in knowledge according to the image of its creator. In that renewal there is no longer Greek and Jew, circumcised and uncircumcised, barbarian, Scythian, slave and free; but Christ is all and in all!

[Roman Catholic: Colossians 3:1–5, 9–11]

GOSPEL *Luke 12:13–21*

Someone in the crowd said to Jesus, "Teacher, tell my brother to divide the family inheritance with me." But Jesus replied, "Friend, who set me to be a judge or arbitrator over you?" And Jesus said to them, "Take care! Be on your guard against all kinds of greed; for one's life does not consist in the abundance of possessions." Then he told them a parable: "The land of a rich man produced abundantly. And he thought to himself, 'What should I do, for I have no place to store my crops?' Then he said, 'I will do this: I will pull down my barns and build larger ones, and there I will store all my grain and my goods. And I will say to my soul, 'Soul, you have ample goods laid up for many years; relax, eat, drink, be merry.' But God said to him, 'You fool! This very night your life is being demanded of you. And the things you have prepared, whose will they be?' So it is with those who store up treasures for themselves but are not rich toward God."

Monday, August 6, 2001

TRANSFIGURATION OF THE LORD

Daniel 7:9–10, 13–14 *I saw the Man of Heaven on the clouds.*

2 Peter 1:16–19 *We are eyewitnesses to God's glory.*

Luke 9:28–36 *Who do the crowds say that I am?*

At the peak of the glory of summer, the Lord shines on the holy mountain. With the law and the prophets, we gaze on God face to face. Yet which mountain is it— Calvary or Tabor? Perhaps they are one and the same.

R E F L E C T I O N

The book of Ecclesiastes is sometimes called the "dark side of the good news." Most people are unfamiliar with this book whose message is so harsh. When the Teacher—identified by name elsewhere as Quoheleth—says that everything is vanity, he is saying that everything—human labor, human wisdom, earthly possessions—really amounts to nothing. The Hebrew word translated as "vanity" here conveys an image of vapor, such as an exhaled breath in frigid air or smoke billowing from a fire. These things are visible for a moment but lack substance; there is really nothing to grab on to. The author reinforces this image by saying that all human deeds are like "chasing after wind."

The rest of the book (today's passage is from the first two chapters) goes on to point out all the terrible things about life. It seems that the book describes life without belief in God. Human life is just vapor or wind if it is lived outside of a relationship with God.

The rich man believed that he was responsible for his own existence, for which he alone could take credit. When he heard God demanding his life, however, he learned that his life was nothing without God. God gave the rich man life and thus can claim it back again.

Jesus reminds us that we are nothing without God. So much of our stress, anxiety, depression and workaholism comes from the belief that we have to rely on ourselves alone. Instead, Jesus calls us to a new set of priorities where we recognize our dependence on God and seek to build up that relationship by sharing with those in need.

■ **When are the times when you feel that all is vanity? What aspects of your life are vanity? How can you change these areas of your life to have substance, meaning?**

■ **Pray with today's gospel parable; insert yourself into the role of the rich man and reflect on your feelings and attitudes as the events unfold. How would this parable be lived out in our modern world? How would you feel about the rich man if you were a peasant listening to this story as told by Jesus? What does this parable demand of you today?**

PRACTICE OF FAITH

TRANSFIGURATION. Tomorrow, many churches keep the feast of the Transfiguration of the Lord. It is ironic that as we remember Jesus, clothed in light brighter than the sun, we also mark the anniversary of the first use of nuclear weapons against human beings. The United States bombed Hiroshima, Japan, on August 6, 1945.

Today, there is less likelihood of a nuclear war. But writer Jonathan Schell interprets this to mean that we have a chance now to dismantle these weapons of mass, indiscriminate destruction. Read his classic *The Fate of the Earth* this week. Then write to your elected representatives.

PRACTICE OF HOPE

JOY AND GLADNESS. I don't know about you, but I enjoy reading vanity license plates. The other day I saw a license plate that was perfectly clear, but thought-provoking all the same. It said: BE GLAD. A few days later, the license plate in front of me advised: BE KIND. It made me wonder about the people driving these vehicles and what prompted them to put such words of wisdom out for all to see. There is no doubt that this rolling encouragement is needed—especially in traffic! We know that our daily diet of stress is bad for us. Studies show that expecting the best is good not only for our mental health, but for our physical health as well. Worry may be part of life, but that doesn't mean we can't BE HAPPY more often.

PRACTICE OF CHARITY

VANITY OF VANITIES. Despite the end of the Cold War, nuclear weapons still threaten the world's security. Many nations seem intent on the vanity of having weapons of mass destruction. The United States has led the way in this, with more stockpiled weapons of mass destruction than any other nation.

The Catholic church's teaching on this matter is clear: "Any act of war aimed indiscriminately at the destruction of entire cities or extensive areas along with their population is a crime against God and [humanity] itself. It merits unequivocal condemnation" (Vatican II, *Gaudium et spes,* 80). Read the U.S. bishops' pastoral *The Challenge of Peace: God's Promise and Our Response,* available from the U.S. Catholic Conference, 3211 4th St. NE, Washington DC 20017-1194; 1-800-235-8722; www.nccbuscc.org. May its challenge enter our hearts and our nation's government.

WEEKDAY READINGS (Mo) Transfiguration, see box (Tu) Numbers 12:1–13; (We) 13:1–2, 25—14:1, 26–29, 34–35; (Th) 20:1–13; (Fr) 2 Corinthians 9:6–10; (Sa) Deuteronomy 6:4–13

READING I *Wisdom 18:6–9*

The night of the deliverance from Egypt was made known beforehand to our ancestors, so that they might rejoice in sure knowledge of the oaths in which they trusted. The deliverance of the righteous and the destruction of their enemies were expected by your people. For by the same means by which you punished our enemies you called us to yourself and glorified us.

For in secret the holy children of good people offered sacrifices, and with one accord agreed to the divine law, so that the saints would share alike the same things, both blessings and dangers; and already they were singing the praises of the ancestors.
[Revised Common Lectionary: Genesis 15:1–6]

READING II *Hebrews 11:1–2, 8–12*

Now faith is the assurance of things hoped for, the conviction of things not seen. Indeed, by faith our ancestors received approval.

By faith Abraham obeyed when he was called to set out for a place that he was to receive as an inheritance; and he set out, not knowing where he was going. By faith he stayed for a time in the land he had been promised, as in a foreign land, living in tents, as did Isaac and Jacob, who were heirs with him of the same promise. For Abraham looked forward to the city that has foundations, whose architect and builder is God. By faith he received power of procreation, even though he was too old—and Sarah herself was barren—because he considered faithful the one who had promised. Therefore from one person, and this one as good as dead, descendants were born, "as many as the stars of heaven and as the innumerable grains of sand by the seashore."
[Complete reading: Hebrews 11:1–2, 8–19]

GOSPEL *Luke 12:32–40*

Jesus said:

"Do not be afraid, little flock, for it is your Father's good pleasure to give the dominion to you. Sell your possessions, and give alms. Make purses for yourselves that do not wear out, an unfailing treasure in heaven, where no thief comes near and no moth destroys. For where your treasure is, there your heart will be also.

"Be dressed for action and have your lamps lit; be like those who are waiting for their master to return from the wedding banquet, so that they may open the door for him as soon as he comes and knocks. Blessed are those slaves whom the master finds alert when he comes; truly I tell you, he will fasten his belt and have them sit down to eat, and he will come and serve them. If the master comes during the middle of the night, or near dawn, and finds them so, blessed are those slaves.

"But know this: if the owner of the house had known at what hour the thief was coming, the owner would not have let the house be broken into. You also must be ready, for the Son-of-Man is coming at an unexpected hour."
[Complete reading: Luke 12:34–48]

Wednesday, August 15, 2001

ASSUMPTION OF THE VIRGIN MARY INTO HEAVEN

VIGIL

1 Chronicles 15:3–4, 15–16; 16:1–2 *David before the ark.*

1 Corinthians 15:54–57 *God gave us victory over death.*

Luke 11:27–28 *Blessed is the womb that bore you!*

DAY

Revelation 11:19; 12:1–6, 10 *A woman clothed in the sun.*

1 Corinthians 15:20–27 *Christ is the first fruits of the dead.*

Luke 1:39–56 *He has raised the lowly to the heights.*

Now we keep the festival of Mary's passover. In time, each one of us will be gathered into the reign of God, shining like the sun, with the moon at our feet.

REFLECTION

Today's first reading is from the book of Wisdom and is part of a larger corpus known commonly as "wisdom literature." In this tradition, wisdom is basically practical instruction about how to live a life that is full and successful. The teachings of the wisdom tradition are often expressed in short proverbs or sayings, many of which are deceptively simple. These teachings are most concerned with justice, right relationships, diligence and self-control. Wisdom literature is unique within the Old Testament because it locates dignity and divine blessing in everyday life rather than solely in the history of the Jewish people and covenent.

Today's gospel reading portrays Jesus as a wisdom teacher in the tradition of the Jewish sages. In fact, Jesus is presented by Luke as wisdom incarnate, reflecting the Hebrew scriptures' personification of a human being when preaching to God's people. Indeed, wisdom is often presented in the Hebrew scriptures as a feminine consort of the God of Israel, and is often equated with the Torah itself. For Luke, these traditions come together in Jesus.

In today's passage, then, Jesus' teaching is full of wise sayings and expressions that fit the everyday life of a Palestinian peasant of this time. Jesus speaks to his audience about such things as giving alms and being dressed and ready for action at all times. He uses such familiar cultural images as wedding banquets, managerial relations and slavery to get his point across.

Even at the time of Jesus, the Jewish tradition had only limited notions of an afterlife or of reward and punishment after death. The faithful Israelite found God in earthly existence. Thus, the wisdom tradition helped people enhance their experience of this life.

■ **What are the sources of wisdom in your life? How can you share your own wisdom with others?**

■ **Do you focus on this life or the next? How can you balance this focus? How can you prepare yourself for being ready and awake in this life for the next?**

PRACTICE OF FAITH

SELL YOUR POSSESSIONS. What an idealist Jesus is! What? Sell my SUV, my DVD and all my CDs? And then what? Give alms. I don't know if I can . . . But wait. Radical discipleship starts with small, simple steps. Try this. Organize a yard or garage sale this week. Begin by putting up for sale all the things you really don't use. Donate the proceeds to a charity that benefits people who are truly down and out. If you don't have enough stuff to sell on your own, team up with neighbors or friends—maybe the whole parish. The important thing is that the money go to the neediest among us. You never know where this may lead.

PRACTICE OF HOPE

MUCH WILL BE REQUIRED. Archbishop Oscar Romero of San Salvador didn't set out to be a martyr. Slowly but surely, he grew into his role as an outspoken opponent of a military that murdered and oppressed the poor people of El Salvador, and a government that showed little interest in the truth. In the end, he paid with his life. Shot to death while celebrating Mass on March 24, 1980, Romero still inspires people in his country and around the world. They continue to hope, because he did: "To believe, to hope: This is the Christian's grace in our time. When many give up hope, when it seems to them the nation has nowhere to go, as though it were all over, the Christian says, 'No, we have not yet begun.'" Romero's birthday is August 15.

PRACTICE OF CHARITY

INVISIBLE PEOPLE. While visiting a friend in a hospital in Knoxville, Tennessee, my father was shocked by the number of people he never saw in his day-to-day life: the poor people of Appalachia, the chronically ill, people of color. For him, it was a revelation. His professional career and suburban home blocked our family's awareness of many people, people whose suffering might challenge our middle-class comfort.

"Sell your possessions and give alms." Jesus' words apply as much to our time as they did to his own. Yet our time has its particular problems: The poor live out of the sight of the wealthy. How does your job, your salary, or where you live keep you from seeing the invisible people around you? Is your heart where Jesus would have it be?

WEEKDAY READINGS (Mo) Deuteronomy 10:12–22; (Tu) 31:1–8; (We) Assumption, see box; (Th) Joshua 3:7–10, 11, 13–17; (Fr) 24:1–13; (Sa) 24:14–29

READING I *Jeremiah 38:4–6, 8–10*

Then the officials said to the king, "This man ought to be put to death, because he is discouraging the soldiers who are left in this city, and all the people, by speaking such words to them. For this man is not seeking the welfare of this people, but their harm." King Zedekiah said, "Here he is; he is in your hands; for the king is powerless against you." So they took Jeremiah and threw him into the cistern of Malchiah, the king's son, which was in the court of the guard, letting Jeremiah down by ropes. Now there was no water in the cistern, but only mud, and Jeremiah sank in the mud.

So Ebed-melech the Ethiopian, an officer in the king's house, left the king's house and spoke to the king, "My lord king, these men have acted wickedly in all they did to the prophet Jeremiah by throwing him into the cistern to die there of hunger, for there is no bread left in the city." Then the king commanded Ebed-melech the Ethiopian, "Take three men with you from here, and pull the prophet Jeremiah up from the cistern before he dies."

[Revised Common Lectionary: Jeremiah 23:23–29]

READING II *Hebrews 12:1–4*

Since we are surrounded by so great a cloud of witnesses, let us also lay aside every weight and the sin that clings so closely, and let us run with perseverance the race that is set before us, looking to Jesus the pioneer and perfecter of our faith, who for the sake of the joy that was set before him endured the cross, disregarding its shame, and is seated at the right hand of the throne of God.

Consider Jesus who endured such hostility against himself from sinners, so that you may not grow weary or lose heart.

In your struggle against sin you have not yet resisted to the point of shedding your blood.

[Revised Common Lectionary: Hebrews 11:29—12:2]

GOSPEL *Luke 12:49–56*

Jesus said:

"I came to bring fire to the earth, and how I wish it were already kindled! I have a baptism with which to be baptized, and what stress I am under until it is completed! Do you think that I have come to bring peace to the earth? No, I tell you, but rather division! From now on five in one household will be divided, three against two and two against three; they will be divided: father against son and son against father, mother against daughter and daughter against mother, and in-laws against one another."

Jesus also said to the crowds, "When you see a cloud rising in the west, you immediately say, 'It is going to rain'; and so it happens. And when you see the south wind blowing, you say, 'There will be scorching heat'; and it happens. You hypocrites! You know how to interpret the appearance of earth and sky, but why do you not know how to interpret the present time?"

[Roman Catholic: Luke 12:49–53]

REFLECTION

The first reading describes Jeremiah's struggle to survive in the muddy cistern where the officials had thrown him as punishment for his prophetic preaching. The severe punishment suggests some great crime; in reality the only thing Jeremiah did was preach faithfulness to Israel's covenant with the Lord. The people were wandering from the law, the military leadership was planning alliances with other nations, the king was weak and cowardly, and the kingdom of Judah was about to be defeated by its enemies. In this time of trouble, Jeremiah calls the people back to covenant faithfulness and fidelity. But speaking the truth leads him into trouble. Jeremiah's suffering foreshadows Jesus' suffering alluded to in today's gospel passage.

The reading from Luke is surprising. Jesus' harsh message that he has come to bring division challenges our notion of him as the prince of peace. In a world where we yearn desperately for families to unite, this is a jolting message indeed.

The passage must be read with sensitivity to the situation in which it was written. Luke is writing to a particular group of Christians who were struggling to follow the way of Christ in the face of much adversity. Becoming Christian meant turning one's back either on one's Jewish heritage or on the pagan society of the Roman empire. So radical was the break that Christians were accused of atheism by their ancient detractors because they refused to support the civil cult. Conversion to Christianity certainly would have brought division and strife to families and communities. The Christians of Luke's community were probably wondering if following Christ was worth so much isolation and suffering. This passage could be a source of comfort and encouragement: Jesus himself expected such division and was himself a victim of it.

■ **What kind of fire if Jesus talking about? How do you experience that fire in your heart? How can you get yourself and others fired up about your faith?**

■ **What have been some experiences of isolation or division you have had because of your faith? How has your faith been affected by these?**

PRACTICE OF FAITH

INTERPRET THE PRESENT. Jesus harshly indicts us: We know lots and lots about all kinds of things, yet when it comes to what we need to know in order to be faithful to our baptism, we fall short. We tend to think of religion as a set of pious exercises (like going to church, reading the scriptures) that have nothing to do with the realities of life: earning and spending money, the work we that we do, our politics. The Second Vatican Council (1962–65) taught that divorcing faith from everyday life is "one of the gravest errors of our time." For help in understanding the signs of the times, subscribe to the magazine *Sojourners*. It offers a good biblical interpretation of current events. Call 1-800-714-7474 or visit www.sojourners.com.

PRACTICE OF HOPE

A NEW SONG. In a perfect world, everyone has value and that value is recognized. The world is not perfect, however, and many people feel invisible. A lesson at Mercy High School in Omaha brought this point home to students. In the morning, each student received a black ribbon or a red ribbon. Those with the black ribbons were "dead" and ignored by the students with the red ribbons. At the end of the day, they shared their experiences.

One "dead" girl said that for the first time she realized what it meant to be overlooked. Fearing that she might have been guilty of that offense, she apologized to the other students. She wasn't the only one singing a new song. The world may not be perfect yet, but with life lessons like those offered at Mercy, there is hope.

PRACTICE OF CHARITY

HOUSEHOLDS DIVIDED. In our age many families are divided not by the gospel but by domestic violence, especially against women and children. The U.S. Justice Department's Violence Against Women Office reports that domestic violence accounts for nearly 18,000 deaths a year in the United States. Estimates of injuries are between four and six million. It is nothing less than an epidemic, one that must be cured in part by an active love that counteracts violence and injury. Support a shelter for abused women and their children in your area. Work to make your home and family a place free of the kind of anger that leads to violence.

WEEKDAY READINGS (Mo) Judges 2:11–19; (Tu) 6:11–24; (We) 9:6–15; (Th) 11:29–39; (Fr) Revelation 21:9–14; (Sa) Ruth 2:1–3, 8–11; 4:13–17

READING I *Isaiah 66:18–21*

I know their works and their thoughts, and I am coming to gather all nations and tongues; and they shall come and shall see my glory, and I will set a sign among them. From them I will send survivors to the nations, to Tarshish, Put, and Lud—which draw the bow—to Tubal and Javan, to the coastlands far away that have not heard of my fame or seen my glory; and they shall declare my glory among the nations. They shall bring all your kindred from all the nations as an offering to the LORD, on horses, and in chariots, and in litters, and on mules, and on dromedaries, to my holy mountain Jerusalem, says the LORD, just as the Israelites bring a grain offering in a clean vessel to the house of the LORD. And I will also take some of them as priests and as Levites, says the LORD.

[Revised Common Lectionary: Isaiah 58:9–14]

READING II *Hebrews 12:5–7, 11–13*

You have forgotten the exhortation that addresses you as children—

"My child, do not regard lightly
the discipline of the Lord,
or lose heart when you are
punished by God;
for the Lord disciplines
those whom the Lord loves,
and God chastises every child
whom God accepts."

Endure trials for the sake of discipline. God is treating you as children; for what child is there whom a parent does not discipline? Now, discipline always seems painful rather than pleasant at the time, but later it yields the peaceful fruit of righteousness to those who have been trained by it. Therefore lift your drooping hands and strengthen your weak knees, and make straight paths for your feet, so that what is lame may not be put out of joint, but rather be healed.

[Revised Common Lectionary: Hebrews 12:18–29]

GOSPEL *Luke 13:22–30*

Jesus went through one town and village after another, teaching as he made his way to Jerusalem. Someone asked him, "Lord, will only a few be saved?" Jesus said to them, "Strive to enter through the narrow door; for many, I tell you, will try to enter and will not be able. When once the owner of the house has got up and shut the door, and you begin to stand outside and to knock at the door, saying, 'Lord, open to us,' then in reply he will say to you, 'I do not know where you come from.' Then you will begin to say, 'We ate and drank with you, and you taught in our streets.' But the Lord will say, 'I do not know where you come from; go away from me, all you evildoers!' There will be weeping and gnashing of teeth when you see Abraham and Isaac and Jacob and all the prophets in the kingdom of God, and you yourselves thrown out. Then people will come from east and west, from north and south, and will eat in the kingdom of God. Indeed, some are last who will be first, and some are first who will be last."

[Revised Common Lectionary: Luke 13:10–17]

REFLECTION

Today's passage from Luke opens with a transitional statement that reminds us that the overall theme of the gospel is Jesus' journey toward Jerusalem. This journey is reminiscent of the Exodus, that long trek of the Israelites to the promised land. Jesus mirrors that sojourn by traveling to the important center of Jerusalem where he will complete his exodus, leaving behind the enslavement of death to enter the promised land of the reign of God.

As the journey unfolds, Luke provides an opportunity for his readers to learn Jesus' teaching on who would be allowed to enter the reign of God. Who will be saved? The question is posed by an anonymous member of the crowd, and Jesus responds with a prophecy.

The question about who will enjoy eternal salvation was apparently common during the first century. There is evidence that other writers of the time tried to deal with it. Jesus' response is that the reign of God is available to all people—people from all four directions—yet they must struggle to enter through "the narrow door." The many must struggle to get through the narrow door, and they must do so quickly. There is a sense of urgency in this teaching: *Now* is the time, and later is too late.

Jesus' parable emphasizes that there is nothing casual about the commitment to make it through the narrow door. Notice that some of those who once ate and drank with the owner of the house now stand outside as strangers knocking on the door. How could it be that those who once shared a table, who once obviously entered, now go unrecognized and barred from entrance? The message may seem harsh: Those who related only superficially with the owner will be turned away. Those who take a casual approach to a relationship with God will not be recognized and will not enter. Salvation demands a commitment beyond convenience or social convention. It demands a decisive, timely decision to pursue a relationship with God before the opportunity passes.

■ **What commitments do you have in your life? Which ones are most fulfilling? Why? What goes into a successful commitment to make it a success?**

■ **What is your "narrow door"? How are you striving to enter through it? How are you successful? In what ways do you need help?**

PRACTICE OF FAITH

DELIGHT IN SUNDAY. The Sabbath—the day of rest—is *Saturday.* The first Christians were Jews, so they kept the Sabbath and they also celebrated the eucharist on Sunday.

Sunday was not at first a day of rest—it was a workday—but it was nonetheless the Lord's day, the day for gathering as church and celebrating eucharist, the day for baptizing and laying on hands. As more people who were not Jews became Christian, Christians stopped keeping Saturday as the Sabbath and transferred many of Saturday's customs to Sunday. Keep Sunday holy as best you can. Make Sunday dinner a special mea. Invite someone to share it with you, even if just once a month.

PRACTICE OF HOPE

OPEN THE DOOR. For members of St. Boniface Parish in Oak Harbor, Ohio, "Open Wide the Doors to Christ" wasn't just another pretty slogan. They took the pope's Jubilee Year 2000 theme seriously by opening the doors to their school in a radical way: They didn't charge tuition for the 2000–01 school year. Parish officials counted on people's goodness to make up for the lost revenue. They also trusted in the Lord. In doing so, they offered a priceless example for the students.

PRACTICE OF CHARITY

ALL YOUR BROTHERS AND SISTERS. Too often people of various languages and races are denied their proper place at the table, even in the United States. Ironically, this nation of immigrants throws up many barriers to those who would like to make a new home and a fresh start here: denial of social services, language barriers, and Byzantine administrative processes that make it difficult for immigrants to achieve legal residency.

Happily, immigrants and refugees have some allies. Diocesan offices of Catholic Charities help settle nearly one quarter of those admitted to the United States each year. These programs rely heavily on community volunteers to help facilitate the immigration process. Contact your local Catholic Charities office to get involved.

WEEKDAY READINGS (Mo) 1 Thessalonians 1:1–5, 8–10; (Tu) 2:1–8; (We) 2:9–13; (Th) 3:7–13; (Fr) 4:1–8; (Sa) 4:9–11

READING I *Sirach 3:17–18, 20, 28–29*

My child, perform your tasks with humility;
> then you will be loved
>> by those whom God accepts.

The greater you are,
>> the more you must humble yourself;
> so you will find favor in the sight of the LORD.

For great is the might of the LORD;
> but by the humble the LORD is glorified.

When calamity befalls the proud,
> there is no healing,
> for an evil plant has taken root in them.

The mind of the intelligent appreciates proverbs,
> and an attentive ear is the desire of the wise.

[Revised Common Lectionary: Proverbs 25:6–7; alternate: Sirach 10:12–18]

READING II *Hebrews 12:18–19, 22–24*

You have not come to something that can be touched, a blazing fire, and darkness, and gloom, and a tempest, and the sound of a trumpet, and a voice whose words made the hearers beg that not another word be spoken to them. But you have come to Mount Zion and to the city of the living God, the heavenly Jerusalem, and to innumerable angels in festal gathering, and to the assembly of the firstborn who are enrolled in heaven, and to God the judge of all, and to the spirits of the righteous made perfect, and to Jesus, the mediator of a new covenant.

[Revised Common Lectionary: Hebrews 13:1–8, 15–16]

GOSPEL *Luke 14:1, 7–14*

On one occasion when Jesus was going to the house of a leader of the Pharisees to eat a meal on the sabbath, they were watching him closely. When he noticed how the guests chose the places of honor, he told them a parable. "When you are invited by someone to a wedding banquet, do not sit down at the place of honor, in case someone more distinguished than you has been invited by your host; and the host who invited both of you may come and say to you, 'Give this person your place,' and then in disgrace you would start to take the lowest place. But when you are invited, go and sit down at the lowest place, so that when your host comes, your host may say to you, 'Friend, move up higher'; then you will be honored in the presence of all who sit at the table with you. For all who exalt themselves will be humbled, and those who humble themselves will be exalted."

Jesus said also to the one who had invited him, "When you give a luncheon or a dinner, do not invite your friends or your brothers or your relatives or rich neighbors, in case they may invite you in return, and you would be repaid. But when you give a banquet, invite those who are poor, crippled, lame, and blind. And you will be blessed, because they cannot repay you, for you will be repaid at the resurrection of the righteous."

Saturday, September 8, 2001

BIRTH OF THE VIRGIN MARY

Micah 5:1–4 *She who is to give birth is born!*

Romans 8:28–30 *We share the image of Christ.*

Matthew 1:1–16, 18–23 *Of her, Jesus was born.*

The words mother—*mater*—and material things—*matter*—are one and the same. In September, Mother Earth gives forth in fruitful abundance our material sustenance. And Mother Mary is born, who in her own fruitful body knit together earth and heaven.

REFLECTION

In the gospel passage for today, Jesus teaches about humility, using two concepts that were taken seriously—honor and shame. To be considered an honorable person was a high compliment. There was a popular notion that there was only so much honor to go around; someone who lost honor was left with a smaller amount and someone else gained what was lost. A loss of honor brought shame. To be considered a shameful person was one of the worst things that could happen.

Jesus uses these two concepts—honor and shame—to teach his listeners about humility. In short, one may gain honor by acting with humility. There is no downside risk to humility; it may bring greater honor but never shame. However, self-exaltation can only bring shame. Claiming the place of honor does nothing to bring honor to a person; in fact it might well bring shame. But humility can never damage honor; it can only increase it.

This message of Jesus' parable would have been difficult one for his audience to accept. Even though they thought honor a great reward and shame something to be avoided, they saw no value to humility. They had no respect for humility; it was a vice and certainly no source of honor. Jesus' teaching was a repudiation of the social hierarchy of his time: Acting humbly is what brings honor, not presuming to exalt oneself.

After the parable on the virtue of humility, Jesus teaches about the virtue of generosity. The custom of the time was for a host to invite guests who could reciprocate in some way. To Jesus' way of thinking, this was not generosity but merely an exchange of wealth for wealth. Jesus exhorts his listeners to invite the poor, crippled, lame and blind—people who not only could not repay their host but whose poverty or disability was considered a punishment by God and therefore shameful. Jesus not only defined true generosity but also dismissed the popular notion that suffering is the result of divine punishment. Jesus challenges his audience to understand that the reign of God is one of inclusion, not exclusion, and that the virtues of humility and generosity are two of the tools that help build God's reign on earth.

■ **In what ways does Jesus' teaching on humility and generosity challenge contemporary social customs?**

■ **What are some ways that you act humbly? generously? How do you integrate those virtues into your life?**

PRACTICE OF FAITH

GIVE A BANQUET. About ten years ago a man in New Jersey decided, a week before the wedding, not to marry. When the woman tried to cancel her reservations for the hall and the caterer, she was told that she would have to pay the full price, whether or not she had the reception. She decided to have the reception, but not with her original guest list. She contacted some social service agencies in New York City, who bused in people from shelters and group homes. This woman penetrated to the heart of Jesus' gospel. You may not be in a position to throw a wedding reception for the poor, but try inviting a single person or widow from the parish for Sunday dinner some week.

PRACTICE OF HOPE

A HOME FOR THE POOR. Who says you can't have a good time while you're helping people? HOPEFEST, a concert to benefit the Chicago Coalition for the Homeless and Willie Dixon's Blues Heaven Foundation, proves that it's possible to do both. Begun in 1990, HOPEFEST has drawn together artists such as Bo Diddley, Chuck Berry and Koko Taylor to raise funds for these worthy causes. It just goes to show you that a little bit of blues can put smiles on a lot of faces.

PRACTICE OF CHARITY

LABOR DAY. Tomorrow the United States observes Labor Day. Some statistics challenge our country to consider the struggle of the "working class."

According to a recent study by the National Priorities Project, 74 percent of new jobs pay less than a living wage. In addition, the most significant factor over the last 20 years in maintaining and increasing family income has been putting two adults into the workforce. On top of this, some 42 million Americans are currently without heath insurance, primarily low-wage workers and their families. Despite the economic boom of the 1990s, many working families are just getting by.

Support initiatives in your area that mandate a living wage, as well as those that mandate health-care benefits for all full-time workers. Write your state and federal representatives and support such legislation, lest the gap between the haves and have-nots in this country continue to grow.

WEEKDAY READINGS (Mo) 1 Thessalonians 4:13–18; (Tu) 5:1–6, 9–11; (We) Colossians 1:1–8; (Th) 1:9–14; (Fr) 1:15–20; (Sa) Birth of the Virgin Mary, see box

READING I   *Wisdom 9:13–18*

For who can learn the counsel of God?
Or who can discern what the Lord wills?
For the reasoning of mortals is worthless,
and our designs are likely to fail;
for a perishable body weighs down the soul,
and this earthy tent burdens the thoughtful mind.
We can hardly guess at what is on earth,
and what is at hand we find with labor;
but who has traced out what is in the heavens?
Who has learned your counsel,
unless you have given wisdom
and sent your holy spirit from on high?
And thus the paths of those on earth were set right,
and people were taught what pleases you,
and were saved by wisdom.

[Revised Common Lectionary: Deuteronomy 30:15–20]

READING II   *Philemon 9–10, 12–17*

I, Paul, do this as an old man, and now also as a prisoner of Christ Jesus. I am appealing to you for my child, Onesimus, whose father I have become during my imprisonment. Formerly he was useless to you, but now he is indeed useful both to you and to me. I am sending him, that is, my own heart, back to you. I wanted to keep him with me, so that he might be of service to me in your place during my imprisonment for the gospel; but I preferred to do nothing without your consent, in order that your good deed might be voluntary and not something forced. Perhaps this is the reason Onesimus was separated from you for a while, so that you might have him back forever, no longer as a slave but more than a slave, a beloved brother—especially to me but how much more to you, both in the flesh and in the Lord.

So if you consider me your partner, welcome Onesimus as you would welcome me.

[Revised Common Lectionary: Philemon 1–21]

GOSPEL   *Luke 14:25–33*

Now large crowds were traveling with Jesus; and he turned and said to them, "Whoever comes to me and does not hate father and mother, spouse and children, brothers and sisters, yes, and even life itself, cannot be my disciple. Whoever does not carry the cross and follow me cannot be my disciple. For which of you, intending to build a tower, does not first sit down and estimate the cost, to see whether there is enough to complete it? Otherwise, when a foundation has been laid and the builder is not able to finish the building, all who see it will begin to ridicule the builder, saying, 'This person began to build and was not able to finish.' Or what king, going out to wage war against another king, will not sit down first and consider whether he is able with ten thousand to oppose the one who comes against him with twenty thousand? If he cannot, then, while the other is still far away, he sends a delegation and asks for the terms of peace. So therefore, none of you can become my disciple if you do not give up all your possessions."

Friday, September 14, 2001

EXALTATION OF THE HOLY CROSS

Numbers 21:4–9 *Whoever gazed on the serpent received life.*

Philippians 2:6–11 *He accepted death on a cross.*

John 3:13–17 *God so loved the world . . .*

As the darkness of another autumn lowers around us, we lift high the shining cross. The means of execution of a criminal has become the means of entering into eternal life. The wood of the cross is the ark that rescues us and the tree that feeds us.

REFLECTION

The letter to Philemon is the only personal letter written by Paul that exists. It is difficult to determine the exact circumstances because of the indirect language of the letter, and the fact that it is only one side of the conversation. Paul is apparently writing from prison to a Christian in Asia Minor. It is difficult to deduce an exact time and place for the writing of this letter, but it is possible that Paul wrote it in the late 50s in Ephesus.

Paul cautiously lobbies Philemon on Onesimus' behalf. Onesimus was Philemon's escaped slave, who apparently sought out Paul in prison for help. Paul helped Onesimus as much as he could, and converted him to Christianity during their time together. Paul now sends Onesimus back to his master with his written request that Philemon take him back "no longer as a slave but . . . a beloved brother" in Christ. Paul uses such diplomacy and tact that it is hard to think of Onesimus as a slave.

We might be surprised that Paul does not condemn slavery outright, but the modern Christian condemnation of slavery took centuries to develop. Slavery was part of Paul's world, and he likely realized the futility of attempting in one letter to change the social structure of his time. Instead, he argues that the faith that Philemon and Onesimus now share overrides social and economic practices; Onesimus might well be a slave, but he is to be accepted "no longer as a slave but more than a slave, a beloved brother."

The letter to Philemon calls upon its modern readers to reflect on their own social and economic relationships. Those that are enslaving must be opened up to the transformation and liberation offered by Christ. While it may be difficult to change unjust social structures, the letter to Philemon encourages us at least to begin to transform such structures by refusing to participate in them.

■ **Do you think that you can change society? In what ways might the small things you do in your life—like not participating in socio-economic structures you consider unjust—make a difference in the world?**

PRACTICE OF FAITH

GIVE UP ALL. Once again Jesus seems to make an impossible demand: "None of you can become my disciple if you do not give up all your possessions." Since the beginning, Christians have puzzled over how to live out this challenge. Consider setting up a trust, naming a charity as a beneficiary. The idea would be that we can use this money and these material things while we are alive, but they ultimately belong to someone else. And thus we are stewards, not owners. For further advice, read John Kavanaugh's book, *Following Christ in a Consumer Society*. If you cannot find a copy in the library, buy one (Orbis Books: 1-800-258-5838), and then pass it along to a friend or donate it to a library.

PRACTICE OF HOPE

A PARTNER. Providing knowledge and encouragement is one way to help a war-torn country rebuild. That is how Loyola University in Chicago chose to help the students at the University of Sarajevo in Bosnia-Herzegovina. According to Catholic News Service, Loyola is providing online education to students half a world away in order to help shape and develop the economy in the region. Courses are taught by Loyola faculty, but the degrees will be awarded by the University of Sarajevo.

War is what happens when people think only of themselves. The agreement between the two universities demonstrates what can happen when people cooperate to create something and care for one another.

PRACTICE OF CHARITY

NOT A SLAVE, BUT A BROTHER. Both the church and the United States have carried the shame of having supported slavery in the past. Slavery no longer exists in North America, but its effects linger. In the U.S., African Americans continue to be at a significant disadvantage to their white counterparts. Poverty rates are higher for African American children than for white, the information age is leaving many people of color behind, and many companies continue to discriminate against certain minorities.

Project Equality is an organization that promotes and encourages diversity at every level of employment. Its buyer's guide can be searched online at www.projectequality.org; its mailing address is 6301 Rockhill Rd., Suite 315, Kansas City MO 64131-1117; 1-816-361-9222. Don't let the dollars you spend contribute to the continuing shame of racism.

WEEKDAY READINGS (Mo) Colossians 1:24—2:3; (Tu) 2:6–15; (We) 3:1–11; (Th) 3:12–17; (Fr) Holy Cross, see box; (Sa) 1 Timothy 1:15–17

READING I   *Exodus 32:7–11, 13–14*

The LORD said to Moses, "Go down at once! Your people, whom you brought up out of the land of Egypt, have acted perversely; they have been quick to turn aside from the way that I commanded them; they have cast for themselves an image of a calf, and have worshiped it and sacrificed to it, and said, 'These are your gods, O Israel, who brought you up out of the land of Egypt!'" The LORD said to Moses, "I have seen this people, how stiff-necked they are. Now let me alone, so that my wrath may burn hot against them and I may consume them; and of you I will make a great nation."

But Moses implored the LORD his God, and said, "O LORD, why does your wrath burn hot against your people, whom you brought out of the land of Egypt with great power and with a mighty hand? Remember Abraham, Isaac, and Israel, your servants, how you swore to them by your own self, saying to them, 'I will multiply your descendants like the stars of heaven, and all this land that I have promised I will give to your descendants, and they shall inherit it forever.'" And the LORD relented concerning the disaster that had been planned for the chosen people.

READING II   *1 Timothy 1:12–17*

I am grateful to Christ Jesus our Lord, who has strengthened me, because he judged me faithful and appointed me to his service, even though I was formerly a blasphemer, a persecutor, and a man of violence. But I received mercy because I had acted ignorantly in unbelief, and the grace of our Lord overflowed for me with the faith and love that are in Christ Jesus. The saying is sure and worthy of full acceptance, that Christ Jesus came into the world to save sinners—of whom I am the foremost. But for that very reason I received mercy, so that in me, as the foremost, Jesus Christ might display the utmost patience, making me an example to those who would come to believe in him for eternal life. To the Sovereign of the ages, immortal, invisible, the only God, be honor and glory forever and ever. Amen.

GOSPEL   *Luke 15:1–10*

Now all the tax collectors and sinners were coming near to listen to Jesus. And the Pharisees and the scribes were grumbling and saying, "This fellow welcomes sinners and eats with them."

So Jesus told them this parable: "Which man of you, having a hundred sheep and losing one of them, does not leave the ninety-nine in the wilderness and go after the one that is lost until he finds it? When he has found it, he lays it on his shoulders and rejoices. And when he comes home, he calls together his friends and neighbors, saying to them, 'Rejoice with me, for I have found my sheep that was lost.' Just so, I tell you, there will be more joy in heaven over one sinner who repents than over ninety-nine righteous persons who need no repentance.

"Or what woman of you having ten silver coins, if she loses one of them, does not light a lamp, sweep the house, and search carefully until she finds it? When she has found it, she calls together her friends and neighbors, saying, 'Rejoice with me, for I have found the coin that I had lost.' Just so, I tell you, there is joy in the presence of the angels of God over one sinner who repents."

[Complete Roman Catholic: Luke 15:1–32]

R E F L E C T I O N

All three readings today form a unified whole with one message: repentance and conversion. In the first reading, the people are given yet one more chance to turn to the Lord, thanks to the prayer of Moses. In the letter to Timothy, Paul prays in thanksgiving for the mercy he received, recognizing that "Christ Jesus came into the world to save sinners." And in the gospel parables, the saving mercy of God is brought out most clearly.

On the Fourth Sunday of Lent, we saw the context in which Luke places these parables. The shepherd and the woman are images of the God of relentless mercy, and these parables are told from that point of view. In the parallel version in Matthew 18:12–14, the sheep "goes astray." Here, Luke says that the man lost one of the sheep to convey a keener sense of loss. He goes after the one sheep *until* he finds it (in Matthew, the phrase is "*if* he finds it"), returns rejoicing and asks those gathered to rejoice with him. Jesus adds that there will be joy in heaven because of the repentant sinner.

Luke's second narrative, which features a woman, is a parable unique to his gospel. This image of God lighting a lamp, sweeping the house and carefully seeking until the coin is found is a very powerful one. The pattern in this parable is the same as in the first one, ending with the woman calling her friends and neighbors together in joy.

In both of these parables (as in the long narrative that follows) the joy explodes into a party. The shepherd calls his friends, the woman calls hers; even in heaven there is the image of a community rejoicing. Luke presents in these narratives one of the essential aspects of the mission of Jesus—to seek and find what had been lost.

■ **How does the description of the shepherd God differ from your own image of God? What image would you choose to describe this God in a society that is unfamiliar with shepherds?**

■ **What do you think of Luke's unique image of God as a woman in search of a lost coin? In what ways does it open up your understanding of our God?**

PRACTICE OF FAITH

GO DOWN! Sing two verses of this African American spiritual this week to remember the scriptural call to seek out the oppressed and set them free:

When Israel was in Egypt's land. Let my people go!
Oppressed so hard they could not stand. Let my people go!
Go down, Moses! Way down in Egypt's land.
Tell old Pharaoh to let my people go.

Oh, let us all from bondage flee. Let my people go!
And let us all in Christ be free. Let my people go!
Go down, Moses! Way down in Egypt's land.
Tell old Pharaoh to let my people go.

PRACTICE OF HOPE

A STEADFAST SPIRIT. The Holocaust has provided so many lessons about prejudice, intolerance and what happens when power goes unchecked. But it also has taught us about hope. One of those lessons has been set to music by Nebraska composer Z. Randall Stroope. The text for his song, "Inscription of Hope," includes words found on the walls of a cellar in Cologne, Germany, where Jews were hiding from the Nazis: "I believe in the sun, even when it is not shining, / And I believe in love, even when there's no one there. / I believe in God, even when he is silent, / I believe through any trial, there is always a way." In the introduction to the song, Stroope notes that "hope was all they had to hold on to; hope was their only bridge to a brighter tomorrow."

PRACTICE OF CHARITY

WELCOMING SINNERS. Among the most scandalous things Jesus ever did was sit down and eat with "sinners": tax collectors, prostitutes, Gentiles. This week (on Friday), the church commemorates Matthew, a tax collector, yet an apostle and evangelist.

Among the most common sins of religious people is a self-righteousness that is quick to look for and condemn the faults of others. Jesus did not deny that the sinners he ate with were in fact sinners, but insisted that those who protested were no less so. Jesus challenged the hypocrisy of the "righteous," showing them their own sinfulness and offering the same forgiveness he offered to everyone else.

When tempted to point fingers and "fraternally" correct, perhaps the supreme act of charity would be keeping one's mouth shut.

WEEKDAY READINGS (Mo) 1 Timothy 2:1–8; (Tu) 3:1–13; (We) 3:14–16; (Th) 4:12–16; (Fr) Ephesians 4:1–7, 11–13; (Sa) 1 Timothy 6:13–16

AUTUMN ORDINARY TIME

Harvest us home to sing your praise!

When the Lord restored the fortunes
    of Zion,
we were like those who dream.
Then our mouth was filled with laughter,
and our tongue with shouts of joy.

Then it was said among the nations,
"The Lord has done great things for them."
The Lord has done great things for us,
and we are glad.

May those who sow in tears
reap with shouts of joy!
Those who go out weeping,
bearing the seed for sowing,
shall come home with shouts of joy,
carrying their sheaves.

—Psalm 126:1–3, 5–6

What tears you cry,
sower God, over us all.
But how you laugh in amazement
and what songs you sing
when there is some harvest.
Your saints from Adam and Eve,
from Moses and Miriam,
from Mary and Joseph,
until our own grandparents and parents,
and we too,
need your tears
and long to hear your laughter.
Harvest us home to sing your praise
forever and ever.

— Prayer of the Season

READING I *Amos 8:4–7*

Hear this, you that trample on the needy,
and bring to ruin the poor of the land,
saying, "When will the new moon be over
so that we may sell grain;
and the sabbath,
so that we may offer wheat for sale?
We will make the ephah small and the shekel great,
and practice deceit with false balances,
buying the poor for silver
and the needy for a pair of sandals,
and selling the sweepings of the wheat."
The LORD has sworn by the pride of Jacob:
Surely I will never forget any of their deeds.

READING II *1 Timothy 2:1–7*

First of all, then, I urge that supplications, prayers, intercessions, and thanksgivings be made for everyone, for rulers and all who are in high positions, so that we may lead a quiet and peaceable life in all godliness and dignity. This is right and is acceptable in the sight of God our Savior, who desires everyone to be saved and to come to the knowledge of the truth.

For there is one God; there is also one mediator between God and humankind, Christ Jesus, himself human, who gave himself a ransom for all—this was attested at the right time. For this I was appointed a herald and an apostle (I am telling the truth, I am not lying), a teacher of the Gentiles in faith and truth.
[Complete reading: 1 Timothy 2:1–8]

GOSPEL *Luke 16:1–13*

Then Jesus said to the disciples, "There was a rich man who had a manager, and charges were brought to him that this man was squandering his property. So the rich man summoned the manager and said to him, 'What is this that I hear about you? Give me an accounting of your management, because you cannot be my manager any longer.' Then the manager said to himself, 'What will I do, now that my master is taking the position away from me? I am not strong enough to dig, and I am ashamed to beg. I have decided what to do so that, when I am dismissed as manager, people may welcome me into their homes.' So, summoning his master's debtors one by one, the manager asked the first, 'How much do you owe my master?' The debtor answered, 'A hundred jugs of olive oil.' He said, 'Take your bill, sit down quickly, and make it fifty.' Then the manager asked another, 'And how much do you owe?' That debtor replied, 'A hundred containers of wheat.' He said, 'Take your bill and make it eighty.' And his master commended the dishonest manager because he had acted shrewdly; for the children of this age are more shrewd in dealing with their own generation than are the children of light. And I tell you, make friends for yourselves by means of dishonest wealth so that when it is gone, they may welcome you into the eternal homes.

"Whoever is faithful in a very little is faithful also in much; and whoever is dishonest in a very little is dishonest also in much. If then you have not been faithful with the dishonest wealth, who will entrust to you the true riches? And if you have not been faithful with what belongs to another, who will give you what is your own? No slave can serve two masters; for a slave will either hate the one and love the other, or be devoted to the one and despise the other. You cannot serve God and wealth."

Saturday, September 29, 2001

ARCHANGELS MICHAEL, GABRIEL AND RAPHAEL

Daniel 7:9–10, 13–14 *A thousand thousand wait upon God.*

Revelation 12:7–12 *The warrior Michael defeated the dragon.*

John 1:47–51 *You will see heaven open and angels descend.*

The transition from summer to autumn represents the battle of sin and death against the kingdom of heaven. Jesus himself uses this mythological language to describe the reality of his battle against evil. And Christ conquers: Michael defeats the dragon, Gabriel announces the kingdom, and Raphael heals the wounded.

R E F L E C T I O N

The reading from the book of the prophet Amos sets the tone for today's liturgy of the word. It is concerned with social justice, equity and the proper use of wealth. Amos condemns the dishonest merchants, noting that they cannot wait for end of the Sabbath and the new moon so they can go back to their crooked trade. Amos denounces those who cheat others to build up wealth for themselves.

At first glance, it seems that Jesus is contradicting the message of Amos. Jesus tells a parable in which a property manager is commended for what seems to be dishonesty. However, there are various interpretations of what the manager was actually doing when he had his master's debtors adjust their bills. Perhaps he was cheating his master, or perhaps the manager was only having the debtors lower their bills by an amount equal to his own commission. Since we will never know whether the manager was in fact stealing from his master, the most we can say is that he is commended for using wealth for the benefit of others. And in so doing, he benefits himself. The manager's actions may seem unsavory, and our sympathies may lie with his presumably defrauded master, but Jesus commends the manager for his easing the burden of others.

The rich master uses his resources only for his own benefit; in fact, he seems to be absentee landlord who uses his property only to build up his own treasury. In this way he is like the merchants in the reading from Amos, who hoard their wealth and scheme for dishonest ways to acquire more. The manager, however, recognizes that there is a value in giving, and that it rebounds to the benefit of the giver.

It is almost certain that, at the time this was written, Luke's community was beginning to work out the place of possessions in the Christian life. It is also certain that there were both rich and poor among the early Christians. In the character of the manager, the Christians of Luke's day had an example: Whoever gives to others will receive life, but whoever fails to give will not receive true riches.

■ **What do you count as your riches? How do you give them away to others? What keeps you from sharing those that you don't?**

■ **In what ways does this parable have an application to our social and economic life as a society? Or does it?**

PRACTICE OF FAITH

GOD AND WEALTH. In their 1998 pastoral letter, *Everyday Christianity*, the U.S. bishops wrote: "Owners, managers and investors face important opportunities to seek justice and promote peace. Ethical responsibility is not just avoiding evil, but doing right, especially for the weak and vulnerable. Decisions about the use of capital have moral implications: Are companies creating and preserving quality jobs at living wages? Are they building up community through the goods and services that they provide? Do policies and decisions reflect respect for human life and dignity, promote peace, and preserve God's creation?"

Ask these questions about your company this week.

PRACTICE OF HOPE

TWO MASTERS. We Americans are very good at compartmentalizing our lives—there is a time for God and a time for work. But what if we did not have to choose? Terry Lemerond, founder and president of Enzymatic Therapy in Green Bay, WI, has made it possible for his employees to have time for both. Lemerond offers workers at his natural supplement company the opportunity to attend an ecumenical prayer service each morning and Mass twice a month. He says he believes in "providing an environment for [employees] to be who they should be." As a result, there is less turnover and absenteeism and more security, freedom and love, Lemerond notes.

PRACTICE OF CHARITY

THE PROBLEM OF WEALTH. In an age of 401(k) plans and individual retirement accounts, Jesus' words against stockpiling wealth or achieving it dishonestly are still words to be heeded. Against the legitimate need to prepare for retirement are the demands of justice. Many mutual funds and other investments commonly used to increase wealth for retirement invest in companies whose actions are contrary to the gospel: sectors of the armaments industry; polluters of the environment; corporations that treat their employees unjustly. "Social investing" is a way to screen one's investments. Visit the Social Investment Forum, www.socialinvest.org, or order the National Green Pages from Co-op America, 1612 K St. NW, No. 600, Washington, D.C. 20006; 1-800-584-7336.

WEEKDAY READINGS (Mo) Ezra 1:1–6; (Tu) 6:7–8, 12, 14–20; (We) 9:5–9; (Th) Haggai 1:1–8; (Fr) 1:15—2:9; (Sa) Michael, Gabriel and Raphael, see box

READING I *Amos 6:1, 4–7*

Alas for those who are at ease in Zion,
    and for those who feel secure on Mount Samaria,
Alas for those who lie on beds of ivory,
    and lounge on their couches,
and eat lambs from the flock,
    and calves from the stall;
who sing idle songs to the sound of the harp,
    and like David improvise on instruments
        of music;
who drink wine from bowls,
    and anoint themselves with the finest oils,
    but are not grieved over the ruin of Joseph!
Therefore they shall now be the first to go into exile,
    and the revelry of the loungers shall pass away.

READING II *1 Timothy 6:11–16*

As for you, who are of God, pursue righteousness, godliness, faith, love, endurance, gentleness. Fight the good fight of the faith; take hold of the eternal life, to which you were called and for which you made the good confession in the presence of many witnesses. In the presence of God, who gives life to all things, and of Christ Jesus, who in his testimony before Pontius Pilate made the good confession, I charge you to keep the commandment without spot or blame until the manifestation of our Lord Jesus Christ, which God will bring about at the right time—God who is the blessed and only Sovereign, the Ruler of rulers and Lord of lords. It is God alone who has immortality and dwells in unapproachable light, whom no one has ever seen or can see; to God be honor and eternal dominion. Amen.

[Revised Common Lectionary: 1 Timothy 6:6–19]

GOSPEL *Luke 16:19–31*

Jesus said: "There was a rich man who was dressed in purple and fine linen and who feasted sumptuously every day. And at his gate lay a poor man named Lazarus, covered with sores, who longed to satisfy his hunger with what fell from the rich man's table; even the dogs would come and lick his sores. The poor man died and was carried away by the angels to be with Abraham. The rich man also died and was buried. In Hades, where the rich man was being tormented, he looked up and saw Abraham far away with Lazarus by his side. He called out, 'Father Abraham, have mercy on me, and send Lazarus to dip the tip of his finger in water and cool my tongue; for I am in agony in these flames.' But Abraham said, 'Child, remember that during your lifetime you received your good things, and Lazarus in like manner evil things; but now he is comforted here, and you are in agony. Besides all this, between you and us a great chasm has been fixed, so that those who might want to pass from here to you cannot do so, and no one can cross from there to us.' The rich man said, 'Then, father, I beg you to send Lazarus to my father's house—for I have five brothers—that he may warn them, so that they will not also come into this place of torment.' Abraham replied, 'They have Moses and the prophets; your brothers should listen to them.' He said, 'No, father Abraham; but if someone goes to them from the dead, they will repent.' Abraham said to him, 'If they do not listen to Moses and the prophets, neither will they be convinced even if someone rises from the dead.'"

REFLECTION

The parable in today's gospel circulated widely during Jesus' time. Stories of the reversal of fortune between a rich person and a poor person are often found in the writings of the time. This often-retold story also took on different forms and qualities depending on the context in which it was told.

In its basic form, the story embodies the message Luke repeats all through his gospel. Those who rejoice in their wealth in this life will suffer in the next, while those who are deprived in this life will be comforted in the next. This simple message amplifies the beatitudes and the woes from the sermon on the plain (Luke 6:17–26).

Luke paints a picture of extremes in his version of the story. The rich man wears purple and fine linens—the customary attire of rich and powerful. Tradition has named this man "Dives," from the Latin for "rich man." Some ancient manuscripts of the gospel of Luke gave the name "Nineveh" for this man, which would have been suitable; this is the name of an ancient city that Luke's readers would have associated with oppression and wealth. The poor man is lying in the street with dogs licking his sores. He longs to have his hunger satisfied. His name is Lazarus, a Greek form of a Hebrew term that means "my God helps me." Throughout the gospel of Luke, as here, the poor are exalted for their reliance on the Lord.

There is an addition to this story of reversal. A lesson for the faithful is given: All that is needed to know how to live justly can be found in the call of the prophets and the teachings of the Torah. The one who is truly rich is the one who heeds this lesson here and now.

■ **What is your view of the life to come? Does a reversal of the type portrayed in the gospel have a place in your view?**

■ **Lazarus longed to eat the rich man's table scraps, and dogs licked his sores. What might this parable teach about the allocation of food and health care?**

PRACTICE OF FAITH

GRIEVED OVER THE RUIN. We cannot be content to lounge before the TV, eat, drink and be merry while people all over the world go without basic food and shelter. The U.S. bishops invite us: "As consumers, believers can promote social justice or injustice. In an affluent culture that suggests that what we have defines who we are, we can live more simply. We can choose to support companies that defend human life, treat workers fairly, protect creation, and respect other basic moral values at home and abroad. We can also make conscious efforts to consume less." (*Everyday Christianity*, 6) Start by crossing one unnecessary item off of your grocery list. Have your children designate one Christmas gift that they will give up and give to a needy child.

PRACTICE OF HOPE

A RICH MAN. Percy Ross knows what it means to be rich—and poor. Over the years he has made and lost three fortunes. Despite two bankruptcies, he found success with the Poly-Tech Corporation, which produced plastic trash bags with recycled materials. He eventually sold the business for $8 million and divided the proceeds among his wife, his two sons, and himself. He didn't keep all the money, though. In 1983, Ross started "Thanks a Million," a syndicated column to help people by giving away his money. It took nearly 17 years. "It has been the most fantastic experience of my life," Ross said in his final column. "In many respects I'm far richer today than when I started."

PRACTICE OF CHARITY

"DOM HELDER." Among the prophets sent from God in our day is Helder Camara, former archbishop of Olinda and Recife in Brazil. "Dom Helder," as he was known by the poor who loved him, was an outspoken advocate of the rights of the poor in Brazil, often angering the military rulers of his country. He was also a voice for the entire world's poor at the Second Vatican Council. "When I feed the poor, I'm called a saint," he once said, "When I ask why the poor have no food, I'm called a communist."

Dom Helder died in 1999, but he left writings to inspire us to justice, respect for the environment and charity. Read *Sister Earth: Creation, Ecology, and the Spirit* by Helder Camara (Hyde Park, NY: New City Press; 1-914-229-0335), and let Dom Helder's example challenge you to greater acts of justice.

WEEKDAY READINGS (Mo) Zechariah 8:1–8; (Tu) 8:20–23; (We) Nehemiah 2:1–8; (Th) 8:1–4, 5–6, 7–12; (Fr) Baruch 1:15–22; (Sa) 4:5–12, 27–29

READING I   *Habakkuk 1:1–4; 2:1–4*

The oracle that the prophet Habakkuk saw.
O LORD, how long shall I cry for help,
    and you will not listen?
Or cry to you "Violence!"
    and you will not save?
Why do you make me see wrong-doing
    and look at trouble?
Destruction and violence are before me;
    strife and contention arise.
So the law becomes slack
    and justice never prevails.
The wicked surround the righteous—
    therefore judgment comes forth perverted.
I will stand at my watchpost,
    and station myself on the rampart;
I will keep watch to see what the LORD
      will say to me,
    and what the LORD will answer
      concerning my complaint.
Then the LORD answered me and said:
Write the vision;
    make it plain on tablets,
    so that a runner may read it.
For there is still a vision for the appointed time;
    it speaks of the end, and does not lie.
If it seems to tarry, wait for it;
    it will surely come, it will not delay.
Look at the proud!
    Their spirit is not right in them,
    but the righteous live by their faith.
[Roman Catholic: Habakkuk 1:2–3, 2:2–4]

READING II   *2 Timothy 1:6–8, 13–14*

I remind you to rekindle the gift of God that is within you through the laying on of my hands; for God did not give us a spirit of cowardice, but rather a spirit of power and of love and of self-discipline.

Do not be ashamed, then, of the testimony about our Lord or of me his prisoner, but join with me in suffering for the gospel, relying on the power of God. Hold to the standard of sound teaching that you have heard from me, in the faith and love that are in Christ Jesus. Guard the good treasure entrusted to you, with the help of the Holy Spirit living in us.

[Revised Common Lectionary: 2 Timothy 1:1–14]

GOSPEL   *Luke 17:5–10*

The apostles said to the Lord, "Increase our faith!" The Lord replied, "If you had faith the size of a mustard seed, you could say to this mulberry tree, 'Be uprooted and planted in the sea,' and it would obey you.

"Who among you would say to your slave who has just come in from plowing or tending sheep in the field, 'Come here at once and take your place at the table'? Would you not rather say, 'Prepare supper for me, put on your apron and serve me while I eat and drink; later you may eat and drink'? Do you thank the slave for doing what was commanded? So you also, when you have done all that you were ordered to do, say, 'We are worthless slaves; we have done only what we ought to have done!'"

REFLECTION

In the opening line of today's gospel, the apostles ask for an increase in their faith. In Jewish thought at the time of Jesus, faith in God meant believing that God was reliable. The Greek word used by Luke and translated as "faith" *(pistis)* did not have a specifically religious connotation, but meant trustworthiness and reliability. In the gospel of Luke, faith in Jesus means believing that he is the reliable incarnation of the Word of God. Faith in Jesus means believing that Jesus' words and actions come from God, and are reliable.

The members of the early Christian community felt the call to invigorate their faith in the gospel, especially as the time between the resurrection of Christ and the second coming grew longer. There was an increasingly urgent felt need to trust ever more firmly that Jesus' words are reliable and that God's reign is indeed dawning through the saving words and deeds of Jesus. Luke is reassuring: Even a tiny amount of faith is enough to see the reign of God come into in the world.

The second story in the gospel builds on the first. The person with faith—no matter the "amount"—should see it as a natural part of life. The example of a servant is given. It was not expected that servants be thanked or even acknowledged for the work they did; they were simply expected to do their assigned tasks. The analogy to faith is that just as serving defines the servant, so faith defines the believer. By definition, a believer has the amount of faith that is needed. Jesus is encouraging his followers to be content with the mustard seed of faith and to let it grow, because it can do great things.

■ **How would you describe your faith? What is your prayer to the Lord about your faith? How can you allow your faith to grow as a mustard seed might?**

■ **What are ways that you live out your faith in your life?**

PRACTICE OF

FAITH

WRITE THE VISION. Keeping a journal can be good exercise in practicing your faith. Buy a notebook or sketchbook with blank pages, or open a new file on your computer. Write daily if you can, or weekly otherwise. Pay attention to what you feel compelled to write. Write it down and then ask, "What is God trying to tell me?" Jot down your thoughts. If you do not feel compelled to write anything, copy a word or phrase from last Sunday's scriptures that seems to jump out at you. After them, write down whatever comes to mind. If you are having a hard time concentrating in prayer, try writing out your prayer. Keep a running list in your journal of people and places and events to pray over.

PRACTICE OF

HOPE

EAT AND DRINK. The Internet has brought people together in ways we never could have imagined. Communication that used to take days can happen instantly now. We have access to vast amounts of information. Chat rooms make our global village that much smaller. A wealth of services and products is available with a few keystrokes and mouse clicks. But there are things the Internet cannot provide, no matter how interactive it becomes—faith and hope. Just as the very nature of our liturgies demands interaction among people taking their full, conscious and active part in the celebrations, faith and hope likewise are transmitted person to person, face to face, not terminal to terminal.

PRACTICE OF

CHARITY

VIOLENCE BEFORE ME. Today marks the third anniversary of the death of Matthew Shepard, a 21-year-old Wyoming man who was murdered primarily because he was gay.

In response to Shepard's murder, two Catholic organizations, Pax Christi USA and New Ways Ministry, published "A Catholic Pledge to End Violence against Gay and Lesbian People": "We pledge to find new ways to bring the peace of Christ to the situation of violence against gay and lesbian people. We call on all Catholics and people of goodwill to look into their hearts and weed out violent perceptions and behaviors. We ask our bishops and church leaders to speak boldly when the rights of gay and lesbian people are destroyed and when they are maligned by politicians and other religious leaders. We pray for both the victims and the perpetrators of violence."

Commit yourself to battling the violence of hatred.

WEEKDAY READINGS (Mo) Jonah 1:1—2:1, 11; (Tu) 3:1–10; (We) 4:1–11; (Th) Malachi 3:13–20; (Fr) Joel 1:13–15; 2:1–2; (Sa) 4:12–21

145

READING I *2 Kings 5:1–3, 9–17*

Naaman, commander of the army of the king of Aram, was a great man and in high favor with his master, because by him the LORD had given victory to Aram. The man, though a mighty warrior, suffered from leprosy. Now the Arameans on one of their raids had taken a young girl captive from the land of Israel, and she served Naaman's wife. She said to her mistress, "If only my lord were with the prophet who is in Samaria! He would cure him of his leprosy."

So Naaman came with his horses and chariots, and halted at the entrance of Elisha's house. Elisha sent a messenger to him, saying, "Go, wash in the Jordan seven times, and your flesh shall be restored and you shall be clean." But Naaman became angry and went away, saying, "I thought that for me he would surely come out, and stand and call on the name of the LORD his God, and would wave his hand over the spot, and cure the leprosy! Are not Abana and Pharpar, the rivers of Damascus, better than all the waters of Israel? Could I not wash in them, and be clean?" He turned and went away in a rage. But his servants approached and said to him, "Father, if the prophet had commanded you to do something difficult, would you not have done it? How much more, when all he said to you was, 'Wash, and be clean'?" So he went down and immersed himself seven times in the Jordan, according to the word of the man of God; his flesh was restored like the flesh of a little child, and he was clean.

Then Naaman returned to the man of God, he and all his company; he came and stood before Elisha and said, "Now I know that there is no God in all the earth except in Israel; please accept a present from your servant."

But Elisha said, "As the LORD lives, whom I serve, I will accept nothing!" Naaman urged Elisha to accept, but he refused. Then Naaman said, "If not, please let two mule-loads of earth be given to your servant; for your servant will no longer offer burnt offering or sacrifice to any god except the LORD."

[Roman Catholic: 2 Kings 5:14–17]
[Revised Common Lectionary: 2 Kings 5:1–3, 7–15]

READING II *2 Timothy 2:8–13*

Remember Jesus Christ, raised from the dead, a descendant of David—that is my gospel, for which I suffer hardship, even to the point of being chained like a criminal. But the word of God is not chained. Therefore I endure everything for the sake of the elect, so that they may also obtain the salvation that is in Christ Jesus, with eternal glory. The saying is sure:

If we have died with Christ,
we will also live with Christ;
if we endure, we will also reign with Christ;
if we deny him, he will also deny us;
if we are faithless, he remains faithful—
for Christ cannot deny himself.

[Revised Common Lectionary: 2 Timothy 2:8–15]

GOSPEL *Luke 17:11–19*

On the way to Jerusalem Jesus was going through the region between Samaria and Galilee. As he entered a village, ten people who had leprosy approached him. Keeping their distance, they called out, saying, "Jesus, Master, have mercy on us!" When he saw them, he said to them, "Go and show yourselves to the priests." And as they went, they were made clean. Then one of them, when he saw that he was healed, turned back, praising God with a loud voice. He prostrated himself at Jesus' feet and thanked him. And he was a Samaritan. Then Jesus asked, "Were not ten made clean? But the other nine, where are they? Was none of them found to return and give praise to God except this foreigner?" Then Jesus said to the Samaritan, "Get up and go on your way; your faith has made you well."

REFLECTION

Today's readings have to do with remembering: Naaman remembered to thank Elisha for his cure, and one of the ten lepers cured by Jesus remembered to turn back and thank his healer. It is in the passage from the second letter to Timothy, however, that remembering is placed center stage.

Paul speaks again of being a prisoner. In the passage read last week, he spoke of himself as being a prisoner of the Lord. Today we hear how he connects his suffering with the gospel. Paul's ministry is literally bound up in his calling as a prisoner of the Lord and in "being chained" to the preaching of the good news. The suffering of Paul, like that of Jesus, is inseparable from the ministry of proclaiming the good news.

Within the good news and its proclamation is a dynamic that provokes a reaction among those who hear it. But if the reaction is one of rejection and the preacher is silenced or imprisoned, the word itself remains unfettered and has not been bound. The poetic insert in verses 11–13 may well be from an early Christian hymn and contains the rhythmic paradoxes of dying and living, enduring and reigning. There is an equation here: If we deny Christ, he will deny us. But there is also a contrast: Even if we are faithless, God remains faithful.

■ **Do you think it is easy to know for certain exactly what a particular passage in scripture is saying? In other words, is it even possible to engage in debates that begin with "the Bible says"?**

■ **Carefully read the remainder of the second chapter of 2 Timothy, paying particular attention to the writer's use of the word "truth." What questions does this reading raise for you?**

PRACTICE OF FAITH

WASHED. The prophet Elisha tells the leprous Naaman to wash seven times in the River Jordan. Later in the Bible, John baptizes Jesus in the same river, sanctifying its water for all time, and unsealing for the church the life-giving fountain of baptism. Like the ten lepers that Jesus cured, we too have been washed clean by baptism. So we should emulate the one of the ten that turned back to thank Jesus and praise God for being healed.

Find out the date of your baptism. (Ask a relative, or write to the church where you were baptized.) Mark it on next year's calendar. Keep the day each year by going to Mass in the morning, renewing your baptismal vows (quietly, or at a meal with your family or friends). Give praise to God for being healed!

PRACTICE OF HOPE

STAND UP. Each November since 1990, women and men of conscience have traveled to Fort Benning, Georgia, to protest the work done at the U.S. Army's School of the Americas. The protesters claim that SOA graduates have been linked to murder and human rights abuses throughout Latin America. They would like to see the school closed. One elderly nun from Nebraska said she made the trip to give witness to lawmakers and to give hope to the people of Central America.

Now the veteran protesters are receiving hope as well as giving it. In the last two or three years, they have been joined by thousands of high school and college students who are ready, willing and able to take up the cause. There fight for justice goes on.

PRACTICE OF CHARITY

LEPROSY. The first and second readings today both recount healings of people with leprosy, a disfiguring illness often mentioned in scripture, one that resulted in the social isolation of its victims. Although one rarely hears about it today, leprosy still strikes people all over the world, even though it is now curable.

Leprosy is not the only curable disease still disabling or killing people. Cholera, influenza and chicken pox continue to kill many, especially children, who lack access to adequate health care. Doctors without Borders is an organization that brings modern medical care to many throughout the world. Make a donation, or contribute your services; 6 E. 39th St., 8th Floor, New York NY 10016; 1–888–392–0392; www.dwb.org.

WEEKDAY READINGS (Mo) Romans 1:1–7 (Tu) 1:16–25 (We) 2:1–11 (Th) 2 Timothy 4:10–17 (Fr) Romans 4:1–8 (Sa) 4:13, 16–18

READING I *Exodus 17:8–13*

Amalek came and fought with Israel at Rephidim. Moses said to Joshua, "Choose some men for us and go out, fight with Amalek. Tomorrow I will stand on the top of the hill with the staff of God in my hand." So Joshua did as Moses told him, and fought with Amalek, while Moses, Aaron, and Hur went up to the top of the hill. Whenever Moses held up his hand, Israel prevailed; and whenever he lowered his hand, Amalek prevailed. But Moses' hands grew weary; so they took a stone and put it under him, and he sat on it. Aaron and Hur held up his hands, one on one side, and the other on the other side; so his hands were steady until the sun set. And Joshua defeated Amalek and his people with the sword.

[Revised Common Lectionary: Genesis 32:22–31]

READING II *2 Timothy 3:14—4:5*

But as for you, continue in what you have learned and firmly believed, knowing from whom you learned it, and how from childhood you have known the sacred writings that are able to instruct you for salvation through faith in Christ Jesus. All scripture is inspired by God and is useful for teaching, for reproof, for correction, and for training in righteousness, so that everyone who belongs to God may be proficient, equipped for every good work.

In the presence of God and of Christ Jesus, who is to judge the living and the dead, and in view of Christ's appearing and his dominion, I solemnly urge you: proclaim the message; be persistent whether the time is favorable or unfavorable; convince, rebuke, and encourage, with the utmost patience in teaching. For the time is coming when people will not put up with sound doctrine, but having itching ears, they will accumulate for themselves teachers to suit their own desires, and will turn away from listening to the truth and wander away to myths. As for you, always be sober, endure suffering, do the work of an evangelist, carry out your ministry fully.

[Roman Catholic: 2 Timothy 3:14—4:2]

GOSPEL *Luke 18:1–8*

Then Jesus told them a parable about their need to pray always and not to lose heart. He said, "In a certain city there was a judge who neither feared God nor had respect for people. In that city there was a widow who kept coming to him and saying, 'Grant me justice against my opponent.' For a while the judge refused; but later he said to himself, 'Though I have no fear of God and no respect for anyone, yet because this widow keeps bothering me, I will grant her justice, so that she may not wear me out by continually coming.'"

And the Lord said, "Listen to what the unjust judge says. And will not God grant justice to God's own elect who are crying out day and night? Will God delay long in helping them? I tell you, God will quickly grant justice to them. And yet, when the Son-of-Man comes, will he find faith on earth?"

REFLECTION

The opening line of the gospel orients us to the parable and echoes the first and second readings' theme of persistence and faithfulness. The two figures, the widow and the judge, act in contrast to what would be expected.

As a widow, the woman is without power. At that time and in that place, women did not speak publicly. They were were required to go through their fathers and then their husbands if they wanted something said. Widows were especially oppressed, and often impoverished. They were frequently taken advantage of financially because they were not included in the laws of inheritance. Yet the widow in today's gospel is not contained by her culture's mores. We are not told who her opponent is or why she is seeking the judge's help, only that she repeatedly insists that justice be done.

Finally, this judge "who neither feared God nor had respect for people" gives in to her relentless pestering and grants her request. If we think of the widow as an example of one who prays always and does not lose heart, we may see this parable as a reminder to remain faithful to our prayer and concern for justice. We are not to allow ourselves to feel powerless. The widow's courage and determination to right the wrong can be a model for us.

The questions at the end of the reading turn our attention to the judge. If even an unjust judge responds to the cry of the widow, how much more responsive is God to the prayers of the people. Jesus is telling his followers to remain faithful: God heeds those who pray.

■ **Many people experience long dry spells in their prayer lives, feeling that God is far from them. What do these readings offer to you during such times?**

■ **The image of a fatigued Moses needing to sit and be supported can speak to us. What do you do when you feel discouraged or feel that your efforts are not enough? Where do you seek the support that allows you to continue?**

PRACTICE OF FAITH

WRESTLE AND BOTHER. Perseverance is necessary for faith. A living faith keeps practicing—one step at a time—the gospel way of life. Remember the widow, who would not stop bothering the judge until receiving justice.

Write again to your congressional representative about a political issue from your faith perspective. (In the United States, you can find the name and address by going to http://www.house.gov/writerep. Or write to your representative at the general address: U.S. House of Representatives, Washington DC 20515.) Wait a month for a reply; mark your calendar. Write again. And again. And again.

PRACTICE OF HOPE

REMAIN FAITHFUL. I moved from Iowa to Nebraska about 10 years ago. Some of my friends still refer to this as when I "changed religions." In gridiron terms, you see, I moved from the land of the Hawkeyes (University of Iowa) and Cyclones (Iowa State) to Big Red Country (University of Nebraska Cornhuskers).

The people in this part of the country take their football very seriously. On game days, red can be seen everywhere and you cannot go into a store, restaurant or house without hearing the play-by-play. I have never seen such devotion—and such hope. At this time of year, anything seems possible in Nebraska. It's a nice feeling—even for those of us who don't know a halfback from a quarterback.

PRACTICE OF CHARITY

UNJUST JUDGES. According to The Sentencing Project, the United States' rate of incarceration is second only to Russia's among the industrialized nations. Mandatory sentencing is increasing the prison population, even though the crime rate has gone down in recent years.

All this is having devastating consequences, especially among people of color. In 14 states, ex-convicts are not allowed to vote, penalizing primarily African American males, 13 percent of whom are already disenfranchised. Thirty-two percent of African American men between the ages of 20 and 29 are under some type of correctional control; forty-nine percent of federal and state prisoners in 1996 were black. For more on the effects of race and poverty on sentencing, contact The Sentencing Project, an organization that advocates for defense-based alternative sentencing programs, 1516 P St. NW, Washington DC 20005; 1-202-628-0871; www.sentencingproject.org.

WEEKDAY READINGS (Mo) Romans 4:20–25 (Tu) 5:12, 15, 17–19, 20–21 (We) 6:12–18 (Th) 6:19–23 (Fr) 7:18–25 (Sa) 8:1–11

READING I *Sirach 35:12–17*

Give to the Most High
    as the Most High has given to you,
  and as generously as you can afford.
For the LORD is the one who repays,
  and will repay you sevenfold.
Do not offer the LORD a bribe,
      for the LORD will not accept it;
  and do not rely on a dishonest sacrifice;
for the LORD is the judge,
    with whom there is no partiality.
The LORD will not show partiality to the poor,
    but will listen to the prayer
      of one who is wronged.
The LORD will not ignore the supplication
      of the orphan,
    or the widow when she pours out her complaint.
[*Revised Common Lectionary* alternate: *Jeremiah 14:7–10, 19–22*]

READING II *2 Timothy 4:6–8, 16–18*

As for me, I am already being poured out as a libation, and the time of my departure has come. I have fought the good fight, I have finished the race, I have kept the faith. From now on there is reserved for me the crown of righteousness, which the Lord, the righteous judge, will give me on that day, and not only to me but also to all who have longed for his appearing.

At my first defense no one came to my support, but all deserted me. May it not be counted against them! But the Lord stood by me and gave me strength, so that through me the message might be fully proclaimed and all the Gentiles might hear it. So I was rescued from the lion's mouth. The Lord will rescue me from every evil attack and save me for the dominion of heaven. To the Lord be the glory forever and ever. Amen.

GOSPEL *Luke 18:9–14*

Jesus also told this parable to some who trusted in themselves that they were righteous and regarded others with contempt: "Two men went up to the temple to pray, one a Pharisee and the other a tax collector. The Pharisee, standing by himself, was praying thus, 'God, I thank you that I am not like other people: thieves, rogues, adulterers, or even like this tax collector. I fast twice a week; I give a tenth of all my income.' But the tax collector, standing far off, would not even look up to heaven, but was beating his breast and saying, 'God, be merciful to me, a sinner!' I tell you, this man went down to his home justified rather than the other; for all who exalt themselves will be humbled, but all who humble themselves will be exalted."

Thursday, November 1, and Friday, November 2, 2001

ALL SAINTS

Revelation 7:2–4, 9–14 *The crowd stood before the Lamb.*

1 John 3:1–3 *We shall see God.*

Matthew 5:1–12 *How blest are the poor in spirit.*

We welcome the winter with a harvest homecoming. All God's people are gathered into the new Jerusalem to begin the supper of the Lamb. The poor, the mourning, the meek and the lowly remove their masks and see themselves as they truly are: the beloved children of God, the saints of heaven.

ALL SOULS

Daniel 12:1–3 *The dead will rise to shine like stars.*

Romans 6:3–9 *Like Christ, we will live a new life.*

John 6:37–40 *I will never reject one who comes.*

In the northern hemisphere, nature shows forth the awesome beauty of the harvest. Yesterday we rejoiced in the harvest of the saints. Today we reflect on what made this harvest possible: self-sacrifice, completed labors and death.

REFLECTION

Knowing more about the two main characters in Jesus' time enhances our understanding of this parable. A Pharisee was a member of a religious sect within Judaism that focused on strict observance of the Law. The Pharisee in the parable would have believed that he was observing the Law by praying as he did. Likewise, those listening to Jesus tell the parable would have thought the Pharisee's prayer was right and good.

The Pharisees looked down on the "people of the land." In fact, the word *Pharisee* means "separated" or "separate ones." It was not unusual for Pharisees to distinguish themselves in public by praying aloud so that all could hear.

Tax collectors were despised as crooked middlemen and traitors to their people. In response, the tax collectors overcharged and skimmed the surplus for themselves.

The Pharisee's prayer is about himself and how perfectly he follows the Law. He says nothing about his need for God, but thanks God for making him so much better than everyone else, especially that disgusting tax collector. The tax collector, on the other hand, stands at the back and bows his head in humility, as he begs God for mercy.

Jesus is clear about who is justified. Jesus is not suggesting a false humility or self-hate. Rather, his concern is for right relationships with one another and with God, in whom we live and move and have our being.

■ **How do you understand humility? How can you be proud of the gifts you have and use well, and yet still be humble? What role does gratitude play in developing humility?**

PRACTICE OF FAITH

BE MERCIFUL TO ME. In the parable about the Pharisee and the tax collector going to the Temple to pray, Jesus commends the tax collector for praying sincerely this prayer: "God, be merciful to me, a sinner." This is a version of a prayer sometimes called the Jesus Prayer, important to Orthodox Christians from the 6th century to this day. The full version of the prayer is "Lord Jesus Christ, Son of God, have mercy on me, a sinner." The practice is to repeat this prayer over and over again. Sometimes, a string of beads like a rosary is used to help in the repetition. Around the 14th century, a set of movements assigned to the prayer: Bow your head, gaze at your heart, breathe in on the first half of the prayer and out on the last half. Try it!

PRACTICE OF HOPE

DEPARTURE. Sometimes hope is a color. The Midwest is ablaze with it right now in the gold, the red, the orange and the brown of the leaves. On a recent concert tour, our choir burst into applause whenever we saw a tree with an exceptionally fine autumn display. Silly? Maybe. But we knew that these colors were the last burst of colorful life before winter took the leaves away entirely and turned the world white and gray. In a few months, we will be filled with hope again as we see the first shoots of new green grass brighten the brown winter turf. Life. Death. Resurrection. The seasons continually invite us to reflect on our lives in Christ.

PRACTICE OF CHARITY

ALL SOULS. Beginning with the feast of All Saints (November 1) and the Commemoration of the Faithful Departed (November 2), November is a time to reflect on death and to remember loved ones who have died. In our time, death is less of a family affair. Many people die in hospitals or nursing homes, often alone, without the comfort of family or friends.

Against this trend is hospice care, which seeks to help patients by managing pain, helping the dying and their families come to terms with death, and making it possible for patients to die at home. Volunteers are an indispensable part of hospice care, required in the United States for a hospice program to receive public funding. Volunteer in a hospice program in your area; volunteers, patients and families all benefit from this holistic approach to dying and death.

WEEKDAY READINGS (Mo) Romans 8:12–17 (Tu) 8:18–25 (We) 8:26–30 (Th) All Saints, see box; (Fr) All Souls, see box; (Sa) Romans 11:1–2, 11–12, 25–29

READING I *Wisdom 11:22—12:2*

The whole world before you, O LORD, is like a speck that tips the scales, and like a drop of morning dew that falls on the ground. But you are merciful to all, for you can do all things, and you overlook people's sins, so that they may repent.

LORD, you love all things that exist, and detest none of the things that you have made, for you would not have made anything if you had hated it. How would anything have endured if you had not willed it? Or how would anything not called forth by you have been preserved? You spare all things, for they are yours, O LORD, you who love the living.

For your immortal spirit is in all things. Therefore you correct little by little those who trespass, and you remind and warn them of the things through which they sin, so that they may be freed from wickedness and put their trust in you, O LORD.
[Revised Common Lectionary: Isaiah 1:10–18]

READING II *2 Thessalonians 1:11—2:2*

To this end we always pray for you, asking that our God will make you worthy of the call and will fulfill by divine power every good resolve and work of faith, so that the name of our Lord Jesus may be glorified in you, and you in him, according to the grace of our God and the Lord Jesus Christ.

As to the coming of our Lord Jesus Christ and our being gathered together to him, we beg you, brothers and sisters, not to be quickly shaken in mind or alarmed, either by spirit or by word or by letter, as though from us, to the effect that the day of the Lord is already here.
[Revised Common Lectionary: 2 Thessalonians 1:1–4, 11–12]

GOSPEL *Luke 19:1–10*

Jesus entered Jericho and was passing through it. A man was there named Zacchaeus; he was a chief tax collector and was rich. He was trying to see who Jesus was, but on account of the crowd he could not, because he was short in stature. So he ran ahead and climbed a sycamore tree to see Jesus, because he was going to pass that way. When Jesus came to the place, he looked up and said to Zacchaeus, "Zacchaeus, hurry and come down; for I must stay at your house today." So he hurried down and was happy to welcome Jesus. All who saw it began to grumble and said, "Jesus has gone to be the guest of one who is a sinner." Zacchaeus stood there and said to the Lord, "Look, half of my possessions, Lord, I will give to the poor; and if I have defrauded anyone of anything, I will pay back four times as much." Then Jesus said to Zacchaeus, "Today salvation has come to this house, because Zacchaeus too is a child of Abraham. For the Son-of-Man came to seek out and to save the lost."

Friday, November 9, 2001

DEDICATION OF THE LATERAN BASILICA IN ROME

Ezekiel 47:1–2,8–9, 12 *Saving water flowed from the temple.*

1 Corinthians 3:9–11, 16–17 *You are God's holy temple.*

John 2:13–22 *Zeal for God's house consumes me.*

Human flesh is God's dwelling place. In November, a season of ingathering, we assemble in the Spirit. Our own flesh and blood is becoming God's holy temple. All creation is becoming Jerusalem.

REFLECTION

The main character besides Jesus in today's gospel is Zacchaeus. He is not mentioned in the scriptures outside of Luke 19, and there is much speculation about him and what he represents. His name is a Greek form of a Hebrew term that means "clean and innocent" or "righteous and upright," and there are stories of his being appointed a leader of the church in Caesarea against his will. His home town, Jericho, was a good place for a tax collector; it was an important customs station. Zacchaeus, a rich man, is shown to be hospitable and humble. It is ironic that he was one of the "poor" whom Jesus continually sought out. However, because of his work as a tax collector, he would have been scorned by his neighbors as a sinner and traitor to Israel. He was "lost." He probably felt like an outcast from his people, despite his wealth and connection with ruling Romans.

The themes of this gospel passage are seeking, seeing and salvation. Zacchaeus made quite an effort to see Jesus. The dramatic expression of his desire to get a glimpse of Jesus is his climbing a tree, which would certainly have caused a stir. Just as it was unheard of in Zacchaeus' culture for a grown man, especially an official, to run in public, it was even more undignified to climb trees in public. Zacchaeus set himself up for even more ridicule by climbing the tree to see Jesus. But Zacchaeus' struggle pays off. Jesus sees him there in the tree and even invites himself to Zacchaeus' home. Salvation is announced as Jesus comes into the house: Jesus declares that the one hated by the townspeople is a "child of Abraham." This is a beautiful acknowledgement by Jesus that Zacchaeus is truly a member of the community. Jesus' listeners would have been shocked; they would have expected the tax collector's exclusion (perhaps calling Zacchaeus something like "child of sin") rather than inclusion.

In this story of Zacchaeus, Luke brings together several characteristic themes: Jesus seeks out and favors some one person despite the complaints of others; hospitality and salvation are paired; Jesus is recognized as the Messiah; and the definition of who belongs to the new Israel is expansive, inclusive and universal.

■ **How do you seek out Christ in your life? How has Christ made the first move in your journey of faith?**

■ **Who are the members of the Body of Christ? How do you define them? Who is included or excluded?**

PRACTICE OF FAITH

TO SEEK AND TO SAVE. Our God is always open to our repentance. And as we read in today's gospel, Jesus actually seeks us out in order to save us. In our own day, we have many ways to experience this saving action of our God. We often begin Mass with a prayer for forgiveness, and in the sacrament of penance we confess our sins and are reconciled with God. Make time this week to consider the need for repentance in your life. Where might you be lost? Then pray the Confiteor ("I confess") from Mass (see page 18), or this Saturday go to your parish church to celebrate the sacrament of reconciliation.

PRACTICE OF HOPE

EVERY GOOD RESOLVE. Our parish communities are rich in talent. There are so many gifted people who want to use those gifts in the service of others. Some already have the training and preparation to do that. For those who don't, Loyola University in New Orleans offers an innovative format for people in ministry to learn and apply their learning in a practical way. The Loyola Institute for Ministry Extension Program allows people to study in small groups where they are, using course materials written by the faculty at Loyola. Each group has a local facilitator to guide the process and an instructor on campus in New Orleans who oversees their work. Reflecting and discerning with a group of fellow believers is the key, according to one graduate. Not only do they affirm each other, but they also call out one another's gifts, he said.

PRACTICE OF CHARITY

ZACCHAEUS. The 1990s saw massive increases in wealth for those who already had much. In 1999, the chairman of Microsoft, Bill Gates, reportedly had a net worth of some $90 billion dollars, an astonishing amount by any standard. To his credit, Gates and his wife, Melinda, pledged one billion dollars for college scholarships for minority students. This, of course, didn't match match Zachaeus' generosity—Gates would have had to pledge 45 billion!

Only a very, very few can give the kind of money that makes headlines, yet tithing has been a Christian obligation since the church's beginning. All of us have treasures to offer others: our time, our skills, our financial resources. As Zacchaeus did, choose a portion of your income to offer to others. Or a portion of your time. Stick to your commitment, and make tithing part of your daily life.

WEEKDAY READINGS (Mo) Romans 11:29–36; (Tu) 12:5–16; (We) 13:8–10; (Th) 14:7–12; (Fr) Dedication of Lateran Basilica, see box; (Sa) Romans 16:3–9, 16, 22–27

NOVEMBER 11, 2001
Thirty-second Sunday in Ordinary Time
Twenty-third Sunday after Pentecost

READING I *2 Maccabees 7:1–2, 9–14*

It happened that seven brothers and their mother were arrested and were being compelled by King Antiochus, under torture with whips and thongs, to partake of unlawful swine's flesh. One of the brothers, speaking for all, said, "What do you intend to ask and learn from us? For we are ready to die rather than transgress the laws of our ancestors."

After the first brother had died, they brought forward the second for their sport. And when he was at his last breath, he said, "You accursed wretch, you dismiss us from this present life, but the Sovereign of the universe will raise us up to an everlasting renewal of life, because we have died for the laws of God."

After him, the third was the victim of their sport. When it was demanded, he quickly put out his tongue and courageously stretched forth his hands, and said nobly, "I got these from Heaven, and because of God's laws I disdain them, and from God I hope to get them back again." As a result the king himself and those with him were astonished at the young man's spirit, for he regarded his sufferings as nothing.

After the third brother too had died, they maltreated and tortured the fourth in the same way. When he was near death, he said to his torturers, "One cannot but choose to die at the hands of mortals and to cherish the hope God gives of being raised again by him. But for you there will be no resurrection to life!"

[*Revised Common Lectionary: Job 19:23–27*]

READING II *2 Thessalonians 2:16—3:5*

May our Lord Jesus Christ himself and God, our Father, who loved us and through grace gave us eternal comfort and good hope, comfort your hearts and strengthen them in every good work and word.

Brothers and sisters, pray for us, so that the word of the Lord may spread rapidly and be glorified everywhere, just as it is among you, and that we may be rescued from wicked and evil people; for not all have faith. But the Lord is faithful, and will strengthen you and guard you from the evil one. And we have confidence in the Lord concerning you, that you are doing and will go on doing the things that we command. May the Lord direct your hearts to the love of God and to the steadfastness of Christ. [*Revised Common Lectionary: 2 Thessalonians 2:1–5, 13–17*]

GOSPEL *Luke 20:27–38*

Some Sadducees, those who say there is no resurrection, came to Jesus and asked him a question, "Teacher, Moses wrote for us that if a man's brother dies, leaving a wife but no children, the man shall marry the widow and raise up children for his brother. Now there were seven brothers; the first married, and died childless; then the second and the third married her, and so in the same way all seven died childless. Finally the woman also died. In the resurrection, therefore, whose wife will the woman be? For the seven had married her."

Jesus said to them, "Those who belong to this age marry and are given in marriage; but those who are considered worthy of a place in that age and in the resurrection from the dead neither marry nor are given in marriage. Indeed they cannot die anymore, because they are like angels and are children of God, being children of the resurrection. And the fact that the dead are raised Moses himself showed, in the story about the bush, where he speaks of the Lord as the God of Abraham, the God of Isaac, and the God of Jacob. Now God is God not of the dead, but of the living; for to God all of them are alive."

REFLECTION

The question the Sadducees ask Jesus is legitimate from their point of view. The Sadducees were a major group in Palestinian Judaism during the late Hellenistic period, but much of what we know about them was written by outsiders, or worse, their opponents. Thus we have very little solid knowledge about them. Some authors think that the name is from a Hebrew word meaning "righteous." Others think that they are named after Zadok, the high priest at the time of David and Solomon. If that is correct, then we can understand the Sadducees as a party of aristocrats related to the high priests.

Sadducees held that there was no resurrection of the dead. They believed that the soul died when the body did. They also believed that the only valid regulations were those in the Torah. According to the Sadducees, a person's only chance of "living on" after death was through offspring. If a man died before fathering a child, then it was the responsibility of a brother of the deceased to marry the widow and have children with her so that the dead man's life could carry on through his children. Thus, the situation the Sadducees set up in their question to Jesus is plausible. They are using this hypothetical situation which is compatible with the Torah to try to prove that the idea of resurrection is not.

Jesus provides a new understanding of resurrection, describing the new life as one of a different age, one that does not involve the same ties as the old life. Luke will continue to teach about resurrection in the post-resurrection stories. The new life of the resurrection that Christ lives is free of earthly confines, giving hope to those on earth who live in fear or pain or poverty. The theme of reversal that continually surfaces in Luke's gospel is also part of the Christian hope in eternal life.

■ **What is your understanding of the resurrection of the dead? How do you understand the Christian church's teaching of resurrection? What is your hope of resurrection?**

■ **What are some beliefs that you would like to ask Jesus about as the Sadducees did? What beliefs would you like to learn more about? How could you go about such learning?**

PRACTICE OF FAITH

MY REDEEMER LIVES. Find a recording of Handel's *Messiah*. It will be good for the season of Advent, too. Listen to the aria "I Know That My Redeemer Liveth" as a meditation on the first reading and gospel that we hear today.

Sing these words to the tune "Praise God from whom all blessings flow" as part of your prayer this week: I know that my Redeemer lives! / What joy the blest assurance gives! / He lives, he lives who once was dead. / He lives, my ever-living head. / He lives and grants me daily breath; / He lives, and I shall conquer death. / He lives, my mansion to prepare; / He lives to bring me safely there.

PRACTICE OF HOPE

INCLINE YOUR EAR. Do you like the sound of your own voice? At some time everyone wishes the whole world would listen to them. Be careful what you wish for. I got a new perspective on that desire when I developed a blockage in my middle ear. For one week I could only hear the sound of my own voice. I couldn't really interact with people, because I couldn't hear them very well. It was especially troublesome when I tried to sing, because I couldn't blend with the people around me. I missed that harmony. I longed for the sound of other voices. Long since cured, I hear differently now. The experience made me more appreciative of what everyone brings to the conversation.

PRACTICE OF CHARITY

THE SECOND COMING. Although we have been waiting for some 2000 years for the return of Christ and his reign of justice, we continue to hope for the advent of the new creation, sometimes called the "eighth day," the day of completion. Prefigured in Christ's resurrection, the eighth day has not yet dawned completely on our world, still laboring toward fulfillment. One organizations seeking to bring the world toward its destiny is the 8th Day Center for Justice, which seeks to be an "alternative voice to the systems that suppress the human community and environment." The Center offers two publications, a Legislative Action Sheet and *Focus*, which highlights special topics. For more information and to subscribe, contact the 8th Day Center for Justice, 205 W. Monroe, Chicago IL 60606; 1-312-641-5151; www.8thdaycenter.org.

WEEKDAY READINGS (Mo) Wisdom 1:1–7; (Tu) 2:23—3:9; (We) 6:1–11; (Th) 7:22—8:1; (Fr) 13:1–9; (Sa) 18:14–16; 19:6–9

READING I *Malachi 3:19–20*

See, the day is coming, burning like an oven, when all the arrogant and all evildoers will be stubble; the day that comes shall burn them up, says the LORD of hosts, so that it will leave them neither root nor branch. But for you who revere my name the sun of righteousness shall rise, with healing in its wings.

READING II *2 Thessalonians 3:6–13*

Now we command you, beloved, in the name of our Lord Jesus Christ, to keep away from believers who are living in idleness and not according to the tradition that they received from us. For you yourselves know how you ought to imitate us; we were not idle when we were with you, and we did not eat anyone's bread without paying for it; but with toil and labor we worked night and day, so that we might not burden any of you. This was not because we do not have that right, but in order to give you an example to imitate. For even when we were with you, we gave you this command: Anyone unwilling to work should not eat. For we hear that some of you are living in idleness, mere busybodies, not doing any work. Now such persons we command and exhort in the Lord Jesus Christ to do their work quietly and to earn their own living. Brothers and sisters, do not be weary in doing what is right.

[Roman Catholic: 2 Thessalonians 3:7–12]

GOSPEL *Luke 21:5–19*

When some were speaking about the temple, how it was adorned with beautiful stones and gifts dedicated to God, Jesus said, "As for these things that you see, the days will come when not one stone will be left upon another; all will be thrown down."

They asked him, "Teacher, when will this be, and what will be the sign that this is about to take place?" And Jesus said, "Beware that you are not led astray; for many will come in my name and say, 'I am the one!' and, 'The time is near!' Do not go after them.

"When you hear of wars and insurrections, do not be terrified; for these things must take place first, but the end will not follow immediately." Then Jesus said to them, "Nation will rise against nation, and country against country; there will be great earthquakes, and in various places famines and plagues; and there will be dreadful portents and great signs from heaven.

"But before all this occurs, they will arrest you and persecute you; they will hand you over to synagogues and prisons, and you will be brought before rulers and governors because of my name. This will give you an opportunity to testify. So make up your minds not to prepare your defense in advance; for I will give you words and a wisdom that none of your opponents will be able to withstand or contradict. You will be betrayed even by parents and family, by relatives and friends; and they will put some of you to death. You will be hated by all because of my name. But not a hair of your head will perish. By your endurance you will gain your souls."

REFLECTION

A prophet, in the Hebrew understanding, is "one who is called" by God for a special ministry to the people. The prophet is also "one who calls" the people back to the covenant way of life. Malachi, whose name means "my messenger," embodies both aspects of the prophetic ministry. He was called by God to warn the people of what could happen if they continued to wander from their covenant with the Lord. The prophet is not a fortune-teller in the sense that he or she would predict the future; a prophet proclaims the current reality in a way that incites a realization of what could happen if the current trend continues unabated.

Jesus is portrayed throughout the gospel of Luke as the perfect prophet. He continually calls his followers to the fullness of life that the covenant offers, and does so with such undivided conviction that he becomes the new and living covenant.

One might misunderstand today's gospel passage and what Jesus is doing in his prophetic ministry. It might be easy to see Jesus as merely predicting the future, but that is not so. Jesus is most concerned with the situation at hand, and not with future events. Luke places these words on Jesus' lips to communicate to Luke's own audience that in their current situation Jesus is present with his people. Luke was writing between 80–85 CE, after the destruction of the Temple, a time when Christians were suffering persecution. Jesus' words are meant to echo the events of Luke's day and offer hope to the persecuted Christians.

For those who worry about the future, it is good to learn through Luke's writing of Christ's word and wisdom living in the present moment.

■ **In what situations do you find it difficult to stay present in the moment at hand? How can you stay focused on Christ in your life today?**

■ **In what ways do you struggle with being a Christian in the world today? Are you ever "persecuted" for your faith? Do you know others who are persecuted for their faith? How can you help them?**

PRACTICE OF FAITH

THE DAY IS COMING. The warning is clear: The end of the world, the end of each of our individual lives, will come unexpectedly, so be ready! Live each day as though it were your last. Practice your faith as though you will be judged this very day!

To help you think through the details surrounding your death, each year use the months of October and November to take stock and make plans. Get a copy of *Now and At the Hour of Our Death* from Liturgy Training Publications (1-800-933-1800), and use it to create a folder of final instructions. Review it each year and make the necessary changes.

PRACTICE OF HOPE

PERSEVERANCE. Prayer works. Care works. Love works. We don't always see the results of our prayer, care and love, but they do have an impact. Anglican Archbishop Desmond Tutu of Cape Town, South Africa, made that clear when he accepted the Vision 2000 Award from Catholic Charities USA. According to a Catholic News Service report, the retired prelate said that it was the prayer and concern of people around the world that sustained black South Africans in their struggle to end apartheid. "Without your support and your help, we couldn't have made it," he said.

Their perseverance was also fueled by faith. "We are forever prisoners of hope," Archbishop Tutu said. "We know, despite all appearances to the contrary, that goodness is stronger than evil, that love is stronger than hate."

PRACTICE OF CHARITY

THE DAY IS COMING. The readings toward the end of the liturgical year warn of the time when God will judge the nations of the world.

Something that the United States will certainly have to answer for is the School of the Americas, called the "School of Assassins" by those who oppose it. This training facility, costing some $20 million a year to operate, trains Latin American military personnel in "counterinsurgency" tactics, many of which are little more than torture. Its graduates have included some of the worst butchers of Latin America's troubled twentieth century.

Join SOA Watch, an organization committed to closing the School of the Americas through non-violent means, PO Box 4566, Washington DC 20017; 1-202-234-3440; www.soaw.org.

WEEKDAY READINGS (Mo) 1 Maccabees 1:10–15, 41–43, 54–57, 62–64; (Tu) 2 Maccabees 6:18–31; (We) 2 Maccabees 7:1, 20–31; (Th) 1 Maccabees 2:15–29; (Fr) 4:36–37, 52–59; (Sa) 6:1–13

READING I *2 Samuel 5:1–3*

All the tribes of Israel came to David in Hebron, and said, "Look, we are your bone and flesh. For some time, when Saul was king over us, it was you who led out Israel and brought it in. The LORD said to you: It is you who shall be shepherd of my people Israel, you who shall be ruler over Israel."

So all the elders of Israel came to David in Hebron; and King David made a covenant with them at Hebron before the LORD, and they anointed David king over Israel.

[Revised Common Lectionary: Jeremiah 23:1–6]

READING II *Colossians 1:11–20*

May you be made strong with all the strength that comes from God's glorious power, and may you be prepared to endure everything with patience, while joyfully giving thanks to the Father, who has enabled you to share in the inheritance of the saints in the light. God has rescued us from the power of darkness and transferred us into the dominion of the beloved Son of God, in whom we have redemption, the forgiveness of sins.

Christ is the image of the invisible God, the first-born of all creation; for in Christ all things in heaven and on earth were created, things visible and invisible, whether thrones or dominions or rulers or powers—all things have been created through him and for him. Christ himself is before all things, and in him all things hold together. Christ is the head of the body, the church; Christ is the beginning, the first-born from the dead, so that he might come to have first place in everything. For in Christ all the fullness of God was pleased to dwell, and through Christ to reconcile to God's own self all things, whether on earth or in heaven, by making peace through the blood of his cross.

[Roman Catholic: Colossians 1:12–20]

GOSPEL *Luke 23:33–43*

When they came to the place that is called The Skull, they crucified Jesus there with the criminals, one on his right and one on his left. Then Jesus said, "Father, forgive them; for they do not know what they are doing." And they cast lots to divide his clothing. And the people stood by, watching; but the leaders scoffed at him, saying, "He saved others; let him save himself if he is the Messiah of God, the chosen one!" The soldiers also mocked him, coming up and offering him sour wine, and saying, "If you are the King of the Jews, save yourself!" There was also an inscription over him, "This is the King of the Jews."

One of the criminals who were hanged there kept deriding Jesus and saying, "Are you not the Messiah? Save yourself and us!" But the other rebuked him, saying, "Do you not fear God, since you are under the same sentence of condemnation? And we indeed have been condemned justly, for we are getting what we deserve for our deeds, but this man has done nothing wrong." Then he said, "Jesus, remember me when you come into your kingdom." He replied, "Truly I tell you, today you will be with me in Paradise."

[Roman Catholic: Luke 23:35–43]

REFLECTION

On this last Sunday of the liturgical year, we celebrate the feast of Christ the King. Luke, the skilled artist, presents a strange picture of a king: Jesus, the prophet, the teacher and healer, hangs from a cross undergoing the death penalty meted out to criminals. The people stood watching, as one would observe a public event. The rulers scoffed, the soldiers mocked, and one criminal railed.

Jesus spoke of salvation, healed, and even raised others from apparent death. Yet now he hangs on a cross in seeming powerlessness. One person in this narrative, one of the condemned criminals, recognizes Jesus' innocence and power and hears the blessed "today" that in Luke's writings conveys a sense of eschatological importance.

The portrait of the kingly messiah outlined in Colossians is more in accord with our usual post-resurrection images of Christ the King. However, underlying the shining Christ is the blood of the cross.

Why such contrasting images? The key may be found in the nature of Christ's mission: The task of Christ is to reconcile all things to God and to establish a state of peace. Reconciliation has to do above all with change and exchange and involves movement and a reversal of the way things are. The kingdom initiated by God in Jesus is founded on change, and there can be no greater change than a crucified king.

The inauguration of the kingdom is watched as a spectator sport, is scoffed at and is mocked and railed at by those who only understand the language of power. Jesus is king and Christ by his endurance and acceptance of the consequences of his faithfulness to initiating the change necessary—the great reversal—that leads to peace and reconciliation.

■ **The concept of "king" and "kingdom" are alien to us, yet they are at the core of the message of Jesus. Reflect on the inner reality behind these terms, translating them into concepts and terms that touch your life.**

PRACTICE OF FAITH

FIERY CROWN. It's over. The year of grace 2001 ends next Saturday at sunset when we begin another season of Advent. Make your Advent wreath this week. Construct or buy an evergreen wreath. With florist's wire, fasten four long lengths of 1-inch velvet ribbon to the wreath. Wire the loose ends together. Some traditions use three purple and one rose candle, some four red candles, some four white ones. Your fiery crown for Christ is ready for when he comes again to judge the living and the dead.

PRACTICE OF HOPE

AMEN. We often say this word at the end of something: a prayer, a statement of belief, a statement of hope. In reality, it is only a beginning. If we mean what we say, if we truly accept what we have heard and received from God, then we are compelled to act. We cannot remain silent. We cannot remain unseeing. We cannot be complacent. Every time we say "Amen!" we pledge to continue our efforts to bring about the kingdom of God here and now.

At the beginning of *Saying Amen: A Mystagogy of Sacrament,* a wonderful book by Kathleen Hughes (available from LTP), there is a poem that explains this eloquently. Barbara Schmich Searle reminds us that "'Amen' makes demands / like a signature on a dotted line. . . / 'Amen': We support. We approve. / We are of one mind. We promise. / May this come to pass. So be it."

Amen. The adventure continues.

PRACTICE OF CHARITY

JUSTLY CONDEMNED, YET FORGIVEN. In his crucifixion, Jesus shows that the supreme act of charity is forgiveness. Our call to charity lies in recognizing, as did the thief, that we are responsible for the condition of our brothers and sisters, that we have failed in our duty to serve and build God's reign, and we stand in need of forgiveness. And so we must forgive generously those who have sinned against us, lest we fail to receive forgiveness for our own failures. In this act of charity, the forgiver and the forgiven benefit equally.

Amnesty International is an organization with chapters in many U.S. cities committed to securing and protecting the rights of all the world's people. Consider becoming a member, or make a contribution. It can be contacted at 322 8th Avenue, New York NY 10001; 1-212-807-8400; www.amnesty.org.

WEEKDAY READINGS (Mo) Daniel 1:1–6, 8–20; (Tu) 2:31–45; (We) 5:1–6, 13–14, 16–17, 23–28; (Th) 6:12–28; (Fr) Romans 10:9–18; (Sa) Daniel 7:15–27

Information on the License to Reprint from *At Home with the Word 2001*

The low bulk rate prices of *At Home with the Word 2001* are intended to make quantities of the book affordable. Single copies are $7.00 each; 5–99 copies, $5.00 each; 100–499 copies, $4.00 each; 500 or more copies, $3.00 each. We encourage parishes to buy quantities of this book.

However, Liturgy Training Publications makes a simple reprint license available to parishes that would find it more practical to reproduce some parts of this book. Reflections (and questions), Practices, Prayers of the Season, and/or the holy day boxes can be duplicated for the parish bulletin or reproduced in other formats. These can be used every week or as often as the license-holder chooses. The page size of *At Home with the Word 2001* is 8 x 10 inches.

The license granted is for the period beginning with the First Sunday of Advent—December 3, 2000—through the solemnity of Christ the King—November 25, 2001.

Note also that the license does *not* cover the scriptures, psalms, or morning, evening and night prayer texts. See the acknowledgments page at the beginning of this book for the names and addresses of these copyright owners. Directions for obtaining permission to use these texts are given there.

The materials reprinted under license from LTP may not be sold and may be used only among the members of the community obtaining the license. The license may not be purchased by a diocese for use in its parishes.

No reprinting may be done by the parish until the license is signed by both parties and the fee is paid. Copies of the license agreement will be sent on request. The fee varies with the number of copies to be reproduced on a regular basis:

Up to 100 copies: $100
101 to 500 copies: $300
501 to 1000 copies: $500
More than 1000 copies: $800

For further information, call the reprint permissions department at 773-486-8970, ext. 268, or fax your request to 773-486-7094, att: reprint permissions.